D1562620

RABBINIC
AUTHORITY

RABBINIC
AUTHORITY

Michael S. Berger

New York   Oxford

Oxford University Press

1998

Oxford University Press

Oxford   New York

Athens   Auckland   Bangkok   Bogotá   Buenos Aires   Calcutta
Cape Town   Chennai   Dar es Salaam   Delhi   Florence   Hong Kong   Istanbul
Karachi   Kuala Lumpur   Madrid   Melbourne   Mexico City   Mumbai
Nairobi   Paris   São Paulo   Singapore   Taipei   Tokyo   Toronto   Warsaw

and associated companies in
Berlin   Ibadan

Copyright © 1998 by Michael S. Berger

Published by Oxford University Press, Inc.
198 Madison Avenue, New York, New York 10016

Oxford is a registered trademark of Oxford University Press

Library of Congress Cataloging-in-Publication Data
Berger, Michael S.
Rabbinic authority / Michael S. Berger.
p.   cm.
Includes bibliographical references and index.
ISBN 0-19-512269-0
1. Talmud—Evidences, authority, etc.   2. Talmud—Inspiration.
3. Bible.   O.T.—Criticism, interpretation, etc., Jewish—History.
4. Tannaim.   5. Amoraim.   6. Rabbis—Office.   7. Rabbinical
literature—History and criticism.   8. Tradition (Judaism)
I. Title.
BM503.B47   1998
296.1'2'00922—dc21   97-36779

1 3 5 7 9 8 6 4 2

Printed in the United States of America
on acid-free paper

To Ellie

Preface

As a general field of inquiry, philosophy of religion is not new. Starting with the Greeks, thinkers, both within religious contexts and outside them, have sought to clarify and explicate the central concepts of religion: God, God's relation to the world, the relationship of human beings to God, the ultimate end of things, to name but a few. To be sure, philosophical reflection about religion has ebbed and surged over the centuries, at times being of only peripheral interest, at others, of genuinely central concern to philosophers. Nevertheless, within Western culture, the field has been conducted almost exclusively within a Christian orbit, seeking either to challenge, defend, or simply analyze Christian belief and doctrine.

Since the middle of this century, there has been a self-conscious effort to reflect philosophically about the nature of religious thought and practice in the same way that philosophy of science and philosophy of history discuss questions of the thought and practice of scientists and historians.[1] Using the tools and insights of analytic philosophy, philosophers–religious and nonreligious alike–have again turned to treat issues in religious thought seriously.[2] More recently, some philosophers have turned to explicating specific concepts, practices, and doctrines in religion such as atonement, prayer, and life after death.[3] Although several religious traditions share some of these concepts, these treatments tend to reflect the Christian context in which most of this inquiry takes place.[4]

While a substantial number of the discussions admittedly cut across denominational lines, at least with respect to monotheistic traditions, two consequences emerge from the overwhelmingly Christian orientation of the discipline.

First, certain concepts are simply absent in Christianity. Two examples will suffice. While Christianity acknowledges certain places as "holy sites," it would be inadequate to characterize the Land of Israel as a very large "holy site" for traditional Judaism. The land not only possesses intrinsic holiness, but it is seen by many Jews to be the land promised to them by God since the time of Abraham. The notions of national homeland and diaspora or exile are central to Judaism, and they have no obvious parallel in Christianity. Another topic that has been neglected in the literature of the philosophy of religion is that of religious law. This omission reflects not only a Christian but especially a Protestant bias in the literature. Religious law is central to the theory and practice of many religious traditions, including various forms of Christianity, but not to Protestantism. The result is an important lacuna in theories of religion.

Second and more subtly, certain concepts, although shared nominally by several religions, do, in fact, assume significantly different meanings within each tradition. The understanding of "atonement" in a religion where God-incarnate died for humanity's sins is not necessarily the same in a tradition which does not share that conviction. Similarly, Judaism, Christianity, and Islam all share the belief in a revealed text, but the notion of a revealed text varies markedly among these religious traditions. In other words, like any other cultural term, a religious concept is embedded in a constellation of other concepts and beliefs that require us to adapt or refine our understanding of it according to each tradition. As the field of philosophy of religion expands to include both non-Christian subjects and students, the maturation of the discipline is inevitable.

This study of Rabbinic authority is a first step in that project. Although many topics could have been chosen, this subject is particularly worthy of attention for several reasons. While every religious tradition has its legitimate and authoritative interpreters, the Sages of the first five centuries of the common era–often referred to reverentially as Ḥazal, a Hebrew acronym for "our Sages of blessed memory"–occupy a central and unrivaled position in traditional Judaism. Their statements, collected in the vast corpus of Rabbinic literature, serve as the basis for Halakhah (the system of Jewish law). Virtually every practical issue taken up by schooled Jewish jurists over the last thirteen centuries begins with an appeal to some Rabbinic text, primarily the Babylonian Talmud, which was compiled and redacted in the fifth to eighth centuries C.E.

However, the acceptance of Rabbinic authority is not limited to this professional class. The Sages of the Talmud continue to be revered and their comments studied by Jewish schoolchildren and adults, in large lecture halls and small study groups, at home and in the synagogue. Many traditional Jewish men can probably cite more names of talmudic Sages than names of contemporary rabbis. Therefore, I have adopted a convention used in popular literature: the word "Rabbis," with a capital R, refers to the talmudic Sages.

As a work in the philosophy of religion, it must be emphasized that this book is not intended either to justify the normative claim that a Jew must obey talmudic law or even to prove that Rabbinic authority is an internally coherent concept. Rather, in the tradition of philosophical inquiry, it attempts to unpack the notion of the authority possessed by the talmudic Sages in Judaism and seeks to lay bare the assumptions that undergird it and the implications that follow from it. This work makes use of historical and sociological data within the course of the argumentation without becoming a historical or sociological study. I will show that Rabbinic authority is a complex notion, a single term that includes a range of claims and ideas, not all of which are neatly correlated or even integrated one with the other. The question, however, of whether one ought to obey Rabbinic authority is left open.

The hope contained in this book is twofold: first, that the notion of Rabbinic authority will be seen to be a rich, sophisticated, and variegated concept rather than the simplistic enforcer of blind obedience that it is often taken to be; and second, that it will stimulate serious philosophical treatment of non-Christian concepts in the academy, as well as encourage the reexamination of certain religious ideas within their more particular, tradition-specific contexts.

Acknowledgments

The notion of authority, in all its many instantiations, has been of lifelong interest to me. Relationships such as parent-child, teacher-student, professional-client, and law-citizen have intrigued and fascinated me in that individuals in such relationships apparently quite willingly give up their autonomy and follow the orders or utterances of another. Inspecting religious authority, or at least one type of it, was a natural extension of this more general interest.

A book is ultimately the product of only one scholar, but no scholar is the product of only one teacher. This long course of study, which originated as a doctoral thesis but which underwent significant revisions as my thinking evolved on the subject, brought me into contact with many individuals who have enhanced, encouraged, and guided my research. They helped form my thinking and provided me with an appreciation for the nuanced diversity of authority relationships, a theme which runs through this book.

First, I must mention my parents, who valued education above all else, instilling curiosity and nurturing critical thinking from early on in my life, coupled with respect and deference. This healthy tension was stressed in every choice I made, and its fruits are in many ways evident in this work.

My years at Yeshivat Har Etzion cultivated the technical and analytic skills necessary to understand the immense Rabbinic corpus and the subsequent centuries of commentary. But above all else, the authority of the talmudic Sages permeated the environment, leading me to ponder its nature and contours.

An initial inquiry into the analysis of the Babylonian Talmud's authority was the focus of my doctoral work at Columbia University, ably guided by Professors Wayne Proudfoot, David Shatz, and David Weiss Halivni. While this book moves significantly beyond that original investigation, it is nevertheless deeply indebted to these scholars, as is evidenced in the many footnotes that cite their comments and work.

My colleagues at Emory University have been a constant source of encouragement, broadening my understanding of religion in general even as they induced me to finish the book. I believe that part III, which is new to my thinking on this subject, could not have been written without the enriching environment of the Religion Department and its faculty at Emory. The University Research Committee also graciously underwrote two summers of intensive revising and writing, without which I would not have been able to see the project to completion.

Rabbis Michael Broyde and Emanuel Feldman carefully read the completed manuscript and offered many helpful suggestions, as did Jim Gustafson, from whose professional companionship I have benefited these last two years. My colleague David Blumenthal of Emory University deserves my deep *hoqarah* for being a constant source of encouragment (and prodding!) throughout the writing of this book. Dr. Joel Wolowelsky has been a mentor and friend for twenty years; my thinking on authority, in many ways, is rooted in our evolving relationship during the last two decades, and I look forward to many more such years.

I would also like to thank the editors and staff at Oxford University Press who have been extremely helpful in guiding me along my maiden voyage in book publishing. They have made an intimidating project manageable and even enjoyable. Responsibility for the final version, of course, lies entirely with its author.

Books have a way of consuming their authors, and such concentration often comes at the expense of those closest to us. My sons Akiva, Hillel, and Yehuda, who bear the names of some of the greatest talmudic Sages, endured a father who had to return to the office or retreat into the study a great deal these last few years. Those separations, which made me cherish the time we were together, also afforded me the opportunity to recognize and reflect on the connection between authority and other aspects of life.

Lastly, it is most fitting that the book be dedicated to Ellie, with whom I have shared my life since beginning graduate school, and who has patiently borne more than her share of responsibilities so that I could be unburdened to finish this book. Her willingness to go wherever my research or career took me and to take care of our children and ease their adjustment to their frequently changing surroundings helped me appreciate even more deeply how so few accomplishments are achieved alone in life. As the second-century Sage Rabbi Akiva said to his students regarding his own wife, *sheli vi-shelakhem shelah hu*: what's mine and yours is hers.

Contents

RABBINIC
AUTHORITY

Introduction

The Challenge to Biblical and Rabbinic Authority

During the last two hundred years of Jewish history, the authority of Jewish law, Halakhah, has been one of the central issues with which many Jews have struggled, particularly those taking their first, often eager, steps into Western culture.[1] For well over a millennium, Jewish society had been guided primarily by Jewish law as it was developed by the talmudic sages, known as "the Rabbis" with a capital R. Although certain groups, such as the Karaites, understood Judaism's prescriptions differently, the majority of Jews continued to affirm their basic loyalty to Rabbinic Halakhah, even if their personal practice fell short of the ideal.[2] To be sure, observance was, for the most part, not a matter of personal preference or choice; it was simply a way of life imbibed mimetically from one's surrounding from earliest childhood.[3] The internal cohesiveness of the Jewish community, coupled with the constant external pressures of a non-Jewish population intent on maintaining economic and social segregation (to varying degrees)[4] essentially made fidelity to Halakhah a given for most Jews, barring exceptional cases.[5]

However, under the influence of Enlightenment ideals in the late eighteenth century and into the nineteenth, western and central European countries began to grant Jews equal rights as full citizens of the state. The invitation extended to the Jews was, in reality, a conditional one: the Jews could join Christian society only if they surrendered all claims of distinctiveness and adopted the cultural norms of the state. As the Count of Clermont-Tonnerre succinctly articulated it during the 1791 debate in France over emancipating the Jews: "to the Jews as individuals—everything; as a nation—nothing." For the first time since Jews had settled on European soil, they had another option, an alternative to their way of life *without the requirement of conversion*; there was another community which would accept them and in which they could pursue their personal goals. The

3

invitation to become full-fledged members of the state meant for many Jews the end of their membership, or at least their exclusive membership, in traditional society.[6]

In response to the offer, many Jews cast off the heavy yoke of Jewish law that often laid obstacles in the path of their complete integration into a Christian society. Those who had been exposed to the German Enlightenment in the intellectual salons of Berlin in the late eighteenth through the early nineteenth century soon assimilated or even converted to Christianity.[7] Nevertheless, many Jews responded to this offer of equality, not by assuming an entirely new identity, but by transforming their Jewish practices in ways that would render these activities both more consistent with their newly held esteem of rationality and propriety and more palatable to their onlooking Gentile neighbors.[8] Some laws, such as the dietary laws, were abandoned as outdated, while others were modified to reflect a more "civilized" mentality; for example, organs were installed in synagogues, and the prayer service was revised to omit any reference to animal sacrifices and to add hopes for a united brotherhood of humanity.[9] While most of these early reformers were motivated as much by sociological as by religious concerns, the intellectual justification of reform was found several decades later in two related assumptions: first, the premise of biblical criticism that the Bible is not of divine origin and is therefore not immutable; and second, that the bulk of Jewish practice is the invention of the Rabbis, primarily those of the talmudic period, who set out to ensure the survival of the Jews in the first centuries after the Second Temple's destruction in 70 C.E. Both these premises allowed for the systematic and often radical revision of Jewish law in the nineteenth century because the two pillars that had held up the edifice of Halakhah for close to two millennia had collapsed: the belief in the Torah as divine revelation and the belief that the Rabbis of the Talmud were its sole legitimate interpreters. For the overwhelming majority of Jews who left the organized and insular Jewish community in this period, Halakhah had lost most of its authority.

Those committed to a maximal level of observance realized the serious extent of this breach and sought to shore it up primarily in two ways, corresponding to and countering the two central claims of the reformers.[10] Nineteenth-century biblical criticism, led by scholars such as Vatke and Wellhausen, had based its claim of the human authorship of the Pentateuch on the literary inconsistencies and variant styles contained in the text. Therefore, if these contradictions and inconsistencies could be resolved, the claim that the Torah is a compilation of documents could be challenged, if not undermined.[11] Of course, this did not, in itself, mean that the Pentateuch *was* divinely authored; secular society still maintained the rationalist bias against all things supernatural. However, arguing for a unitary, consistent text minimally weakened the evidence *against* the belief that God did, in fact, reveal the text.[12]

However, acceptance of the Torah's divine origin could not, on its own, logically impose a traditional lifestyle on the believer. In reality, traditional Jewish practice was based less on the Pentateuch than on the interpretation of that text by the Sages, that group of scholars in Palestine and Babylonia who were active during the first five centuries of the common era, and whose views and pronouncements were preserved in the Mishnah, the Palestinian and Babylonian Talmuds, and other Rabbinic texts. The authority of the Torah was mediated through *their* understanding of it—an understanding which seemed, at times, far from the plain, simple meaning of the text. Superfluous words, juxtaposed sentences, and even variant spellings were all legitimate grounds for legal inference, even to the extent of supplanting the simple meaning of the verse entirely.[13] Out of a firm belief in the divinity of the Torah text and hence in the significance of every word and letter, the Sages inferred "mounds and mounds of laws," which became the basis of all Jewish religious practice.[14] It was not biblical but Rabbinic Judaism that was normative, and the reformers' challenge to the Sages' authority was as fatal to the Halakhah as much as the challenge of biblical criticism was.

To be sure, the Rabbis of the talmudic period were themselves aware of the distinction between the written text and their understanding of it.[15] They articulated a sophisticated notion known as the dual Torah—the Written Torah and the Oral Torah—where the latter was a self-conscious, *contemporaneous* exposition of the former.[16] The Rabbis considered both bodies of law to have been revealed, to varying degrees, at Sinai, rendering Rabbinic interpretation of the Torah as divinely grounded as the revealed letters themselves.[17] The nineteenth-century challenge, at least in the realm of ideology, was staged, then, against both these Torahs: the biblical critics' assault on the Written Law and some reformers' attempts to reject elements, or all, of the Oral Law expounded by the Sages of the Talmud.

Several strategies were employed to counter this latter challenge.[18] The simplest was to concede that only that which was divine was indeed authoritative but to deny that Rabbinic exegesis was a human distortion of the Pentateuch's simple meaning. To the contrary, it was actually a *loyal reflection of it*. By carefully examining the grammar of the original Hebrew and other lexical issues, the Sages' interpretations were seen to be the accurate expression of the text's plain meaning, if only one understood the subtle nuances of biblical Hebrew. In other words, the Oral and Written Torahs were conflated: the oral tradition merely unpacked and explicated what was implicit in the written text, but it certainly did not distort it.

This approach was, however, inherently limited, for although the Sages of the Talmud engaged in biblical exegesis, a significant portion of Rabbinic law was based not on derivations from verses but on sheer legislative authority. This realm of Rabbinic enactment, while nominally part of the Oral Law, was clearly historically based and postbiblical. Even were one to admit that the Rabbinic interpretation of a verse was binding because it was merely transmitted from the time of Moses to the present, such a normative ground could not be applied to Rabbinic decrees and enactments, such as observing two days of a holiday outside the Land of Israel[19] or taking the four species of plants during prayer services for all seven days of the holiday of Sukkot rather than the biblically prescribed first day.[20] In this realm, Rabbinic authority would presumably have to be justified another way.

More traditional figures in the nineteenth century actually pursued the ambitious (and counterintuitive) strategy of claiming that, in fact, *all of Rabbinic law* — exegesis, decrees, and even custom — had indeed been revealed at Sinai.[21] Every statement of the Talmud is merely a record of *transmitted* divine law, direct and unadulterated from Moses at Sinai.[22] However, this maximalist view ran counter not only to the historical consciousness of the nineteenth century but even to the evidence of the Talmud itself, which attributed legislative enactments to several Rabbinic leaders of the first two centuries C.E. While this strategy presently enjoys widespread support in the Ultra-Orthodox community, it was originally voiced only by the most extreme elements and was eschewed by most traditionalists as oversimplified and, in some instances, simply false.[23]

The awareness of the historical evolution of Judaism, quite obvious and undeniable to those with a thorough knowledge of the Talmud and the history of Halakhah, was perhaps the most potent weapon in the arsenal of the reformers. They argued that if the Sages had formed a postbiblical Judaism in response to the catastrophes of the Temple's destruction in 70 C.E. and the failed Bar Kokhba Rebellion in 135 C.E., even if only in the realm of decrees and enactments, then this was clear evidence that the system included, even sanctioned, change. The more moderate traditionalists, who were reluctant to reduce all Rabbinic activity to a maximalist notion of revelation, were thus faced with defending two positions that were inherently in tension: that, on the one hand, the Sages did indeed develop elements of Judaism as we know it today, but that, on the other hand, we are, to a great extent, permanently bound to those laws, no longer free to modify or change them. A theory had to be found which could admit that the talmudic Rabbis were, indeed, the source of much of Jewish law, but which could, at the same time, prevent or at least moderate any major tampering with that evolved tradition.[24] For those Jews committed both to their traditional practices and to participating *intellectually* in modern Western culture, this was the central problematic.[25]

The Nature and Scope of This Inquiry

This brief historical survey provides the social context of this work. One student of political science has astutely observed that if authority requires justification, that is the first sign that it has ceased to exist.[26] As stated in the preface, it is not the aim of this book to engage in a defense or grounding of Rabbinic authority for normative ends. However, the fact that today's Jews are often classified — even in their own eyes — by their level of commitment to halakhic practice invites a closer examination of one of the concepts which forms the basis of this commitment, at least theoretically. Whether one feels bound by Rabbinic authority wholly, partially, or not at all, it is appropriate for those who see themselves in conversation with a tradition to understand more thoroughly one of its basic tenets. And for those who stand outside the tradition but are interested in understanding Judaism more fully, Rabbinic authority, as one of traditional Judaism's cardinal features, is certainly a reasonable place to begin.[27]

The aim of this book, therefore, is to explore the notion of Rabbinic authority by inspecting various theories of the grounds for that authority. This is not, however, a historical survey of explanations actually proffered by Jewish scholars over the last several hundred years. As a work in philosophy of religion, it will seek to establish a *typology of justifications* for the authority of the Sages, developing these theories in such a way as to lay bare their assumptions, their scope, and any other implications which may flow from them. As a work in Jewish scholarship, it is important to be in conversation with the tradition of reflection on this subject. I will therefore cite ancient, medieval, and modern scholars, traditional and academic, who have dealt with this issue. This citation should not be construed, however, as an effort to see that particular thinker as an instantiation of the specific model under discussion or to show that the theory being described accurately represents the view of the scholar cited. That would be a historical project, and although extremely interesting, it is beyond the scope of this book to ascertain the view actually held by any individual writer.[28] In fact, I will cite Maimonides' writings under more than one model, for several of his statements often capture most closely and succinctly the notion I am trying to develop. I do not mean either to suggest that Maimonides changed his mind from one work to another or to prove that he actually held multiple views on the subject. But his wording often captures the essence of the particular model under discussion.

Admittedly, the question of the authority of the talmudic Sages is somewhat artificially circumscribed. Although the ideological debate begun in the mid–nineteenth century between traditionalists and reformers centered on the authority of these Rabbis of antiquity, it could not remain there for long. The issue naturally extends itself to two, broader issues. One is the authority of Halakhah in general, as it has evolved over the centuries since the Talmud's redaction. While this legal system certainly finds its roots in the statements of the talmudic Sages, accepted Jewish practice is based on the history of the Halakhah's codification, all the way from the decisions of the medieval scholars who applied talmudic opinions to the very recent handbooks on particular areas of the law, such as Sabbath observance or mourning practices.[29] In other words, normative Jewish law is grounded not so much in the talmudic Sages' authority but in theories of authority relating to a more developed and historically evolving legal system which includes both widely accepted codes and the constant need to apply these codes to the contingencies of daily life.

The second related issue is that of rabbinic authority—with a lowercase *r*. The Jewish community has always included a scholarly elite well versed in Jewish law, who guided the laity in the practical application of Halakhah. Whether it was the leading scholar in the academy or the officially appointed rabbi of the community, the question of rabbinic authority was always a real one: why should someone obey the decisions of another person? There are many valid reasons to defer to someone else's authority; in the following section, I will show how authority relationships pervade the structure of our smaller and larger societies such that normal life could not be conducted without them. In fact, several models of authority that I will use to understand Rabbinic (with a capital *R*) authority will be applicable to the case of subsequent scholars or some community rabbis as well.

Given the natural extension of the question to these two broader issues, I should say a word about why the topic is so delimited. As in every book, there is the concern for manageability. Limiting the subject to Rabbinic authority is not a denial of the other, highly relevant issues; it is merely an admission that this is only a first step in understanding the notion of authority in Judaism, which is, without doubt, multifaceted and complex. Halakhic authority is a rich, multidimensional issue that can be approached in many ways. I have simply chosen to discuss what could arguably be called one of its fundamental foundations, the other being the authority of the Torah. But this work should, in no way, be seen as an exhaustive or comprehensive treatment of a complex and composite subject.

Pragmatic concerns aside, there are more substantive reasons to single out Rabbinic authority from other instances of authority in Judaism. First and perhaps foremost, the other cases of authority are, to a great extent, derivatives of Rabbinic authority. If one were to formulate the inquiry into authority as a series of successive questions of "Why should I do/believe that?" then in a relatively short time, most series would regress to the question of Rabbinic authority. For example, if a local congregational rabbi (with a lowercase *r*) is approached about the halakhic permissibility of a certain food mixture, the rabbi will often apply a well-known rule or set of rules in the realm of *kashrut* (Jewish dietary laws). If the person who posed the original question asks the rabbi, "Why should I believe your answer?" the rabbi would most likely respond, "Because that is the Halakhah in this matter." Pressed further, the rabbi may cite recent sources, which are, in turn, based on late medieval codes, which themselves navigate among early medieval sources, which are, finally, interpretations of talmudic sources. In many (but not all) cases, the chain of questions will eventually lead to one about the Sages' authority, even if the total answer will need to address some equally significant, but in the end second-order, questions as to the authority of medieval scholars, sixteenth-century codes, and recent responsa.

Second, while in the untrained popular perception, a scholar is someone who knows a lot about a subject, and while the title "rabbi" technically confers equivalent status on all who bear it, the truth is very different. The Sages' authority cannot be reduced to an instance of rabbinic authority, for in very real terms, they do not do the same thing. Primarily, there are three differences. The first is that with respect to normative practice, the interpretation of the Pentateuch ceased with the Sages. After them, no scholar went back to the primary text of the divine revelation to interpret what God's will was. Subsequent scholars, as great as they were, were in the derivative position of interpreting the interpreters, whether with respect to explaining the talmudic case or limiting its application. In either case, the post-talmudic scholars did not revisit the Torah but restricted their analysis to the second-order activity of explaining the Talmud.

The second difference is in the quality of interpretation. As noted earlier, at times the Sages interpreted a verse far beyond what we would assume was the plain and simple meaning. Despite the efforts in the last one hundred and fifty years to defend Rabbinic exegesis, we nevertheless sense in reading the Talmud that the Sages often inferred from the divinely revealed text laws of major significance that seem barely rooted (if at all) in the original. In contrast, post-talmudic scholars engaged and engage in a genuinely text-based enterprise, seeking the meaning of talmudic statements according to textual arguments and rules of inference that are more similar to the strategies we use today to understand a text. While there is a tendency, developed to the level of commitment by the medieval tosafists, to find significance in every talmudic line as if it were another Torah, not every superfluous letter in the Talmud serves as the basis of a legal inference. Context and the logical flow of an argument are canons of medieval interpretation in ways that the talmudic exegesis of the Pentateuchal verse cannot always claim. It is a gross oversimplification to state that the post-talmudic scholars did to the Sages what the Sages did to the Torah; while both treated their subject reverentially and attributed significance to every word or letter, the respective methodologies—and what counted as a legitimate inference—were vastly different.

Third, the opinions registered in a talmudic discussion in many cases effectively exhaust the range of views that can be legitimately maintained within the tradition. To be sure, medieval or even later interpretation can so limit the talmudic position as to leave open the possibility of other decisions. However, this is never presented as a *rival* to the talmudic options; every scholar must deal first with the positions staked out by the talmudic Sages.

Aside from these practical and substantive reasons, there is another, admittedly sociological reason to limit this study to the Sages. Any review of the later literature, in any period, shows that the talmudic Rabbis continued to occupy a unique position in Jewish law and lore. An aura surrounds them, both in the popular image and in the circles of scholars. While individual rabbis over the last fifteen centuries have certainly possessed considerable degrees of authority, and even today are carefully studied and cited, only the talmudic Sages are venerated *collectively*, without exception. Any scholar cited in Rabbinic literature from that period is, ipso facto, deemed to be of exceptional piety, extraordinary intellect, and impeccable character. Ḥazal, an acronym for *ḥakhameinu zikhronam livrakhah* (our Sages of blessed memory), is a term which studs centuries of halakhic and aggadic literature and, when cited in some traditional circles, immediately instills awe and reverence in the reader or listener.

I have therefore chosen to focus this work exclusively on the talmudic Sages' authority for *subsequent* generations.[30] In the final chapter, some of the implications of my analysis for the other, related forms of authority will be addressed. However, given these pragmatic, methodological, and substantive reasons, it is wisest to maintain a more limited focus for the book. It is my sincerest hope that the analysis will invite or even provoke further reflection on a topic so central to contemporary Judaism.

A Brief Analysis of Authority

The authority of the talmudic Sages is, of course, a particular instance of the general category of authority. Therefore, in order to discuss our subject in any analytic depth, it is appropriate to review, however briefly, the major themes in the philosophical analysis of authority, which began in earnest in the 1950s. This introduction will equip the reader with a philosophical vocabulary sufficiently rich and nuanced to reflect the inherent complexity of Rabbinic authority.

Given that the Sages as individuals are inseparable from the texts that convey their statements to us, we will analyze the nature of both a person's authority, and the authority of texts.

Institutional and Personal Forms: In *Authority* and An *Authority*

In a significant paper on the subject of authority, R. S. Peters distinguished between two senses of the term.[31] The first, which is one frequently encountered in political life, is the authority of someone holding office or rank. Although such a person may be able to demand compliance with his or her orders, the authority wielded is more accurately taken to be the authority of the office itself and not of the individual occupying it. In other words, the authority stems from the institutional framework in which both the officeholder and the underling find themselves. The system they are in, whether from nine to five Monday through Friday or on an ongoing basis, determines the rules regulating the responsibilities of both parties and the scope and intensity of their relationship. Thus, a colonel and a private are in positions whose interactions are frequently determined by the rules of that particular army, and other rules, in turn, dictate the relationship of the colonel to his superior. Peters calls this being *in* authority, where the person is in a particular post or position that defines his or her role and relationships to others. The clearest indication of the context dependence of this sort of authority is when the two individuals step out of their rule-governed framework. In an office, for example, it is clear that a secretary must do what the chief executive officer says. But if the two find themselves in line for a movie or playing a game of tennis, then the secretary is not expected to obey what the executive says, unless there are personal, noninstitutional reasons for doing so. These "political" relationships, of course, exist whenever we find ourselves in an institutional setting, such as school, work, or any organizational structure.

In contrast, some people possess authority for personal reasons, such as competence or expertise. Peters calls this a case of someone being *an* authority, whereby authority is based on an individual's personal qualities: a doctor is *an* authority for a patient, and a professor is *an* authority for her students in a particular field. No institution regulates these relationships, but the *domain* of expertise determines the scope of the person's authority: for the doctor, it is medicine (or a specific area of medicine), and for the professor, it is her area of specialization. What must be underscored is that in being *an* authority, the ground of the authority is *relational*: it is one person's assessment of another's qualities. This insight explains two important and related facets of personal authority which distinguish it from being *in* authority:

1. *Personal authority is inherently provisional in nature.* As long as the trust of the subordinate party remains intact, the authority relationship exists and is justified. If someone else captures the trust of the individual, or if the advice

offered leads to failure, then personal authority is either reduced or nullified. Of course, some relationships defy verifiability, such as charismatic authority; in the event the person's stature is challenged by reality, then so much the worse for the facts. But in general, a personal authority relationship is fluid, being either reinforced or weakened by actual experience. This is in sharp contrast to the *comparatively* static nature of institutional authority.

This aspect of personal authority is related to the fact that, very often, being *an* authority is relative: a native English speaker may be an authority on the English language while in Russia, but not necessarily in the United States or England. Similarly, medical school students often become initial authorities on medical issues for their friends, even though no doctor, or even a more advanced medical student, would see them as authorities.

2. *Personal authority is evaluated by external standards.* Since assessment is the ground of personal authority, independent criteria must exist by which to conduct the evaluation. As just stated, simple experience may serve as the bar at which the authority is judged: if the doctor's prognosis does not lead to an improvement or, worse, provokes a deterioration of the patient's condition, then his medical authority is compromised *with this patient*, if not entirely forfeited.[32] The standards of an academic discipline are used to evaluate a professor's views, although an uninitiated student may not yet be in a position to make such an assessment intelligently. In this regard, being *an* authority is similar to being *in* authority in that an appeal is made to an external source, such as the institutional framework or the recognized criteria of truth within a particular discipline. However, this does not change the basic dynamic character of personal authority, in that it is still in flux compared to the more stable form of authority of the political model.

To be sure, personal authority can be based less on skill or knowledge than on other, less quantifiable or verifiable qualities. Thus, speakers who are inspirational or leaders who are charismatic may be authoritative for their audiences in ways that cannot be reduced to simple, concrete criteria. As its name implies, there is an important *personality* component to this category of authority; gurus or cult leaders exhibit this element much more than doctors or professors do, although many holders of personal authority partake of it to some degree.

Peters's classification affords us an insightful and fruitful way for understanding human authority, but we should be aware of its limits. First, the distinction between being *in* or *an* authority should not be seen as a hard and fast one. While the typology is convenient, and in many cases the models obtain in their pure form, we encounter cases in real life that do not fit neatly into one or the other category. Often, an individual who possesses some internal quality also occupies a position of authority, such as a brilliant researcher who heads a laboratory that conducts medical tests[33] or a charismatic leader who assumes a political post.[34] Second, this analysis is seemingly exhaustive only with respect to persons possessing authority; ideas or other abstract notions that we recognize as authoritative are not all reducible to these categories (even if they emerged in that manner) and require independent analysis.[35]

Lastly, Peters's discussion does not deal with what the notion of authority entails *normatively*: strict deference, where the authority figure's instructions are obeyed, or simply giving the judgments or opinions of the authority a certain priority, such as initially pursuing an avenue of research or line of thinking suggested by an expert. Intuitively, this last distinction seems to depend on Peters's own analysis: a person *in* a position of institutional authority should be obeyed, but one who is *an* authority simply captures our initial attention, even if it is never superseded. However, the range of authority relationships among people is too complex to be understood as the simplistic difference between a veto or a vote. We intuitively recognize that not everything said by persons who are in superior positions to us, even within institutional settings, demands obedience, nor is it the case that all the statements of those in personal authority should be construed as mere suggestions. Consistent with our initial analysis, the normative implications of authority must be examined according to the specific circumstances of the particular case.

The Authority of Texts

Peters's analysis set the tone and even the terms for the discussions of authority conducted in the 1960s and 1970s. But his focus on the authority of persons, whether *in* or *an* authority, was soon seen to be inadequate because it omitted the rather large realm of authoritative texts, an omission picked up rather quickly by those who sought to understand the authority of law.[36]

To be sure, one is inclined to locate the authority of texts prima facie in their authors, an observation already made by Hobbes.[37] If we see the person as the central locus of authority, then verbal or written communications are equally valid methods of expressing that person's ideas. The only difference is that writing, to varying degrees, includes the inherent doubt of hearsay, which direct interlocution lacks. Except in the case of documents written in the author's own hand (and even then, we may suspect forgery), we must *believe* that a particular text is the genuine reflection of a person's statements. This is true whether the document is a memo of a company vice-president (sometimes initialed by the writer for precisely this reason) or a scientific paper sent to a journal for publication; both are taken as accurate reflections of their authors' minds.

However, such an analysis hardly exhausts the realm of the written word, particularly when it comes to law. When a bill is drafted, it is correctly seen as the expression of the view of a particular legislator or team of lawmakers. However, once passed, legislation is not authoritative because of its authors; it possesses some form of institutional authority in its own right—as a duly constituted law.[38] If we grant any independent standing to the law, its authoritativeness correctly derives from its institutional setting; it is not the expression of anyone's mind, except in the most derivative sense of being the will of the people as expressed by their duly appointed representatives.

Nevertheless, certain legal texts cannot be adequately described even by this sense of independent standing, for their authoritativeness is based on much *more* than simply the legal validity pertaining to a law's authority. I am referring, of course, to foundational legal texts, such as a country's constitution. In the case of the United States, the Constitution is studied, quoted, interpreted, and enforced in a way that brings it closer to the status of a sacred text.[39] It is the center of virtually all legal studies, and its every word is analyzed and frequently hotly debated for potential implications regarding contemporary legal situations. The entire American legal community—judges, lawyers, legislators, and scholars—sees it as its central text, the document that defines its members' goals and serves as the context for their activity. It is therefore not surprising that so much attention has recently been given to understanding the nature of this document's authority.[40]

This sort of unique, irreducible authority can be extended to other texts as well. Literary classics, which constitute a canon for students of literature,[41] possess some sort of special status that is not "authoritative" in the generally accepted sense of the term and certainly is not an expression of their authors' personal authority. Rather, they maintain a grip on a particular part of our culture which deems these texts worthy of close reading and constant analysis. In a similar way, certain reference texts, such as dictionaries and encyclopedias, cannot be understood either as the products of particular authors or even as a sort of canon within a larger, rule-governed system. Rather, they are texts that live in their *usage* by a culture: how often they are consulted, cited, and used to decide other issues. If we are unsure of the meaning of a specific word or its etymology, we turn to certain dictionaries and look it up, thus clearing up any doubt. Although actual lexicographers wrote the dictionary, we sense that consulting a reference text is qualitatively different from simply asking those people in person.[42] For some texts, the nature of their authority is that they are embedded in the *way of life* of a particular community, whether construed narrowly, as in a group of lawyers and legal scholars, or broadly, as in the society as a whole.[43] To be sure, this is a contingent state of affairs, and within a specialized community, one text can potentially supersede another as the focus of the community's activity. Nevertheless, the more integrated the text is into all aspects of a particular way of life, the less likely is that text to be supplanted or rendered irrelevant, as long as that community remains vital and active.

Thus, although Peters's analysis was helpful for appreciating the nature of a person's authority, we see that the nature of the authority of texts cannot always be reduced to the authority of their authors. At times, books assume a life of their own, cited and consulted for a variety of reasons. Moreover, the relationship can be reciprocal; authors may gain greater "authority" in various circles because the texts they have written achieve a certain standing in society, not always or exclusively on the merits of the books' contents.

This brief review underscores that any analysis of authority must appreciate—and account for—the diversity and complexity of the notion. Our inquiry will utilize the themes laid out in this introduction to unpack and analyze one of the twin pillars of traditional Jewish thought and practice: the authority of the Sages.

Outline of the Book

Before we can actually inspect various models for understanding Rabbinic authority, we must clarify the parameters of our subject more thoroughly in two respects. One is the elaboration of the inherently diverse realm of Rabbinic activity, from straightforward exegesis of biblical verses to revolutionary enactments in the socioreligious realm. The second is the ways in which Rabbinic law is demarcated from the Torah, the other pillar of Jewish tradition, which locates its ground in divine revelation. The relationship between the Oral and the Written Law is a complex subject, with a variety of theories available within the tradition to explain it. The first chapter will therefore be devoted to establishing the parameters and laying out the terrain on which the ensuing discussion will be carried out.

R. S. Peters's fundamental analytic distinction between being *in* authority or *an* authority suggests a convenient division for our inquiry. In part I, we will explore several institutional models of Rabbinic authority. In all these theories, the weight of the argument for the Sages' authority rests on understanding it within a larger institutional nexus; the Sages, by "occupying" that position (in whatever sense), constitute simply a particular instance of the authority of that post. This strategy can be largely distilled into two general models, one of which further divides into two:

1. There is a divine command in the Torah to obey the leading scholars of any generation, which the Sages represent (chapter 2).

2. As in any legal system, some judiciary organ must be empowered to interpret and apply the laws of that system. Whatever undergirds the system as a whole therefore serves as the ground for the judiciary's authority. In Judaism, that could be either (*a*) the Sanhedrin, a collective body of seventy or so scholars (chapter 3); or (*b*) ordained individuals, who trace their authorization in a direct line back to the original prophet-lawgiver, Moses (chapter 4).

In all these models, two things will have to be proved: first, the theoretical claim that these institutions genuinely draw their authority from another source, and in what ways; and second, the quasi-historical claim that the Sages of the talmudic period are, in fact, the embodiment of that particular institution.

Part II will deal with seeing the Sages as authorities themselves, possessing personal qualities which grant them special standing, such as the requisite expertise in their field (chapter 5) or a unique level of divine assistance or guidance (chapter 6).[44]

Authority, as we have seen, is a complex notion, and understanding it can involve more than searching for transcendent reasons which endow certain people with authority. Since we are examining the Sages' authority for subsequent generations, in part III we consider Rabbinic authority as "authority transformed." Chapter 7 explores the possibility that although the Sages may initially have served as the local judges of the Jewish communities of Palestine and Babylonia, deciding laws through the authority vested in local courts, these decisions ultimately became part of the people's tradition. What began as "Rabbinic authority" was transformed into the authority of accepted practice, even as it continued to bear the original name. Chapter 8 modifies this approach but limits itself to discussing the transformation of authority within a legal community, particularly one in which transmission was oral. What began as the authority of Sages such as Rabbi Akiva, Rabbi Samuel, and Rav Ashi was later transformed into the authority of a "text," in the sense that their utterances achieved a status within the academy and were studied a certain way. The Babylonian Talmud, which impressively and comprehensively collected the statements of hundreds of Sages, served as the basis for the juridic community's analysis of virtually every issue—an accepted procedure expressed by the term "Rabbinic authority."

The concluding chapter evolves rather naturally from the previous one and continues to inspect the role of the community in understanding Rabbinic authority. Using Stanley Fish's analysis of interpretive communities and the "authority" they exert in the process of reading and interpreting, chapter 9 suggests that we must rethink what we mean when we invoke the notion of "Rabbinic authority." Rather than a normative claim to obedience which must be justified by reasons somehow "outside us," "Rabbinic authority" is more accurately a way of describing an interpretive community (broadly construed) that fashions its "form of life" in accordance with the laws, commentaries, and insights of the talmudic Sages. Each denomination of American Judaism then constitutes its own interpretive community, in that each "sees" and interprets the Rabbinic legacy differently. Rabbinic authority, in the end, cannot be proved or disproved, because it is a notion that describes distinctly different ways of understanding what it means to be a Jew in the modern world.

In that last chapter, we will also review some of the salient points of our inquiry, most prominently how a community of interpreters both shares in the authority of the text they interpret and contributes to the centrality of the primary text. What indeed emerges from our study is not only that the Sages' authority in Judaism is a complex, nuanced notion but also that no thorough understanding of their authority can focus on that subject alone to the exclusion of an examination of the more complex relationship of text and interpreter.

ONE

The Domains of Divine Revelation and Rabbinic Activity and Their Relationship

Any analysis of the authority of the Sages must be preceded by a clarification of the domain of Rabbinic activity. Unless the precise contours of the subject are outlined first, any attempt at understanding the grounds of Rabbinic authority will prove futile, for we will not know what sorts of activity—legislative, interpretive, or otherwise—are being justified.

This effort at definition entails two separate goals. The first is to bring the diverse areas of Rabbinic activity into sharper focus for the reader. Taken as a whole, Rabbinic literature confronts the student as an unsystematic collection of a wide variety of legal statements, some anonymous and others attributed to specific Sages, artfully woven into various literary forms. However, these utterances and transmitted historical traditions can be cataloged into relatively distinct categories, so that a clear picture emerges of the diversity of the Sages' activity. As will be seen, some statements are connected to the Torah or to other parts of the Hebrew Bible through simple elaboration or complex exegetical techniques, and others are entirely independent of the divinely revealed text.

Given this variety, it will be necessary as a second goal to establish the relationship between the Torah and the Rabbinic project. In the introduction, we mentioned that this is far from a settled issue; even within the tradition itself, several theories have been advanced to explain with some precision how the Sages' Oral Law saw itself with respect to the Written Law, the divinely revealed Torah. While we will not reach any specific conclusion on this thorny subject, it is important to realize the inverse relationship existing between these two domains and its consequences for our discussion. If one's view of the original revelation is maximalist, such that most, if not all, Rabbinic utterances are only the final stage in a long line of transmission back to Sinai, then the domain of Rabbinic activity that needs to be justified independently is quite small (although their role as transmitters will need to be examined). Conversely, the more one sees the Sages as playing an active, even innovative role in the transcription and unfolding of the Oral Law, then the greater must be the efforts to justify their considerable authority. So the question of the relative domains of divine revelation and Rabbinic activity will directly impact our study. As we consider each model in turn, we will revisit this issue, explaining whether the particular theory lends itself more appropriately to a maximalist notion of revelation or to a maximalist notion of the Sages' authority.

Before setting out to accomplish these two goals, a word on methodology is important. The period of the Sages spans roughly the first five centuries of the common era, from a generation or two before the destruction of the Second Temple in 70 C.E. until the death of Rav Ashi about the year 500. Although modern scholarship sees the redaction of the Babylonian Talmud as having continued for some time after that by anonymous redactors known as Stammaim (and possibly others),[1] for centuries Jewish tradition saw Rav Ashi as the scholarly "endpoint" of the Talmud.[2] Even the anonymous portions of the text were attributed to Rav Ashi, although some editing continued through the next two generations, until the death of Ravina. Therefore, for all intents and purposes, the category "the Sages" within the tradition includes all those scholars mentioned by name in Rabbinic literature.

From a historical standpoint, there is no doubt that the role and function of the Sages did not remain static throughout this time period. The changing realities of the political, social, and economic landscape, both in the Land of Israel and in Babylonia, often had direct impact on the realm of Rabbinic activity.[3] Nevertheless, from within the tradition, the Sages are generally viewed as a single collective, with few historically based distinctions drawn between scholars. There is an acknowledgment that some Sages were ordained and others were not; even among the ranks of the ordained, certain individuals were granted greater authorization.[4] But outside the realm of judicature, tradition sees little basis to apportion Rabbinic activity among different groups of Sages. Rabbinic literature is seen largely as one single cloth, and so is the Rabbinic enterprise, although it does admit of its distinction from the Written Law, as will be discussed below.

The Range of Rabbinic Activity

Although the following catalog of the scope of the Sages' activity[5] is sufficiently diverse to reflect the variety of Rabbinic statements and actions, there will necessarily be some that do not fall neatly into one, or even several, categories, and others will be subsumed under several. Recognizing the inherent limitations on this sort of endeavor, we may classify the range of Rabbinic activity as follows.

Clarification of Biblical Law

Very often, the Pentateuch's formulation of a particular commandment is extremely brief. Questions about the definition of words, scope of application, and exemptions and exceptions required resolution. The Sages therefore explained the law by providing details where they were lacking in the text.

One example will suffice. In Lev. 23:42, the Torah states tersely: "You shall dwell in booths [*sukkot*] for seven days." This short prescription prompted a host of questions:[6]

> What constitutes a "booth"? What are its requisite dimensions, both minimally and maximally? What materials can be used in its construction?
> What does "dwell" entail—all one's activities or only certain ones? Is a complete transfer of one's possessions from the home into the booth required or not?
> Who is obligated to do this? Every Jew? Are there any exemptions, such as infirm adults or nursing children? What about the person traveling on the road?
> Must one dwell there for the full seven days (all or nothing), or must one do whatever is in one's ability?

All these facets of the law required clarification so that God's will, as revealed in the Torah, could be fulfilled.

A variety of techniques were employed in this effort to clarify doubtful points of law, including *analogical reasoning*, where another case that *is* elaborated in the law serves as a paradigm for the case in question; *exegetical arguments*, on the premise that the Torah was literally dictated by God to Moses, so every aspect of the text—extra letters, juxtaposition of unrelated laws, identical words used in different contexts in order to link them, etc.—was significant and disclosed God's law in greater detail; *logical reasoning*; *transmitted traditions*, which a scholar has received from his teacher, but which are not necessarily grounded in the text; and *accepted practice*, where the common manner of performance is evidence of a long-standing tradition, even if there is no explicit basis in the revealed text.[7] Occasionally, not only ambiguities but contradictions within the Pentateuchal text demanded clarification, yielding a variety of solutions as well.

It should be emphasized that these various strategies were not necessarily intended to uncover the plain, simple meaning of the text—the *peshat*. The Sages' commitment to the literal meaning of the text is the subject of considerable debate,[8] but their interpretations of the Torah's verses are certainly *not limited by* the plain meaning of the words.

Resolution of Disputes

Not all Sages agreed on the proper application of these techniques or even on which strategy should be employed in a particular situation. Obviously, when logical reasoning was employed, mutually exclusive inferences could be persuasively argued. At other times, two scholars were simply heirs to differing traditions from their own teachers. The Sages therefore frequently voiced differing opinions on a subject, as inspection of virtually any page of the Talmuds will verify. The existence of more than one view often, although certainly not always, forced subsequent scholars to adjudicate which view was to be deemed normative.

Legislation

The Sages were engaged not only in interpreting the law but also in creating it. This self-conscious effort to legislate for the community was usually expressed in two forms. By means of the ordinances (*gezeirot*), the Sages sought to distance the people from biblically prohibited transgressions due to either habit or confusion. Thus, the Rabbis created a legal category called *muktzeh*, which forbade on the Sabbath virtually all contact with objects whose normal use was forbidden on the Sabbath. This new prohibition was intended to prevent individuals from sinning inadvertently on the Sabbath. The second type of legislation, regulations (*taqqanot*), was motivated by socioreligious concerns, such as the proper mourning for the Temple's destruction or the improvement of the lot of socially disadvantaged groups, such as orphans, divorcees, and debtors.

The somewhat anomalous category of custom (*minhagim*) was sometimes considered simply the accepted practice of a particular location and at other times was either implemented or sanctioned by the local Sage(s). In either case, the fact that the custom is recorded in the Talmud grants it a significant measure of authoritativeness.

Nonhalakhic Biblical Exegesis

A very large realm of Rabbinic literature consists of nonlegal interpretations of the Torah's text—the Aggadah. God's revelation was taken to be the ultimate source of truth, and its verses could yield a range of insights as wide as the full spectrum of human experience. The employment of exegesis for homiletic ends is integrated within the talmudic text side-by-side with the legal sections, giving the reader the *impression* that for the Sages, there was little difference between the two enterprises, at least in terms of their methodology.[9] For centuries, traditional scholars have debated the authority of these utterances, with views ranging from mere allegory to a strict literalism. In any event, their content meant that they had relatively little impact on the development of Jewish law, which relied almost exclusively on halakhic statements. But the aggadic interpretations continue to hold a prominent position in Jewish religious life and consciousness.

Rabbinic Advice on Nonlegal Matters

Closely connected with the last category is the vast number of Rabbinic statements that are not strictly legal or linked to any biblical text. They range from suggestions on how to act in a variety of social settings[10] to home remedies for an assortment of ailments.[11] There are also Rabbinic accounts of historical events, many of which are employed for homiletical purposes or other, nonhistoriographical ends. Since the time of the Talmud, the authoritativeness of the Sages in these *nonhalakhic* realms has been hotly debated.[12]

This brief inventory of Rabbinic statements underscores the inherent difficulty of understanding Rabbinic authority. If the Sages' activity is characterized by such variety, we would hardly expect explanations of their authority to be either simplistic or unsophisticated. While the mind, understandably, sometimes yearns for the straightforward and simple argument, most issues involving human beings are too complex to be packaged in neat theories.

The Relationship of Divine Revelation and Rabbinic Activity

The catalog above clearly portrays the rich diversity of the Sages' enterprise, collectively known as the Oral Law. Nevertheless, the Sages were deeply aware that their project was distinct from the Written Law, believed to be revealed in its entirety to Moses at Sinai.[13] This deceptively simple distinction worked well when applied to Rabbinic legislation, but what was one to do with some of the other categories, such as biblical exegesis? On the one hand, the Rabbinic inference derives from a verse, thus placing it within the realm of Written Law. On the other hand, it was the Sages who drew out this derivation, going far beyond (in some cases, against) the simple meaning of the verse. These opinions therefore should be classed more suitably within the realm of Oral Law, based as they are on Rabbinic authority.

A variety of theoretical models exist which explicate the precise relationship of the expansive Oral Law, expressed by the Sages, and the original divine revelation at Sinai. As stated earlier, these two domains exist in a rather strict inverse relationship: the larger the domain accorded to one, the smaller the domain of the other. And for the purposes of our study, the greater the initiative displayed by the Rabbis, the more fundamental and far-reaching the theory of their authority must be.[14]

Before laying out these models, it should be clear that, for the sake of exploring Rabbinic authority, this book assumes that a law derived from a divine source demands obedience. Rabbinic authority, not divine authority, is under examination. While independent arguments must be advanced to justify obedience to divine command, the focus of this book is more narrow and assumes that within Judaism, divine origin entails adherence.

There are many ways to view the complex relationship between divine and Rabbinic domains in the area of exegesis. I will plot them along a spectrum of sorts, from a minimalist notion to a maximalist notion of revelation. Schematic sketches will be used to show graphically how the Rabbinic project relates to the original revelation.

Minimalist Notions of Revelation

Rabbinic exegesis, as noted, employs a wide array of hermeneutical strategies to make a finite revealed text yield a virtually infinite number of laws. In theory, these hermeneutical "tools" could produce a wide variety of results (as evidenced by the Rabbinic literature itself),[15] but only the legal rules and principles deduced by the Sages—and more specifically, those which emerge victorious from the talmudic debate—have a normative character. There are several theoretical possibilities regarding the status of these hermeneutical principles, which in turn determine the status of the resultant laws and the nature of the Sages' role.[16]

The Minimalist Position   Only the Written Torah, as we have it, and some elements of the oral tradition were divinely revealed at Sinai. The hermeneutical principles by which other laws are derived from the Torah are either logical or are simply the accepted (contemporary) tools of the trade of the Rabbinic academies and could, in theory, have been different. The resultant laws, the product of applying these exegetical techniques to the Torah, would then all be candidates for acceptance, and the Rabbis, using some agreed-upon procedure, would have to choose one as normative. Those laws which have no basis whatsoever, exegetically or otherwise, within the Torah, are part of the Oral Law revealed to Moses and faithfully transmitted over the generations until their codification in Rabbinic literature.

According to this model, the Sages' role includes determining the proper hermeneutical rules; applying the hermeneutical rules to the Torah to yield legal inferences; choosing which derived law will be normative when applying hermeneutical rules yields several inferences; and transmitting the Oral Law accurately. As can be seen, the role of the Sages is quite extensive in this view of revelation, and the term "Oral Torah" actually encompasses divinely revealed as well as Rabbinically inferred laws.

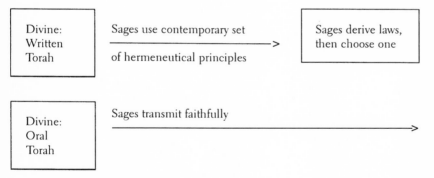

Intermediate Position 1   Not only was the Written Torah given to Moses but so were the hermeneutical principles needed to properly derive laws from its verses. However, the actual inferences were not revealed; they are valid simply by being the result of a divinely validated procedure.[17]

As any student of law knows, rules of inference can be applied in a variety of ways, all equally valid. By applying the revealed rules of inference, the Sages would generate one or possibly several legitimate inferences from the revealed Torah. They would then have to choose from among the "candidates" one position that would be taken as normative. There would, once again, be a set of transmitted oral traditions which make no claim to be derived from the Written Torah, but which are nevertheless divinely revealed.

| Divine:
Written Torah AND
hermeneutical principles | Sages apply revealed
——————————————>
hermeneutical principles | Sages derive laws,
then choose one |

| Divine:
Oral Torah | Sages transmit faithfully
————————————————————————————————————> |

Inclusion of the hermeneutical principles in the body of the revealed tradition prima facie elevates the status of the resultant laws, possibly to the level of "implicit divine law." However, since the application of the hermeneutical principles is a human enterprise, evidenced by the diversity of Rabbinic opinions, the legal positions inferred from the text still partake of human involvement, requiring some ground for Rabbinic authority.

In this configuration of the revelation, then, the Sages' role would include applying the revealed hermeneutical rules to the Torah to yield legal inferences; choosing which derived law will be normative; and transmitting the Oral Law accurately.

Intermediate Position 2   The hermeneutical principles *as well as their locus of application* were revealed at Sinai. For instance, God revealed that an analogy is to be made between two sets of laws, based on a linking word. However, the extent and scope of the analogy — are the two to be compared in all respects? in both directions? — are subject to Rabbinic refinement, thus leaving open the possibility of debate. Of course, once again, only one position must, in each case, be chosen to be the law.

| Divine:
Written Torah,
hermeneutic principles,
and where to
apply them | Sages apply revealed
——————————————>
hermeneutical principles | Sages derive laws,
then choose one |

| Divine:
Oral Torah | Sages transmit faithfully
————————————————————————————————————> |

By "adding" the ingredient of a divinely revealed locus of application, the resultant law gains in its level of divine authority. The role of the interpreting Rabbis is becoming increasingly that of a very skilled "technician." Presumably, knowing where to apply a revealed hermeneutical technique would reduce the likelihood of debate regarding the resultant law. However, clear evidence of this is presently unavailable in Rabbinic literature.[18]

According to this model, the Sages' role includes applying the revealed hermeneutical rules at the predetermined loci in the text, yielding legal inferences; choosing which derived law will be normative; and transmitting the Oral Law accurately.

Maximalist Notions of Revelation

Maximalist Position 1   In an extension of the previous model, both the hermeneutical principles and their correct application *in every respect* were given as part of the revelation at Sinai.

```
┌──────────────────────────────────────┐
│ Divine:                              │      Sages transmit faithfully
│ Written Torah, hermeneutic principles,│      ────────────────────────────
│ and their correct application;        │                              >
│ Oral Torah                            │
└──────────────────────────────────────┘
```

Obviously, as the domain of the divine revelation expands, the Rabbinic role shrinks proportionally. At this point on the spectrum, the role of the Sages is strictly one of transmission. Given this passive role, two things require explanation: the pervasiveness of debate in Rabbinic literature and the need of revealing the hermeneutical principles if the laws which flow out from them are themselves revealed and preordained.

Maximalist Position 2   A slightly more refined model of the maximalist version, intended, in part, to answer some of the objections to the prior model, is one where the Oral Torah, also revealed at Sinai, consisted of a large body of laws not contained in the Written Torah. The Rabbinic project then was not only to transmit this extensive set of laws but to find linkages (*asmakhtot*) to the Pentateuch, in essence integrating the "two Torahs." This is the function of the hermeneutical principles: not to derive new law but to determine the textual basis of an existing, orally transmitted law.

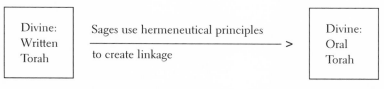

Several motives for finding such linkage may exist. One may be part of an effort to verify an opinion. If there had been an error in transmission, and several opinions (all but one mistaken) had now been orally transmitted, then hermeneutic arguments could be used to help arbitrate the dispute: the law more thoroughly grounded in the Written Torah must be the more authentic. To be sure, the legal ground of all law—written and oral—is its divine origin; the connection to the Written Torah is merely a means of deciding which position is genuine.

This explanation, however, obtains only when there is more than one opinion on a particular issue. In Rabbinic literature, we frequently find that uncontested views are exegetically supported as well. This may have been done simply as a mnemonic device, to assist people in remembering the various laws making up the Oral Torah. There may be yet another, more significant, motive in this process of linkage: with both Torahs deriving from the same divine source, the Sages sought to integrate the two for no other reason than to give substance to the claim that they were both given at Sinai (or were of equally divine origin). Particularly in cases where the oral tradition was contrary to the literal meaning of the text, the Rabbis used these hermeneutical devices to resolve the inconsistencies, principally by showing how the Written Torah does not always mean what it says but speaks through the somewhat elliptical language of exegesis. Thus, the project of linkage has its own rewards, aside from any practical or adjudicatory function.

According to this model, the Sages' role is primarily to transmit all the elements of the Oral Law; and find, wherever possible, a connection to the Written Law. The range of possibilities raised by the other views regarding the origin of the hermeneutical techniques applies mutatis mutandis to the maximalist version as well.

Rabbinic Legislation

What has been left out from all these models is the realm of Rabbinic legislation (the gezeirot and taqqanot) mentioned earlier. By their very definition, these enactments should be understood as the Sages' innovation and thus are not directly subsumed under this category of Oral Law understood as transmission. Nevertheless, for those models that sought to reduce the Rabbinic project *entirely* to one of transmission, these legislative enactments had to be recast either as an esoteric tradition that had been disclosed to Moses and faithfully passed down throughout the generations or as a sort of contingency that was revealed to Moses but that became relevant only later, such as when an event occurred or a situation arose. Thus, the holiday of Hanukkah, instituted at some point after the Maccabean victory over the Seleucid Greeks and the rededication of the Temple in the second century B.C.E., was in reality part of the original Sinaitic revelation, which called for the creation of a holiday if such events ever transpired.[19] Of course, there can be no verification of this; if the Sages instituted a law, then according to the more maximalist understandings, we must view their legislation as the disclosure or application of a prior revealed "contingency." The important point for us is that the question of whether the Rabbinic role was one of transmission or creation is not inherently limited to cases of exegesis but may be extended even to cases of Rabbinic legislation.

Thus, the question of Rabbinic authority, certainly in the realm of legal exegesis but perhaps even in legislation, depends in large measure on the function one sees the Sages fulfilling. If their role is primarily to *transmit* a fully formed Oral Law, then certain sorts of appeals to authority are more appropriate; if the Sages are more involved in *creating* that law, then other models of authority are perhaps more suitable. I am not suggesting that one view of Rabbinic activity is more correct, nor am I favoring a particular theory justifying their authority. The purpose of this chapter is simply to show that the Sages were engaged in a variety of interpretive and legislative projects and that even their exegetical role is subject to various conceptual formulations, depending on one's view of the extent of the original divine revelation.

With such a complex issue as our subject, we can only anticipate, at this point in our inquiry, the corresponding complexity of the notion of Rabbinic authority.

PART I

INSTITUTIONAL AUTHORITY OF
THE TALMUDIC SAGES

Three aspects of our subject incline us toward an institutional model of Rabbinic authority: the nature of the authority itself, the types of Rabbinic activity, and the fact that this notion is limited to the scholars of a specific period.

First, the Sages' understanding of Jewish law has been normative for the traditional community for over fifteen hundred years. For centuries, scholars and laymen alike have closely analyzed their pronouncements, examining every word recorded in their name. No decision is ever rendered without some reference to their opinions and deliberations; certainly no traditional scholar ever openly challenged their positions on his personal authority alone. This sort of enduring authority over traditional Jewish society, broadly construed, is more characteristic of institutions: decisions of a court are binding within a system until they are overturned, and a law that is officially "on the books" is valid law until a duly constituted legislature repeals it. Given the authoritativeness of Rabbinic law for almost two millennia, an institutional model suggests itself more readily when attempting to understand that authority.

Second, the Sages fulfill primarily two functions: interpretive and legislative. Their decision making regarding Jewish law and textual exegesis is more aptly characterized as a judicial function, whereas their enactments and ordinances, which are similarly authoritative, are correctly described as expressions of a legislative role. Within human society, these functions are generally performed by those working within some institutional framework. This is not to deny that individuals can act in these capacities outside an institutional context; history is full of such examples, and the history of religion is certainly no exception. Nevertheless, these functions lend themselves more readily to institutional models of justification. Talmudic references to "taking a vote and deciding,"[1] Rabbinic rulings in the contexts of judicial proceedings,[2] and the preference for the opinion of the many against that of the individual,[3] all combine to make a prima facie case for characterizing Rabbinic authority as institutional.

Last, the period of the Sages is seen by tradition as spanning roughly five centuries, from one or two generations before the Destruction of the Temple in 70 C.E. to the death of Ravina and Rav Ashi about 500 C.E. Since our subject is relegated to a specific time period, we are inclined to understand it in institutional terms, for institutions have *histories*: they begin and end.

Personal authority, in contrast, can emerge at virtually any time, whenever an individual exhibits those characteristics. That certain legal options are foreclosed if they are not endorsed by the Sages attests to the enduring authority of the talmudic Rabbis and to the final closure that can no longer be overcome. Thus, portraying the Sages as possessing some form of institutional authority is rather logical.

We will therefore begin our analysis of the Sages' authority by examining several models of institutional authority in Judaism. Because the Torah is the foundational document of Judaism, taken by traditionalists to be the literal record of God's revelation, it was naturally seen as the proper ground for all subsequent institutions. Indeed, if God is the ultimate authority in Judaism, then all temporal forms of authority should ideally derive their legitimacy by some appeal to divine authorization. In the time of the Bible, certain judges were divinely chosen, and prophets at God's bidding, were anointed kings. The Sages' authority to legislate and interpret God's law should logically be connected with some form of divine authorization. Chapter 2 will examine the notion that a Torah commandment in Deuteronomy compelling obedience in matters of law to "the contemporary authority" refers to the talmudic Sages; since they filled that function during their time, the Torah demands obedience to them.

According to the accepted history of the late Second Temple period, the Sanhedrin, as the High Court in Jerusalem was known, apparently served as the supreme judicial and legislative authority in Judaism. Indeed, the Sages saw this venerable institution as existing already from the earliest phases of Jewish history, having been created during the Israelites wandering through the Wilderness of Sinai after they left Egypt. Nevertheless, the clearest profile of this body comes from Rabbinic literature. Several passages in the Talmud suggest that even after the Temple's destruction in 70 C.E., the Sanhedrin continued to function and that its members were none other than the Sages. In chapter 3, we will therefore examine the model that the Rabbis of the talmudic period constituted a formal Sanhedrin which possessed the judicial and legislative authority associated with that body.

According to tradition, the members of the Sanhedrin had to be ordained, a status conferred on a particular Sage by his teacher. This chain of ordination (*semikhah*) was seen as going directly back to Moses, who ordained Joshua as the next leader of the Jewish people and the next link in the oral tradition.[4] Therefore, chapter 4 will inspect an alternative model of authority which is located less in the strict framework of the Sanhedrin as an institution and more in the personal authorization that ordination confers. This will serve as a convenient transition from the institutional model to the personal one, for although ordination grants a certain authoritativeness to a *person*, the status is technically conferred by a framework external to the individual. Those without it, even if objectively quite erudite, are simply not authorized in the same way as the ordained scholar.

The amenability of this approach should not mask certain difficulties. An institutional conception of Rabbinic authority implies that institutionality itself validates the various acts and rulings of the body. In a constitutional form of government, the decisions of the supreme judicial body are, *by definition*, legal and constitutional; for example, the U.S. Constitution authorizes the Supreme Court to decide how the law should be interpreted. Nevertheless, an entire tractate of the Talmuds, Horayot, is devoted to the *errors* a Sanhedrin may commit in their juridical decisions, particularly those affecting the entire Jewish nation. This seemingly anomalous phenomenon of a supreme judicial body committing an error will be dealt with in the concluding section of part I.

TWO

---

*"The Judge in Charge
at the Time"*

Rabbinic Authority as Divine Command

The Torah, viewed by the tradition as the unadulterated revelation of God, is the most appropriate place to begin our inquiry. If the Sages' authority can be portrayed as an instance of divinely sanctioned authority, then our subject is in fact a secondary one, relying on the fundamental axiom of divine authority. The weight of our analysis will rest solely on showing that it was indeed the talmudic Sages who were so authorized to interpret and legislate for all time.

Given that no legal system can encompass every situation that might arise, it necessarily must provide for the means to resolve untreated cases. The Torah is no different, and the famed passages dealing with this anticipation of future legal uncertainty are found in Deut. 17:8–13.

Background

The Pentateuch contains hundreds of instances where God tells human beings what he expects of them. In Genesis God communicates his instructions to people directly through speech,[1] vision,[2] and dreams,[3] but beginning with the Book of Exodus, disclosure is almost exclusively through the agency of a prophet, in this case Moses. After choosing the Children of Israel to be his "kingdom of priests" (Ex. 19:6), God reveals an extremely vast array of laws to Moses (Ex. 20–23). These commandments deal both with interpersonal situations, such as torts and criminal law, and with what we might artificially call today "religious law," such as holiday ritual and Temple sacrifices.[4] Many other laws are subsequently revealed at Mount Sinai, whether on the mountain or in the Tent of Communion ('Ohel Mo'ed), but some are revealed later, as the Israelites travel through the wilderness for forty years. On several occasions, situations arise which do not fall under any existing law, so Moses faithfully turns to the divine Lawgiver himself for guidance.[5]

However, as Moses' death draws near, the aging leader expresses anxiety about how, and by whom, the people will be led after his portended passing. Moses is no ordinary leader; he is at once the people's military and political leader, God's prophet, and the head of the judicial system which governs the people. In fact, these many roles will no longer be found in one person. Joshua is to take the political and military reins,[6] while divine counsel will be available to him through the "Urim" of High Priest Elazar, who succeeded his father, Aaron. In addition, Moses promises the people that other prophets will arise in the nation to inform them of God's will,[7] although they need to be wary of false prophets.[8] As for the day-to-day management of the people and the adjudication of their disputes, presumably the seventy elders appointed in Numbers 11 to assist him administratively would continue in their duties, as would the judicial hierarchy proposed by Jethro and implemented by Moses in Exodus 18. However, the top position in this judicial hierarchy held by Moses ("the difficult matter they would bring to Moses")[9] would be left vacant after his death. In Deut. 17:8–13, Moses designates a formal institution specifically for filling this vacuum:

> 8If a case is too baffling for you to decide, be it a controversy over homicide, civil law, or assault—matters of dispute in your courts—you shall promptly repair to the place that the Lord your God will have chosen, 9and appear before the levitical priests, or the judge in charge at the time, and present your problem. When they have announced to you the verdict in the case, 10you shall carry out the verdict that is announced to you from that place that the Lord chose, observing scrupulously all their instructions to you. 11You shall act in accordance with the instructions given you and the ruling handed down to you; you must not deviate from the verdict that they announce to you either to the right or to the left. 12Should a man act presumptuously and disregard the priest charged with serving there before the Lord your God, or the judge, that man shall die. Thus you will sweep out evil from Israel: 13all the people will hear and be afraid and will not act presumptuously again.[10]

The Torah makes clear that the ruling handed down by the priest or judge is to be unswervingly obeyed; the full weight of the law descends upon one who is defiant. Moses, as a prophet able to speak to God directly, spoke with divine authority; the judge's decisions, in a parallel fashion, are backed by a Torah commandment for Jews to obey them.

These verses then provide a prima facie case for the Sages' authority: the Sages function in the capacity of a supreme court that is divinely authorized to explain all ambiguous points of Jewish law.[11] Jews must obey their decisions because *God commands them*.[12]

The burden of our analysis is to show that the verses indeed apply to the talmudic Sages of the first five centuries, such that their interpretation of Jewish law is normative *for all time*, not just for those who lived then. Can these verses sustain an *ongoing* commandment to heed the rulings of ancient scholars?

On a fundamental level, we must first determine whether the passage can genuinely be applied to the Sages. Do the talmudic Rabbis fit any definition of "judge"? And if so, do the verses authorize them to function (or Jews to obey them) in the various realms of Rabbinic activity we reviewed in chapter 1?

Applicability of Deuteronomy 17:9 to the Talmudic Sages

Jurisdiction

At first glance, the Torah limits the jurisdiction of the High Court to civil and criminal law cases which were "too baffling." If a lower court which was at a loss to resolve a case based on existing interpretations or principles of the law, the matter made its way to the High Court.[13] This function should not be confused with the appellate role of the Supreme Court of the United States, to which an appeal is made to *challenge* a lower court's ruling; in the Jewish case, it is the *absence* of a lower court's ruling that allows a case to reach the High Court. (Like the Supreme Court, the Jerusalem High Court also had initial jurisdiction over a limited number of cases.)[14]

This relatively limited notion of jurisdiction seems unable to encompass most of Rabbinic law for several reasons. First, given the vast number of laws covered in Rabbinic literature, it is highly unlikely that each law actually came before the High Court. Much of the law seems to be treated theoretically, without reference to actual cases. Second, Deut. 17:8 refers to civil and criminal law; while this is certainly a significant portion of Rabbinic law, the Sages' rulings extend far beyond that, to the realm of ritual law, matrimonial law, etc. To be sure, some laws, such as marriage and divorce laws, can be seen as civil matters in that they often involve property or assets. Nevertheless, a considerable amount of Rabbinic law defies being classified as dealing with "controversy over homicide, civil law, or assault."

It is possible to see the broad range of Rabbinic activity included in this verse if we shift our focus to other parts of verse 8: "*If a case is too baffling for you to decide,* be it a controversy over homicide, civil law, or assault—*matters of dispute in your courts* . . ." Both the italicized phrases can be interpreted strictly or loosely: "a case . . . too baffling for you to decide" may be an actual case which has confounded the lower courts, or it may refer more broadly to any aspect of the law which requires explication. "Matters of dispute in your courts" may narrowly mean a real lawsuit between two litigants or to any disagreement among religious scholars regarding interpretation of the law. In other words, since from a Jewish perspective, all laws—whether civil, criminal, or ceremonial—are expressions of God's will, then the court could deal with *every* legal matter that might be confusing, not just civil or criminal cases. (This interpretation is admittedly dependent on understanding the subsequent clause, "be it a controversy over homicide, civil law, or assault," not as delimiting the prior domain but merely offering some examples.)

Moreover, in the American legal system, higher courts (usually at the state level) not only deal with real-life cases which may arise to "test" the constitutionality or interpretation of a law but also take up theoretical issues and resolve them *before they come in front of the court* so as to preempt any misunderstanding or misapplication of the law. The Sages' discussions did not necessarily have to be practical or in response to an actual state of affairs; any ambiguity or dispute in the academies may have been sufficient warrant, even within the parameters of the biblical verse, to explicate or resolve the matter immediately.[15] This determination of the law *before* confusion arises is particularly urgent in Judaism, where law is seen as an expression of the divine will; for every law, there is presumably always a right way and wrong way to fulfill it.[16]

Therefore, Rabbinic activity, *at least as regards explication of divine law*, can be construed as falling under the rubric of this verse. Decrees and ordinances (*gezeirot ve-taqqanot*), which are legislative in character (see chapter 1), seem to fit less comfortably within this particular model.

However, it is once again more prudent to distinguish between the various types of rabbinic legislation before admitting that this entire domain sits outside the present schema. We recall that the original context of the passage in Deuteronomy was the civil and criminal lawsuits between individuals, including "matters of dispute," that is, legal tensions that may exist between people (although we broadened it to any matter of dispute, even between legal scholars in the schools). Parallel to our understanding of the possibility of "anticipatory exegesis" within the domain of decision making, the role of social legislator may also be accommodated by broadening the notion of treating tensions between individuals within society. The court may choose to be reactive, redressing each wrong once it is committed, or it may prefer to deal with the societal problem in general by trying to prevent the commission of such crimes in the future.[17]

For instance, commercial transactions are without doubt within the scope of the High Court's jurisdiction. Let us say a person buys a certain amount of grain and pays the vendor, but expects to pick it up the next day when his wagon will be available. That night, however, a fire breaks out in the vendor's warehouse, and the grain is consumed. The buyer claims that he is still owed his merchandise, but the vendor claims that since the grain was paid for already, it was the *buyer's* grain that was destroyed, and he therefore owes nothing. To prevent this sort of disagreement arising every time this situation occurs, the Court rules *pre-emptively* that a transaction is completed when the transfer of goods is completed, and not simply when the money is paid. This may not be a formal "decision" in the juridic sense, nor does it necessarily arise as the explication of a verse. But it does notify the public what the Court's view of a legal transaction is and the implications that follow from that.[18] Other examples can be found in the realms of family law (marriage and divorce), inheritance, and others.[19]

However, when we cross into the world of religious ritual, it is difficult to conceive the Sages' decrees and ordinances (*gezeirot* and *taqqanot*) as falling within the Court's jurisdiction. Decrees intended to prevent more serious religious infractions and ordinances which promote certain religious values (such as remembering the destroyed Temple) are plainly pure legislative acts.[20] Areas of genuine Rabbinic innovation, such as the post-Pentateuchal holidays of Purim and Ḥanukkah, or the entire realm of prayer, cannot properly be understood as *judicial* activity, however broadly construed.[21]

The Sages as "the Judge"

Of greater concern to us is the identification of the Sages with the term "the judge" (*ha-shofet*) in the passage. It is, on all accounts, an ambiguous term: it may refer to a single judge, a group of judges, or a judicial institution. What is logically unavoidable is that the Sages themselves *cannot* be authorized to interpret this word, for it is that very authorization which we are seeking. For the Sages to claim that the passage refers to them is both circular and self-serving.

Of course, when dealing with an element of the oral tradition, we must be cognizant of the distinction raised in the previous chapter: whether the Oral Law is something the Sages inferred from the Torah, or whether it had its origins at Sinai and was merely transmitted loyally from teacher to teacher down through the ages. It is certainly possible that the details of this passage were told to Moses and handed down as part of the Oral Law, which the Sages faithfully conveyed generation to generation, until it was written down during talmudic times. What would emerge from this approach would be that the Sages transmitted the referent of "the judge" intact from Moses, and this oral tradition in turn authorized the Sages to interpret all *other* passages in the Torah. This model avoids the logical flaws of the simpler version by locating the source of Rabbinic authority outside the realm of Rabbinic interpretation, but at the cost of shifting the weight of the argument to a faith-claim. We must *believe* that this detail of the Oral Law was passed down intact from Moses to subsequent generations and suffered no alteration at the hands of those who stood most to gain from it. Normative legal interpretation requires *authorization*, but proper transmission is, at bottom, a matter of *trust*.[22]

Believing that the Sages have faithfully preserved the Oral Law is insufficient as a ground for their own authority. Logically speaking, justifying their authority requires a theory that excludes them entirely from any of the critical premises of the argument. It is circular to claim that we must obey the Rabbis in their transmission of the Oral Law because it is divinely ordained and at the same time to admit that it is they who claim that this is what the Oral Law says. It would be similar if our inquiry concerned the grounds for obeying God's Torah and we used the Torah as proof of the divinity of the text.

The divine command theory of rabbinic authority thus seems to be caught on the horns of a dilemma. To be of divine origin, a commandment must be either explicit or interpreted. If it is explicit but unwritten, then it must be transmitted orally. If it is implicit and needs to be interpreted, then someone must do the interpreting. If the Rabbis are the transmitters, then the transmitting Sages inform us that the passage authorizes them, and the argument is circular. If the Rabbis are the interpreters, then the interpreting Rabbis reveal to us that they are divinely sanctioned to interpret, and the question begs who authorized them to interpret. Only an explicit, written statement by the divinity would seem to break the circularity and allow a valid justification of Rabbinic authority based on divine command to stand.[23]

If we must search for a model that leaves out the Sages entirely, then the passage itself is our only recourse. The expression in the Torah "the judge in charge at the time" is indeterminate; as we noted earlier, no specification is offered as regards number, qualifications, and so on. Now it is true that in a revelational context, ambiguity is prima facie regrettable, for contrary to human law, "original intent" is essential. God's will, as expressed through the inherently limited vehicle of language, is specific; if we perform what *we* take to be the meaning of the passage, it is possible that the divine will has not been fulfilled for God meant something else.[24]

However, this is problematic only if we assume that there is but *one way* for God's intention, as expressed in the passage, to be satisfied. It is entirely possible that the indeterminacy is built into the very essence of the commandment. In our case, the phrase "in charge at the time" is not a temporal modifier of little consequence; to the contrary, it is the very source of the judge's authority. Earlier in Deuteronomy, (16:18) the Torah required the Israelites to set up "judges and police" (*shofetim ve-shoterim*) in every city to administer justice locally. Once again, no clear criteria or specifications were set forth; the Torah required only that a juridical system be set up immediately upon entering the land. The person or persons deemed to be *the* judge of the country in that generation are thus authorized by our passage. Indeterminacy is not a flaw but a deliberate aspect of the law: God wanted only that there be a final arbiter of the law, but the makeup of that ultimate authority was not crucial.[25]

Of course, some quality control was required. The word I translated as "judge" (*shofet*) is an office that demands, at least ideally, certain qualifications: "capable men who fear God, trustworthy men who spurn ill-gotten gain" (Ex. 18:21); "men who are wise, discerning, and experienced." (Deut. 1:13). And certainly, aside from personal qualities, a judge must be guided by God's law in his deliberations.

Moreover, the notion of "in charge at the time" invites reflection on the source of the judge's authority. As it is written, it seems that the de facto judge is, by definition, the de jure judge; if he or they are in charge, then the Torah authorizes their decisions as final and binding. Assuming that some measure of quality is maintained, the one who in fact is seen by the Jews as their final judge in matters of law is the duly authorized judge. "Jephtah in his generation is as Samuel in his generation" goes the oft-cited Rabbinic adage.[26] Every generation has at its head the best that it can produce, even if that leader, compared to others from different times, is vastly inferior. The centuries covered by the biblical books of Judges and Samuel testify to the range of talent which, in all instances, "judged Israel." If the people recognized that person—king, priest, prophet, or court[27]—as its judge, then his pronouncements were authoritative based on this verse.[28]

This presentation should not be taken as a license for every generation to cast out the institutions of its predecessors and establish its own from scratch.[29] In any society, authority structures tend to become integrated into the fabric of life, evolving into features of the social and political landscape in a way that grants them a measure of longevity. This is not to say that they are immune to any change; precisely because they are interwoven with other aspects of society, they will be affected by significant social and political forces. Nevertheless, these institutions tend to be stable and constant within most cultures, evolving slowly over time and only occasionally undergoing radical revision.

On this indeterminate reading of the verse, then, we can claim that the talmudic Sages constituted "the judge in charge at the time," and therefore their pronouncements on the wide range of Jewish law were authoritative. Obeying them could be an instance of the divine commandment to heed the words of the contemporary judge.

Implications of an Interpretation of Indeterminacy

However, although we have gained in offering a model of the Sages' authority grounded in God's commandment, we have sacrificed a more crucial element of our claim: the *ongoing* authoritativeness of the Sages. If the talmudic Rabbis were "the judge" for their *contemporary* generations, then they could not be for *subsequent* generations. During the Middle Ages, another "*shofet* in charge at the time," whether a local town rabbi, a world-renowned scholar, or a chief rabbi appointed by the secular authorities, would presumably be backed by the Torah.[30] The Sages may be divinely authorized, but that authorization is limited to their own time period: to those Jews who lived during the first five centuries of the common era. In what way could the Sages retain authority for ensuing generations while remaining under the rubric of the Torah's commandment?

At first glance, they cannot, for the expression "at the time" which formed the basis of our theory of authorizing the talmudic Sages inherently limits that authority to their own time period. It would seem that any effort to establish ongoing authority will have to search in other quarters for a satisfactory answer.

Nevertheless, let us examine more closely the claim that the Sages were authoritative for their own period. Given that we are referring to a period of five centuries, what could this mean? In what way was Rabbi Meir—a second-century scholar in the Land of Israel and clearly a "Sage" in the technical sense—authoritative for Babylonian Jews in the fifth century? Or let us take the example of Rav (Rabbi Abba), who came to Sura from Palestine and established a major academy there in the third century. In what way can we see him as authoritative for his own community in Sura two or three hundred years *later*? The truth is, these Sages were not authoritative in the sense that their literal pronouncements continued to be deemed law by all Jews. Rather, the legal community, which *was* authoritative for its contemporaries, continued to study these scholars' statements, analyzing them, sharpening them, and applying them to new situations. This is what is meant by being in a legal tradition; one studies the legal views and opinions of prior scholars and advances that study by expounding and clarifying those views, fleshing them out so that the underlying principles are clear and can be used in other situations. Legal systems are not invented anew every generation but "accrue" over time; like cities, they contain older sections and newer ones, revitalized sections and some neglected ones. This is what a living tradition in *any* field is like, and law—even religious law—is no exception.

Asking what Rabbi Meir's or Rav's authority was for later generations yields a more profound understanding of authority: not necessarily a strict adherence to a particular set of pronouncements but a community that consults, examines, and fine-tunes a set of inherited traditions so that they continue to be applicable to the present generation. Thus, for example, the medieval scholars were indeed "the judge in charge at the time" for the communities of Spain, Provence, Franco-Germany, and Egypt.[31] But because they would never render a decision without consulting the vast legacy of the Sages, because they analyzed every subject using talmudic concepts and cases, and because their scholarly pursuits centered on the continued elaboration of the Sages' views, the talmudic Rabbis retained an authoritativeness for the Jewish community that is still intact today for traditional Jews.

As authoritative as the Sages are, however, it would be hard to apply our verse to them; they are simply no longer "in charge at the time." Rather, their authority is derivative and contingent: it is derivative because the Sages' interpretations are not *directly* authoritative for the average Jew but are mediated through the authority of the contemporary rabbi, scholar, or even legal code, who *are* authorized by the verse as the contemporary judge(s). Moreover, our analysis suggests that this authority is largely contingent, for subsequent scholars' dependence on the Sages and refusal to discuss issues independently of the Talmud seem to be primarily an academic convention rather than a well-grounded or justified practice. In other words, we could imagine a community of contemporary scholars who chose to deviate from some Rabbinic pronouncements (a total or even major departure might destroy any resemblance to the older tradition) but who would nevertheless be authoritative for the community as "the judge in charge at the time" if the people deemed them their judges. If we insist on the indeterminate approach to the verse in Deuteronomy, then we must conclude that the Sages' authority was indeed grounded in this verse during their own lifetimes. But subsequently, as the mantle of judicial leadership passed from the Sages to their medieval heirs, these medieval scholars derived their own authority from the Torah. The Sages' authoritativeness evolved into one of a different sort: it became the primary foundation of a living legal tradition. Through this complex combination, the Sages' interpretations and decisions continue to be normative for the traditional Jew. This approach will be examined further in chapter 7.

However, presenting the Sages' authority as mere convention does not accurately capture the role of the talmudic Sages within this legal tradition. While jurists of the eighteenth century are theoretically able to disagree with medieval scholars, both groups are in general restricted from challenging Rabbinic exegeses and pronouncements.[32] Legal opinions, as logical as they may be, have virtually no standing if not grounded or connected in some way to a passage in the Talmud. Again, this may be mere convention, but the deference to the Sages which permeates the Jewish legal community suggests a deeper obligation than just the accepted custom of a particular discipline.

There is certainly more to say about a legal tradition's authority for a particular community. In the case of the Sages, their legal opinions did not remain part of an oral tradition of a small scholarly community but were collected and redacted *into a text*, or more accurately several texts, among them the Mishnah, Tosefta, and the Palestinian and Babylonian Talmuds. The Sages' legacy was thus collectively embodied in documents that bestowed on it a certain canonical status that independent, orally transmitted statements generally do not share. This issue will be discussed in greater depth in chapter 8.

Summary

Grounding the talmudic Sages' authority upon the passage from Deuteronomy regarding judicial authority proved difficult on several fronts. In terms of scope of law, the sorts of cases mentioned in verse 8 were not broad enough to encompass the wide range of Rabbinic activity, even if we allowed anticipatory exegesis and preemptive Rabbinic legislation under those categories. More important was the problem of having the verse refer explicitly to the talmudic Sages without need of their interpretation. This was accomplished by seeing the term "the judge at the time" as deliberately indeterminate, but this in turn similarly authorized the scholars of each generation for their own time period. The Sages' authority would then be mediated through the contemporary religious leaders who might be employing Rabbinic law.

We have explored the possibility of using this passage in Deuteronomy as a ground for Rabbinic authority, but the Talmud itself sees it as referring to the Sanhedrin in Jerusalem, an institution which for part of the Second Temple period was the seat of religious and, at times, political authority for much of world Jewry. Its functions, which ranged from judicial interpretation to social legislation, seem, in many respects, to have been carried out later on by the talmudic Sages. Given this functional equivalence, we will next explore the possibility that the Sages embodied the institutional authority of the Sanhedrin.

THREE

The Sages as
the Sanhedrin

In the last chapter, the ground for the Sages' authority was sought in a divine commandment, namely, the verses in Deuteronomy requiring obedience to the decisions of "the judge in charge at the time." Despite my conclusion that only a very indeterminate reading of the passage could apply to the Sages, Rabbinic literature historically saw this verse as specifically referring to the High Court in Jerusalem, known as the Sanhedrin. In this chapter we will examine the claim that the Sages' authority is, in fact, that of the Sanhedrin. This is a form of ex cathedra authority: the office is authoritative for various reasons, and these persons—the talmudic Sages—occupy that office.

This approach invites an immediate question: what do we hope to gain from this strategy? If the Sanhedrin's authority is, in the end, based on Deut. 17:9, then seeing the Sages as possessing the Sanhedrin's authority does not move us appreciably beyond the conclusions of chapter 2! This would be a legitimate query were the Sanhedrin's functions exhausted by the passage in the Torah. However, a historical sketch of the Sanhedrin shows that it in fact functioned in a wide range of judicial and legislative roles, far beyond the limited scope of Deut. 17:8–13. It is not the aim of this chapter to closely and critically examine whether the Sanhedrin was truly authorized to fulfill all the roles it did. However, since it performed these roles and since the Sages' rulings and enactments were similarly diverse, this model suggests itself as an appropriate one for understanding Rabbinic authority.

A priori, there are two ways to cast this model. One is to say that the talmudic Sages themselves constituted the Sanhedrin of their day: they were its members, they followed its rules and procedures, and they enjoyed the privileges and authority attendant to it. Certain difficulties inhere in this "stricter" version, chief among them the fact that according to most scholars, the formal Sanhedrin in Jerusalem ceased to exist sometime during the Jewish war against Rome (66–70 C.E.), before most of the talmudic Sages flourished. This objection inclines us to inspect a "looser" form of the proposal, where the Sages are seen as the *heirs* to the Sanhedrin or as its *agents*, substituting in some way for that institution and therefore authorized to function in its wide range of roles. Both versions of the model will be inspected in this chapter.

It must be emphasized that this model is not meant to determine the basis of the authority of those traditions which were, indeed, established by the Sanhedrin while it existed. No doubt, a considerable amount of textual interpretation and legal decision making were performed by the Jerusalem High Court, and their results are binding on Jews by virtue of the authorization of the Court. Provided we admit frankly that this involves the added belief that the Sages faithfully transmitted this material, a fair amount of Halakhah is authoritative based on the Sanhedrin's authority, not on that of the talmudic Rabbis. The aim of this chapter is to ground those exegeses and ordinances which *originate* with the postdestruction Sages in a particular conception of their authority as that of the Sanhedrin. Of course, the extent and scope of this domain depend on our discussion in chapter 1; if all laws were revealed, and the Sages merely passed them on, then once again it is not the Sanhedrin's "authority" per se that is the ground of Jewish law but our trust in the Sages as faithful transmitters.

One methodological note is in order before we begin: unlike the last chapter, which was almost entirely theoretical in nature, in this chapter certain historical claims will be made regarding an institution that did, in fact, exist. This implies that while our inquiry is largely philosophical, appeal to historical fact must necessarily inform the discussion, although it will not exhaust it. Establishing the parameters of the Sanhedrin's powers, when it functioned, and so on, are thus important prerequisites to any attempt at characterizing the Sages as either the embodiment or the continuation of the Sanhedrin.

An Overview of the Sanhedrin: History and Functions

Our main sources for the nature and function of the Sanhedrin are the Rabbinic material (which is often difficult to date), the writings of Josephus, the Apocrypha (especially the Books of Maccabees and Judith), and the Christian Bible, especially the Gospels and the Book of Acts. These sources often provide inconsistent, if not contradictory, information, and in all four (but in the Christian case in particular), the details may be part of a narrative written with an intention other than a purely historical one.[1] Thus, a clear image of the historical Sanhedrin is elusive, leaving it the subject of great scholarly debate.[2] For our purposes, though, it is important to focus on the Jewish sources, as their perception of the nature and role of the Sanhedrin will determine whether it is possible to conceive of the Sages as its heirs, if not its actual members.

Even within the Jewish sources, we are faced with a variety of names, such as *beit din ha-gadol* (the Great or High Court), *beit din shel shiv 'im ye'ehad* (the Court of Seventy-one), and Sanhedrin, leaving us to wonder whether the sources are indeed referring to the same institution.[3] Most, although certainly not all,[4] scholars accept the identity of these terms, attributing the shift to the spread of Greek terminology as a result of hellenization[5] or to the social and political vicissitudes the institution underwent over time.[6] It is most likely that only one institution existed during the late Second Temple period.

The name *beit din ha-gadol* suggests that it was primarily the supreme court of the land, serving as the final arbiter in all matters of Jewish law, whether there was doubt or a dispute among scholars.[7] Its decisions were seen to be binding on all Jews, whether in the Land of Israel or in the Diaspora.[8] The court also had initial jurisdiction in cases involving a tribe, the high priest, or a false prophet.[9] Moreover, the Sanhedrin exercised legislative authority, imposing decrees (usually intended for a limited time) or enacting ordinances either as new situations arose or as social and political conditions affected the continued practice of existing laws.

The High Court comprised seventy-one scholars, who were, in the ideal depiction, well versed in the law and in many other disciplines. They were the most talented scholars in Israel, having moved up a specified judicial ladder based exclusively on merit, not seniority (although in most cases, the oldest members were the most learned). Until 70 C.E., when the Temple was destroyed, the Sanhedrin as a body sat in the Lishkat ha-Gazit, or Chamber of Hewn Stone, which was in the northern wall of the Temple precincts. This was in fulfillment of the verse in Deuteronomy that one with a legal puzzlement should "promptly repair to the place that the Lord your God will have chosen" (17:8). The Torah apparently insists on this locale by repeating in verse 10 "And you shall carry out the verdict that is announced to you *from that place that the Lord chose.*" The Sanhedrin thus sat in close proximity to the two other seats of authority: the high priest in the Temple and the king in his palace in the capital.[10]

With the major social and political upheavals brought about by the Great War against Rome in 66–70 C.E., the Jerusalem Sanhedrin was dissolved. Shortly after the Temple's destruction, Rabban Yohanan ben Zakkai organized the surviving scholars into a body which he called the Sanhedrin and which was located in Yavneh (Jamnia).[11] As time went on, and particularly in the days of Rabban Gamliel, the Sanhedrin at Yavneh evolved into the central seat of religious and political authority, initially for Palestinian Jewry and then for world Jewry.[12] This Sanhedrin continued to function with varying degrees of religious and legal authority, depending on the political situation with Rome. At times, such as immediately after the Bar Kokhba Rebellion in the 130s, it was officially banned, although it seems to have continued to operate at a de facto level until official recognition was again granted by the Roman authorities.[13] Throughout this period, it performed several of the roles of the original Jerusalem Sanhedrin, particularly in the realm of explicating Jewish law, and even enacted specific rules and ordinances as the need arose. Its ranks were filled with scholars whose opinions are recorded in Tannaitic literature, culminating in the Mishnah of Judah I, the most significant and influential patriarch of this period.[14]

According to most scholars, the Sanhedrin as an institution ceased to exist around the year 70 C.E.[15] What Rabban Yohanan founded was a body of scholars who performed many of the same functions as the original Sanhedrin but who composed an entirely different institution.[16] Given the Jerusalem Sanhedrin's

physical and theoretical linkage to the predestruction institutions of the priesthood and the Temple, it is reasonable to see the Sanhedrin at Yavneh as at best
a pale imitation of the original;[17] the Rabbis themselves admit that it did not
enjoy all the prerogatives of its predecessor, such as the power to impose capital
sanctions.[18] The mere fact that it was not in Jerusalem, in "the place that the
Lord your God will have chosen," as the Torah prescribed, already compromised
its standing. Therefore, we will begin by inspecting the notion that the Sages
served as substitutes for the Sanhedrin.

The Sages as Substitutes for the Sanhedrin

Presenting the talmudic Sages as standing *in lieu of* the original Sanhedrin seems
to satisfy two desiderata: it supplies prima facie justification for the wide range
of Rabbinic activity, both exegetical and legislative, while at the same time avoid-
ing the pitfalls of any historical claim that the Sages embodied an institution
which many historians claim had ceased to exist by 70 C.E. Yet its practical
attractiveness should not mask some of the difficulties that emerge as soon as we
examine the claim more closely.

What does "substitute" mean? One possible understanding is that through
some formal procedure, one person or entity is *designated* to represent someone
else, to varying degrees. This designation may be done by the represented party
or by a third party;[19] granting power of attorney is the best example in our
contemporary legal lexicon. If for any reason (e.g., health, competence, or simple
inability to be present), a person cannot participate in a certain activity, the
designated substitute acts in the other person's stead. This sort of substitution is
construed as *agency*. When applied to the Sages, the claim would be that the
talmudic Rabbis, both in Palestine and in Babylonia, are the substitutes for the
dissolved Jerusalem Sanhedrin.[20]

How was that substitution effected? Since this model of agency normally
requires some formal designation, we would need either the Sanhedrin itself
actually designating the Sages as its substitutes or a third party performing the
designation. Both are historical claims. As regards the former, we have no record
that the Sanhedrin, in its final days in Jerusalem, ever acted in such a way. It is
conceivable that a third party made the appointment (the Sanhedrin, being de-
funct, was "incapable"), but who would that third party have been? There are
only two possibilities: God, as the authority behind the entire halakhic system;
or the people.

Were God to do it, God could naturally communicate this appointment
through prophecy; Jewish tradition, however, maintains that prophecy ended
during the early days of the Second Temple period, shortly after the Jews returned from Babylonia.[21] In any event, it does seems odd that if God was already
communicating his will to the people, he would designate the Sages as a *substitute* for the Sanhedrin rather than authorizing them directly. It is also possible
that some interpretation of the Torah may provide this designation; however, if
it involved a Rabbinic exegesis, it would be caught in the same circularity we

encountered in the last chapter. If the Sanhedrin, while still extant, interpreted a Pentateuchal verse to apply to the Sages, then such an interpretation would be valid, provided we assume the Sages faithfully transmitted it. Nevertheless, we have no record of such an interpretation.[22]

The other "third party" to whom we might turn is the Jewish people. Recall that in the last chapter, we claimed that the Torah's phrase "in charge at the time" in essence legitimized whichever judge the people accepted at the time. In the same vein, we may claim that the people simply accepted the Sages' interpretations and ordinances in place of the Sanhedrin's pronouncements. This approach suffers from two weaknesses, one historical, one theoretical. While the people's authorization is certainly possible, we must once again assume it, with no evidence that it actually occurred. Moreover, the question raised regarding a divine appointment must be raised here as well: why should the people designate the Sages as the Sanhedrin's replacement when they can accept Rabbinic authority *directly*?[23] We will explore this last possibility in chapter 7. For now, we must admit that while it is conceivable that the people authorized the Sages to act as the Sanhedrin's agents, there seems little logical reason to grant the Sages authority in this indirect way, and even less historical basis for maintaining the claim altogether.

Alternatively, we may assume that substitution is defined functionally rather than formally: whoever or whatever performs the duties of the Sanhedrin is its substitute.[24] The High Court in Jerusalem decided all doubtful matters of Jewish law; the Sages acted in the same capacity. The Jerusalem Sanhedrin enacted certain legislation which applied to all Jews; the same was true of the talmudic Rabbis. Of course, this is merely descriptive: in the absence of a particular institution, a certain group of scholars stepped in and filled the void. However, such an understanding of substitution in no way carries with it the claim that the substitute possesses the same *authority* as the original entity. If *anyone* performing these functions was seen as the Sanhedrin's substitute and viewed as equally authoritative, then the Babylonian Geonim of the early Middle Ages,[25] or even certain internationally acknowledged Torah authorities in the modern period, would be endowed with the Sanhedrin's mantle of authority.

The effort, then, of seeing the talmudic Sages as the original Sanhedrin's substitutes cannot satisfy the relatively strict demands of our inquiry. If the substitution is essentially agency, then we would have to assume that either the Jerusalem Sanhedrin itself or the Jewish people at the time designated the Sages as the Sanhedrin's substitutes. Regrettably, there is no record that either event ever took place. Moreover, claiming the people appointed the Sages to sit in the Sanhedrin's place raises the possibility that the Rabbis' authority rests ab initio on the people's agreement, although seeing them as an ex cathedra authority might prevent a subsequent withdrawal of consent.

The alternative notion of functional substitution turned out to be *too* inclusive, unable to discriminate between the talmudic Sages and later authorities unless some other, external consideration is imported. But we are searching for a self-sufficient model of Rabbinic authority, and this does not satisfy.

Given the inherent difficulties of any broad definition, we must return to the possibility that the talmudic Sages were indeed a *continuation* of the Jerusalem High Court. Although we cannot deny that some historical obstacles exist to this view, we must also admit that the Sages were historically most proximate, indeed contiguous, to the original institution in Jerusalem. We therefore turn to examining the model of the Sages as actually embodying the Sanhedrin and therefore possessing its authority.

The Sages as a Continuation of the Sanhedrin

I have already pointed out that the postdestruction Sanhedrin at Yavneh, by not being in Jerusalem, was already deprived of certain powers, particularly in the realm of capital punishment. Those who ruled contrary to its decisions were not subject to the same disciplinary measures as those who opposed the Jerusalem High Court.[26] How, then, should we view this "displacement"? Is the judge's presence in "the place that the Lord your God will have chosen" a sine qua non of a court's authority, or is it a detail incidental to a court's being the "chief court," which is *functionally* defined? This disjunction is, however, overly simplistic; it suggests that the Sanhedrin is either duly authorized *in every respect* or ceases to be a Sanhedrin. Take, for example, the following Rabbinic exegesis:

> From where do we learn that execution can take place only when the Temple is standing? From the verse: "Even from My altar shall you take him, that he may die" (Ex. 21:14). It follows that if there is an altar you may put [a convicted person] to death; if there is no altar, you may not.[27]

In other words, the ability of the judicature to execute criminals depends on the existence of an altar; without it, the court system is deprived of meting out a certain penalty, but there is no suggestion that the court is therefore illegitimate.

Or take the following example, which broadens the linkage to the Temple to *all* punitive sanctions of the court:

> Scripture says, "You shall come to the levitical priests or to the judge in charge at the time" (Deut. 17:9)—from which I deduce, at a time when there is a [functioning] priesthood, there is judgment (i.e., the power to impose penalties); but when there is no priesthood, there is no judgment.[28]

Imposing sanctions was certainly one function of the High Court, particularly in the cases in which it had initial jurisdiction. However, the very case that is the Torah's context for a High Court—a matter of doubtful or disputed law—does not seem compromised by the absence of a functioning priesthood or an altar. Therefore, it is possible to suggest that the Sanhedrin-qua-court may have been suspended or dissolved with its move to Yavneh after the destruction but that its role as social legislator or interpreter of the law remained intact.

This theoretical attempt to untangle the intertwined functions of the Sanhedrin and treat them separately may have precedent in two biblical episodes which were seen by the Sages as prototypes of the actual Jerusalem Sanhedrin: the appointment of judges in Exodus 18 and the appointment of seventy elders in Numbers 11.

In the first case, after seeing Moses adjudicate all the Israelites' disputes himself, his father-in-law, Jethro, recommends instituting a judicial hierarchy whereby judges presiding over ever larger groups of people should serve as the people's primary judges. If a matter was unclear to a judge at a lower level, he would take it to the judge at the next level, and so on until the matter reached Moses if no one knew precisely how to rule. Moses, of course, was sure to have an answer, either as the lawgiver or as the prophet with direct access to God.[29] It is clear from the Talmud that this judicial system was the forerunner of, if not the first, hierarchy of courts in Israel, parallel to the one the Mishnah describes.[30] Thus, on several occasions, laws relating to the contemporary courts, with respect to either their makeup or their procedures, are derived from the verses related to this episode.[31]

The other episode, more critical to our argument in that it seems to foreshadow the Sanhedrin directly (and not the system of courts generally), is that related in Numbers 11. After the Israelites complain about the manna sent daily from heaven, Moses returns to God with a plea that the burden of the people is too great for him to bear alone, to which God responds by ordering Moses to assemble seventy elders from all the tribes of Israel who will share in the burden of the administration of the people.[32] In a unique event at the Tent of Communion, some of Moses' spirit is bestowed on the seventy and they begin prophesying.[33] Far from functioning in a judicial capacity, these elders were to assist Moses in the leadership of the people, most likely in a sociopolitical capacity. In Rabbinic literature, this body of seventy serves as the prototype of the Sanhedrin and possibly constitutes the first High Court.[34]

Thus, the contemporary Sanhedrin of which the Tannaim spoke, and which is presented, if only exegetically, as the ideal, is an institution that is a combination of both the supreme court of the people (Ex. 18) and a major administrative, legislating body (assisting the king; Num. 11).[35]

What is interesting for our discussion is that the biblical "models" or prototypes of the Sanhedrin were both outside the Land of Israel, and obviously outside Jerusalem. Moreover, Jewish tradition saw the Sanhedrin as an institution with an uninterrupted history since Moses, which meant that until David picked Jerusalem as his capital and the site of the Temple, the Sanhedrin existed outside Jerusalem. While this fact does not rule out a *subsequent* requirement to be in Jerusalem once that city was chosen,[36] it strongly suggests that many of the High Court's functions were not necessarily tied to its presence in Jerusalem. Some of its powers of sanction may indeed have been compromised, but this is not to say that once it left the "chosen place," the Sanhedrin was bereft of much of its authority.[37]

However, while a legitimate Sanhedrin is conceivable outside its ideal home, the question remains how far this notion can be extended. What other requirements may be deemed unessential so that a valid "Sanhedrin" still exists? Take, for instance, the Torah's reference to "levitical priests" (Deut. 17:9). Is the presence of at least one priest and one Levite critical for the validity of the Sanhedrin *as a body*? This question was raised in the Sifre on the very same verse:

> "To the levitical priests" — it is a religious duty [*miṣvah*] that there be priests and levites [in the High Court]. Is it not possible that it is a religious duty, but if there are no [priests and levites, the Court] is invalid? Scripture therefore teaches "or to the judge" — even though there are no priests or levites, it is valid.[38]

The question was resolved in the negative: another apparent stipulation of the verse is rendered nonrequisite, perhaps by insisting that the letter vav at the beginning of the phrase *ve-'el ha-shofet* should be understood in the disjunctive, rather than the conjunctive, sense ("or" rather than "and"), a legitimate interpretation of the Hebrew. Yet how far can we extend a definition of the "Sanhedrin"? If we remove all formal elements — location, membership, number of judges, etc. — then we have reduced the notion of the institution to its mere function, which was, in essence, the argument in the previous chapter: "the judge in charge at the time." It was hoped that this model would depict the Sages as embodying the Sanhedrin in a formal sense so that the institution's powers and authority would automatically extend to them. Once again, we find ourselves on the horns of a dilemma: if the text is interpreted too narrowly (e.g., it must be in Jerusalem), then the talmudic Rabbis are excluded; if it is understood too broadly, then there is no internal mechanism for limiting the Sanhedrin's authority to the Sages; subsequent scholars would possess the same authority as well. Moreover, the Rabbinic exegeses which understood the Torah as including the Sanhedrin at Yavneh in its scope are problematic since it was the Sages themselves who either transmitted that extension or interpreted it from the text, yet it is their very authority that we are trying to ground.

There is, however, an intermediate approach between these two extremes, although it is, admittedly, only partially supported by the text. Up to this point, we have referred to the Sanhedrin as a *body*, a collective entity made up of many scholars; the number seventy found its source in the narrative of Numbers 11. This is not simply a judge or court that happens to be "in charge at the time"; the Sanhedrin drew much of its prestige from being composed of dozens of great scholars, and the authoritativeness (not authority) of its decisions stemmed in no small measure from the fact that those scholars debated and then took a vote. The decisions of a singularly brilliant yet individual judge rarely achieve the same level of credibility in the legal community as do rulings that emerge from scholarly discourse and consensus.[39] Thus, in spite of the singular *shofet* (judge) used in Deut. 17:9, *every verb* in connection with the judges is *plural*, strongly suggesting that the "judge" in the verse is in reality a court made up of several judges.[40] In this sense, the Sanhedrins at Yavneh, Usha, Sepphoris, and other places all shared with the Jerusalem High Court the image of an assembly of Sages whose decisions reflected the scholarly consensus.[41] In that respect, the Sanhedrin really did continue for several generations past the destruction.

It is not hard to imagine why this might be a central requirement of a divinely authorized High Court. A conciliar approach to both legal interpretation and legislation increases the likelihood that the decision will be sound and justified and given the approval of the legal community. Diversity of opinions and interests virtually ensures that ordinances are not rashly adopted and implemented but are cautiously accepted only after being thoroughly examined for their costs and benefits.[42] Debate among the most talented minds in a field is a rich source of both bold creativity and reasoned restraint. The decisions that emerge from this consensus are therefore, in principle, on sound juridical and legislative footing and are rightly deemed authoritative. The High Court is then not a strictly functional organ, which can be constituted by an individual scholar but must be one that is aggregate in nature and reaches decisions collectively.

A second possible requirement of this High Court is the quality of its members.[43] Unquestioned scholarship is, understandably, a criterion for anyone who sits at the top of a field which requires extensive knowledge. But in the Jewish case, we must add that the judges must also be *part of a tradition*; given the dual nature of Jewish law, their knowledge had to encompass both the Written and the Oral Law. We need not enter into the thicket of the precise extent and scope of the Oral Law; the fact that it existed at all required the chief judges of the Land of Israel to also be heirs to an orally transmitted tradition, from whichever school or master. We will explore this facet of being heirs to a tradition in greater depth in the next chapter. For now, as we attempt to ascertain the essential character of the High Court, we may say that the passage in Deuteronomy implies an assembly of erudite scholars well versed in the Written and the Oral Law.[44] The talmudic Sages appear to fulfill these criteria.

Applying this portrayal of the Sanhedrin to the talmudic Sages is limited in several respects. First, it is not clear historically whether the Sages were always constituted collectively, particularly during the period immediately after the Bar Kokhba Rebellion, when Rome strictly forbade any Jewish institutional infrastructure among Palestinian Jewry, and much of the learning and discussion was probably conducted clandestinely and in small groups. Under the Severan Caesars (193–235 C.E.), the position of the Sanhedrin, and that of the Patriarchate in particular, improved dramatically, both in terms of official recognition by Rome and the prestige they enjoyed among the people. As we move more deeply into the third century and the Amoraic period, the picture of the Sanhedrin as a central institution in Jewish life becomes significantly blurred. There is extensive debate among scholars whether bodies under different names (*bet ha-va'ad, metivta, yeshivah*, etc.) were in essence continuations of the main assembly of scholars known in Tannaitic times as the Sanhedrin, or whether these were other, smaller institutions that were more local and did not exercise the same authority as the Sanhedrin had before them. The present scholarly consensus is that the central body ceased to exist in the early–mid third century C.E., and although local academies of scholars sometimes adopted the name, they never exerted the same sort of authority as the original Sanhedrin in the days of the Tannaim.[45]

Second, while the notion of a "consensus" certainly applies to those talmudic laws introduced by the phrase *nimnu ve-gamru*, "they took a vote and decided," the number of such laws found in the Rabbinic corpus is negligible.[46] The only

way to preserve this model is to assume that even though many Tannaitic statements were preserved as the opinion of an individual scholar, they were in fact
brought in front of the entire convention of scholars.[47] Moreover, one must
accept as axiomatic that the view accepted as halakhically normative was voted
on by the assembly and reflected the majority opinion. I am, in no way suggesting
that these are unreasonable or far-fetched assumptions; all I am saying is that to
maintain that the Sages' (or at least the Tannaim's) authority is grounded in
their constituting the contemporary Sanhedrin, one must accept several *additional* assumptions:

> The Sages usually gathered and discussed their opinions on matters of law
>   collectively so that each view received a proper hearing.
> A formal vote was taken to decide which opinion would be normative.
> This normative view is indeed reflected in the Mishnah or later texts.

We are beginning to see that this model, like most others, is not entirely self-
sufficient; it requires other historical or theoretical claims to obtain in order for
this construct to ground the authority of the Sages.

The Babylonian Amoraim and the Sanhedrin

As an institution, the Sanhedrin (for however long it lasted) never existed in the
Diaspora.[48] Babylonian scholars met either in academies or in small circles,[49]
and although individual scholars maintained their own courts, or possibly held
their academies open for judicial purposes, their jurisdiction was generally quite
limited.[50] Of course, one need not posit a continuous Sanhedrin; there may have
been periods in the history of the Babylonian Amoraim when scholars gathered,
possibly in some sort of synod, and voted to adopt the positions of certain scholars
as normative, even though no Sanhedrin sat regularly. Perhaps at the very *end*
of the Amoraic period, as the Talmud began to take form, such conventions
were held to decide the Halakhah from among the range of views expressed by
generations of scholars. To be sure, this portrayal of events is highly speculative,
and no trace of such meetings remains anywhere in Rabbinic literature.
Therefore, to insist on seeing the Babylonian scholars as constituting a Sanhedrin
requires a considerable set of historical assumptions, ranging from the very feas-
ibility of a Sanhedrin outside the Land of Israel to a collective configuration of
Sages in some institutional form.

   This genuine dissimilarity to the pre-Diaspora Sanhedrin is crucial if we assume that the Sages' legal formulations are authoritative only because of the
formal procedure followed in reaching these decisions. However, this assumption
oversimplifies the scholarly enterprise of the Rabbis and treats Amoraic activity
as identical to that of the Tannaim. Whereas the Tannaim were engaged in the
exegesis of the Torah and enacting ordinances, often preserved orally in the form
of short, apodictic phrases,[51] the central Amoraic task was to *elaborate* on the
Tannaitic corpus, explicating the juridic principles contained therein and reconciling discrepancies when such were detected.[52] The Amoraim engaged in-

creasingly in debate and in the articulation of arguments rather than in the novel interpretation of Torah and bold legislation of their predecessors.[53] Of course, the Amoraim were not entirely subservient to the traditions they inherited; they too engaged in some Pentateuchal exegesis and original legal formulation. Nevertheless, the overall framework in which the Amoraim functioned was derivative and interpretive of the antecedent Tannaim.

What results from this distinction is that if it is somewhat simplistic to merge the Sages into one indistinguishable group, then it is similarly simplistic to ground their authority in the Sanhedrin. It is possible that the Sanhedrin is indeed an appropriate model with which to understand the Tannaim and their activity, yet the Amoraim's authority, especially those in Babylonia, must be grounded in some other notion.

Before abandoning any hope of extending the Sanhedrin model to the Babylonian Amoraim, we should explore one other possibility, raised in the Talmud itself. Based on a Rabbinic exegesis of the word *Elohim* in Ex. 21:6 and 22:7–8, it was determined that only judges who were ordained as *mumhim* (experts) could administer penal justice and decide monetary cases involving loans.[54] Since ordination was conferred in Palestine alone, most Babylonian judges lacked this status and therefore were technically unauthorized to mete out penalties or render decisions in these cases. However, in order to promote lending among Jews,[55] as well as in suits where there is actual monetary loss due to an occurrence of some frequency, such as damage caused by an animal, non-ordained Babylonian judges were permitted to judge, acting as the agents of the Palestinian courts (*avdinan shelihutaihu*).[56] This notion of agency, of course, is akin to what we discussed earlier in this chapter—that the talmudic Sages are agents of the original Sanhedrin—but it differs in several significant respects.

First, the talmudic notion does not specify for whom the Babylonian courts are serving as agents. It might be the existing Sanhedrin or the entire Palestinian judicature;[57] it does seem, however, to refer to a concurrent agency, where the Babylonian judges are acting in lieu of *existing* Palestinian judges, not prior ones.[58] Since Palestinian judges, by dint of their ordination, had jurisdiction over all Jews,[59] Babylonian judges saw themselves as acting in the stead of their Palestinian counterparts, at least as long as a Jewish judicature existed in Palestine. This would force us to answer the historical question of when the Sanhedrin was finally dissolved. It is possible to argue, nevertheless, that this agency ought be construed transhistorically, but then such a justification would extend to all subsequent scholars applying the laws of their predecessors,[60] and would not be limited to Babylonian Amoraim.

Second, the talmudic notion is confined to a limited and rather specific range of cases. While the reasons for this restriction may be debated, the talmudic notion of agency will in any event be unable to bear the weight of the full range of functions exhibited by the Sages, which included the interpretation of verses, legislation, etc. (see chapter 1). We may want to explain the limitation of this agency to frequently occurring tort cases by seeing the Palestinian courts as responsible in some way for maintaining Jewish society worldwide, but it is nevertheless difficult to have this version of agency encompass the full range of the Sages' activity.

Moreover, if the Talmud sees Amoraim acting as agents of the original Sanhedrin, then such agency would include Palestinian Amoraim as well. However, not only does the Palestinian Talmud not make any mention of this, but the talmudic discussion explicitly limits the notion to Babylonian judges. In any event, where the Talmud records cases that came before the Babylonian courts and the decisions that were rendered, these rulings could be seen as authoritative expressions of law, grounded, to a degree, in the authority of the Palestinian courts.

Summary

In this chapter, we explored the model of Rabbinic authority that sees the Sages as some sort of Sanhedrin. The appeal of this model lies in the fact that the pre-destruction High Court acted judicially and legislatively in ways quite similar to the subsequent Sages. Nevertheless, efforts to see the talmudic Rabbis as either substitutes or agents of that original institution either lacked historical evidence of such appointment or proved too inclusive of later rabbinic scholars as well. The Tannaim could be portrayed as a continuation of the Sanhedrin if we assume their configuration to be a collective body reaching consensual decisions, but the Amoraim were not so constituted and would require a separate basis for their authority. Some Babylonian courts saw themselves as agents of the contemporary Palestinian judicature, but this is insufficient to ground the broad authority of the Babylonian Amoraim.

We noted that any conception of a High Court would necessitate that it be composed of competent scholars, in terms of both intellectual acumen and being the bearers of an oral tradition. This sort of competency, upon which one's eligibility to be a member of the Sanhedrin depended, was normally certified by ordination. Through this procedure, individuals were invited into the ranks of the Sanhedrin and could register their opinions during the course of debate on an issue. More important, the fact that ordination continued until the end of the fourth century makes this model particularly fruitful as a possible basis for Rabbinic authority as many Rabbis would be included. In the next chapter, we will explore whether this conferral of status is a useful model for conceiving the Sages' authority.

Ordination

Standing in the Sandals of Moses

As we saw in chapter 3, the effort to portray the Sages as a continuation of the Sanhedrin was successful only to a limited degree. The idea was comprehensive enough to include both judicial and legislative functions and could even sustain broader geographical parameters beyond Jerusalem, but it ran aground as soon as the talmudic Rabbis ceased to be configured in the institutional framework of a collective body abiding by established procedures of decision making. Compared to the Tannaim in the land of Israel, who could realistically be conceived as functioning together as a single organ, the Palestinian, but especially the Babylonian, Amoraim are portrayed much more individualistically; the Talmud shows the Amoraim working in multiple academies with distinct and differing traditions. Assuming that the anonymous apodictic laws in the Mishnah represent the majority's view, the Babylonian Gemara in contrast is *not* a record of collective decisions.

Given the more atomistic and highly discursive presentation of Amoraic views, it is worthwhile to examine another institutional ground of authority which similarly operates at the level of the individual: *semikhah*, or Jewish ordination.[1] In fact, our prior discussion of the Sanhedrin demands this investigation, for we noted that to be a member of the High Court, a scholar had to be sufficiently erudite and well versed in both the Written and the Oral Torah. *Semikhah* accomplished this sort of accreditation, and while it did not guarantee actual membership in the Court, it did certify the person's eligibility.[2] This, then, is a potentially fruitful avenue of inquiry, on several scores. First, by being continuous (at least from the traditional viewpoint) until the fourth or even fifth century C.E., *semikhah* links most Sages to an earlier form of authority while at the same time limiting that status to the talmudic period. Second, as a certification only of eligibility, it is not intrinsically tied, either geographically or temporally, to a formally constituted Sanhedrin. This raises the theoretical possibility that *semikhah* could continue beyond the formal existence of a High Court (whenever that might have occurred), as well as include the Sages in Babylonia, although, to be sure, the Sanhedrin could still convene only in the Land of Israel. This model, then, appears quite promising as a ground of Rabbinic authority.

As in the previous chapter, our discussion is necessarily restricted by the historical evidence since we are speaking of an actual institution in Jewish history. Its true origins are shrouded in mystery, and modern scholars debate whether the original *semikhah* was discontinued in the latter part of the fourth century, during the time of Hillel II, or even later, ca. 429 C.E. with the death of the last patriarch, Gamliel VI.[3] In either case, we are faced with a terminus ad quem for this model of authority, which is roughly coterminous with the period of the talmudic Sages.

In this chapter we will examine what sort of authority *semikhah* confers and to what extent this authority accords with the normative status claimed for Rabbinic pronouncements. However, I will first give a brief summary of the relevant laws governing *semikhah* and the precise parameters under which it operates.[4]

A Brief Overview of *Semikhah*

The sole ordination in the Torah is that of Joshua by Moses (Num. 27:22–23), although the episode of the seventy elders (Num. 11:16–17, 24–25) certainly contains the conferral of status by some other means. Tradition takes this investment of Joshua and of the original (or proto-) Sanhedrin as the beginning of an uninterrupted chain of ordination down to the time of the Second Temple and beyond.[5] Although the biblical story about Joshua's ordination contained an actual "laying on of hands," the Rabbinic tradition understood the ceremony as entailing only an oral or written conferral of the title "rabbi."[6]

The Rabbinic sources offer a fair number of details regarding *semikhah*. According to the Talmud, conferral could be limited in either scope or duration; a scholar may be authorized to render decisions in religious cases but not in criminal cases, and the authorization may be limited to the length of his stay in a specific place.[7] Ordination as a judicial appointment was a formal juridical act, requiring the presence of three elders,[8] only one of whom had to be himself ordained (although not necessarily an active member of the High Court).[9] After Rabban Yoḥanan ben Zakkai, it was decided that all ordinations should obtain the consent of the patriarch out of respect for that office (or for the Davidic ancestry of the patriarchs); later, the patriarch's ordinations reciprocally required the approval of the Sanhedrin.[10] At the ceremony, the ordinand wore special garments and received songs of praise; at times, he even offered a public discourse.[11]

Ordination was performed only by those scholars residing in the Land of Israel;[12] an ordinand needed only to be present in the land at the time of his ordination and could leave the country subsequently.[13] Once ordained, however, a scholar could exercise his full authority outside Palestine, perhaps, as suggested in the last chapter, as an agent of the Palestinian courts.[14] This distinction is noted in the talmudic convention of giving the title *rabbi* only to Sages who were ordained;[15] most scholars in Babylonia, particularly in the later Amoraic period, possess only the title *rav*.[16]

Being ordained rendered a scholar eligible to join the ranks of judges, hence the term *minui* (appointment) employed by the Palestinian Talmud, which is the equivalent of the Babylonian term *semikhah*.[17] The ordinand could be part of either the courts of twenty-three, whose jurisdiction included most criminal and civil cases, or the High Court in Jerusalem. According to the Mishnah, three rows of scholars sat before these courts, and when it was necessary to add a judge, the highest ranking scholar was ordained and joined the court.[18] Other rabbinic functions requiring ordination included intercalating the calendar, annulling vows, deciding whether a firstborn animal was disqualified from sacred status by a blemish, and issuing a ban of excommunication individually.

Following the Bar Kokhba Rebellion, Hadrian abolished the Sanhedrin and outlawed ordination; the Talmud tells in chilling detail how Rabbi Judah ben Bava clandestinely ordained five students and then ordered them to run and hide, slowing the pursuing Roman soldiers with his own body.[19] The Talmud credits him with preserving the ability to judge cases involving penalties, a prerogative reserved for ordained judges. As noted earlier in the chapter, the precise date of the end of ordination has not been conclusively determined, although the formal end of the Patriarchate in 429 is a reasonable hypothesis, given the patriarch's traditional role in the granting of *semikhah*.

The term *semikhah* has since been applied to various forms of academic certification or rabbinic licensing, although it no longer signifies the unbroken continuity or transmission of oral traditions which the original notion conveyed.[20] There have been several attempts to revive *semikhah* since talmudic times, the most famous being the sixteenth-century effort in Palestine, which actually succeeded in ordaining four scholars, although it was not widely recognized as a legitimate restoration of the venerable institution and was not continued.[21] The creation of the State of Israel in 1948 and the restoration of Jewish sovereignty were seen by some as an opportunity to renew *semikhah* and reinstitute the Sanhedrin, but it remained only theoretical.[22]

Equipped with this general sketch of the laws of *semikhah*, we may now begin a thorough analysis of its nature. For heuristic purposes, I will discuss several present-day examples of certification and licensing, using them to zero in more precisely on the character of the Jewish *semikhah*, which many of the talmudic Sages, including all the Tannaim, possessed.

The Nature of Semikhah

Semikhah, like most types of conferral of status, is multidimensional. In respect to the practice of Jewish law, we may distinguish, a priori, two functions that ordination performs: certification and licensing. The cases of lawyers and doctors will serve as good examples, since our contemporary society has found it convenient to separate these two functions and delegate them to different organs or agencies.

Today, aspiring professionals attend schools that, through their respective curricula, prepare candidates with the broad education deemed necessary for performing the duties of a particular field. Thus, law school acquaints its students with the various areas of legal theory and procedure which are presently practiced in this country. Schools certainly vary quite widely in their curricular focus, but in the end, the students who successfully complete the requisite course of study emerge with a doctorate in jurisprudence. Their diplomas represent the institution's verification that they have indeed acquired sufficient aptitude in the discipline of law. (State or national organizations in turn certify the institution, in what is called accreditation, to ensure standards in professional or academic preparation.) Similarly, medical schools subject their students to an intensive curriculum of anatomy, physiology, pharmacology, etc., all subjects deemed indispensable to the proper current practice of medicine. The student who passes all the courses graduates as a doctor of medicine.

However, these certified students are not allowed to enter their fields immediately upon their graduation. They must then receive governmental licensing, which will permit them to practice their profession in a particular state. In the United States, each state's board of examiners in the fields of law and medicine administers tests that establish the competency of the candidate to practice in that profession. Technically speaking, a person who has successfully completed an accredited program is already certified, to some degree. Nevertheless, given the diversity of schools, teachers, and, most significantly, the grading system, it would be virtually impossible to guarantee the quality of each and every professional-school graduate. The state, therefore, charged with protecting citizens in its jurisdiction from either physical or legal harm, prefers to directly examine each graduate's competency through standardized tests and measures.[23] This is the essence of licensing.

Certification and licensing not only are theoretically separable but are differentiable on the practical level: once one has earned a certificate or degree, it generally cannot be revoked or withdrawn, as it merely attests to the completion of a course of study. Licensing, on the other hand, is inherently contingent on the ongoing approbation of the licensing institution and can be revoked at any time and reinstated later. Since a license is the permission a state grants to an individual to perform certain functions, the state has the right to constantly monitor these practitioners to ensure the quality of service being rendered. (In this respect, the accreditation of an institution by an agency is a form of licensing.)

Moreover, a license issued by a professional group, private or otherwise, also constitutes an offer to someone to join its ranks. As a practicing attorney or physician, that person, by dispensing services to the public, also represents the profession as a whole; as in a guild, a professional's performance reflects not only on him or her but on the field as a whole. Licensing is not strictly quality control by an external source from a paternalistic interest to protect the public; the profession is self-motivated to ensure that its image remains untarnished and that the public sees those in that field as policing themselves. Therefore, incompetence, unprofessional conduct, or unseemly behavior are legitimate grounds for revoking someone's license. In fields where individuals are asked to entrust that which is most precious to them to others—in the case of medicine, their health, and in the case of law, their property or freedom—that trust must be earned by a quality control strictly enforced by the practitioners themselves.

Prima facie, *semikhah* accords with this multivalent notion of licensing and includes certification of a candidate's knowledge, his competence to render legal decisions (which may include a certain skill as well), and his formal eligibility to serve on a Jewish court.[24] There is certainly the aspect of possessing the requisite knowledge, coupled with a sensitivity and judiciousness in application. This is why an individual may be ordained in particular fields but not in others. Moreover, the Talmud's examples of reasons why licensing may be withheld— for example, concern that the public will misconstrue the overly delicate distinctions one rabbi would make, or that an older rabbi's dignity may be bruised by the arrival of a younger colleague who would outshine him[25]—are all evidence of a guildlike profession's concerns for both its actual practice and the reputation of its practitioners. Licensing for a short time, or only as long as a certain Sage was absent, is similarly consistent with this image; it is normal practice for a license to expire or require renewal. The Sages, who served as the local judges for Jews in Palestine and Babylonia, sought to control those who could both properly administer justice to Jews and admirably represent the entire system of Jewish law and judicature to the public.[26]

The geographical limitation of *semikhah* to the Land of Israel is, in this light, also understandable: the system of Jewish courts was centered in the national homeland, with the High Court at its apex. Given the centralized notion of Jewish judicature that existed at the time, ordination was confined to that area, even though the ordinand could then leave the country. Perhaps the notion of *shelihutaihu ka 'avdinan* (we are their emissaries) mentioned at the end of the previous chapter is similarly based on seeing the Palestinian courts as the only legitimately authorized judiciary.[27] Maimonides' position requiring the unanimous consent of scholars in Palestine to restore *semikhah* similarly reflects the licensing aspect of ordination and the role of the contemporary professional community in sanctioning it.[28]

Licensing may indeed be a helpful model for understanding *semikhah*, but it apparently does not exhaust it, for it leaves unexplained the tradition's insistence that ordination be an uninterrupted chain from Moses down to the talmudic Sages. Our contemporary understanding of the licensing of professionals does not appear to include the claim that the inductee is joining the ranks of great doctors or lawyers of the past, or that she constitutes the next link in an ongoing chain of professionals. *Semikhah* seems to possess an added historico-religious dimension that licensing cannot describe.

Moreover, licensing is the method by which one *joins* a profession and is permitted to practice it; it does not explain the *ground* of the profession's authority. When we claim someone is licensed to practice medicine, that license *stands for something*: it says that this person has been judged by colleagues in the field and deemed competent to treat patients medically. The genuine source of the *doctor's* authority is her knowledge of the field and her ability to heal a patient or help him deal with a particular condition; licensing by peers is simply the method our society has collectively accepted to ascertain the presence of that competence. It is the public's trust in those colleagues or state-appointed boards and their ability to measure someone else's qualifications upon which the authority of *licensing* truly rests. And those colleagues, in turn, are measured by their successful practice of medicine and the respect their field accords them. In choosing to examine *semikhah*, the hope was that it would provide an actual *ground* for the Sages' authority, not just a certification that they were deemed by their peers to be competent judges or even be eligible to serve on the Sanhedrin. Viewing ordination as more generally signifying a scholar's entry into the august ranks of "the Sages" does not, in any way, ground that authority.

Lastly, licensing is largely an authorization of *contemporary* authority, certifying those who are presently engaged in the practice of law or medicine. No doubt this was true of the Sages as well; through *semikhah*, their contemporary communities were assured that competent scholars were adjudicating their cases and resolving their questions on Jewish law. But we are searching for a model that will grant *continuous* authority to the Sages, such that later generations, or simply scholars who lacked *semikhah*, are compelled to defer to the talmudic Rabbis. If ordination is merely licensing, then it cannot adequately ground the notion of ongoing Rabbinic authority.

Ordination as Substitution

Semikhah *in the Pentateuch*

Joshua's *semikhah* from Moses may be a model of ordination, but it is not the only time the act of "laying on of hands," designated by the verb s.m.kh., appears in the Torah. The primary Pentateuchal context for laying one's hands on something else is in connection with the sacrifices:[29] However, it also appears in two other cases: before a criminal's execution, the witnesses must place their hands on his head,[30] and when the Levites were designated to serve in the Tabernacle as assistants to the priests, the Israelites put their hands on the Levites' heads.[31] An inspection of these cases suggests that *semikhah* is fundamentally an act of substitution: one person or thing is to take the place of another.[32]

On the paradigm of the *akeidah* (the binding of Isaac—Gen. 22), where, in the end, Abraham offers a ram in lieu of his son, the ideational premise of the sacrificial system seems to be substitution.[33] This seems to be the underlying logic of expiatory sacrifices: in the commission of an act against God's will, a transgressor forfeits his or her life; God, however, mercifully accepts an animal in that person's stead. Even in the case of voluntary sacrifices, the talmudic Sages and medieval commentators sought some correlation to violations of the law.[34] The Levites, too, are substitutes for the firstborn among the people,[35] and the blasphemer bears his own guilt as well as the guilt of the witnesses who convicted him, for during the trial, the two witnesses were forced to repeat the impious expression they heard.[36] In this sense, Moses' laying his hands on Joshua was an act not merely of authorization but of substitution, signifying to all those assembled that Joshua would be taking Moses' place as leader of the people.[37] Thus, it seems clear that the laying on of hands represents some type of substitution.[38]

Returning then to *semikhah* as ordination, the question obviously arises: for whom is it a substitution? In the limited, local sense, a disciple who has learned from and lived with a teacher for many years may truly be thought of as a substitute for his master, since he has absorbed and now embodies his teacher's erudition and analytic approach.[39] This does not mean he is merely a parrot, repeating only what his teacher said; he may also contribute his own opinions. Nevertheless, to a large degree *semikhah* can be seen as the master allowing the disciple to take his place, to assume a position on the academic stage; it is at once the acknowledgment of the student's mastery as well as the granting of permission to the disciple to decide matters on his own. Such an understanding explains the talmudic case of awarding *semikhah* for a limited time: R. Yohanan allows R. Shaman to decide cases "until [he] returns to us."[40] In other words, once the disciple is again in the sphere of his teacher, there is no need for a substitute. This goes far in explaining the Talmud's concern for rendering legal decisions within the vicinity of one's teacher: substitution is justifiable only if the one being "replaced" is not present.

Nevertheless, one need not take the notion of substitution so literally; it may be, not actual replacement, but merely allowing one to function in the same capacity as the one authorizing the *semikhah*. Viewed this way, ordination is a sort of agency, discussed in the previous chapter, although there it was in the institutional context. In *semikhah*, the one who ordains does not necessarily surrender all or any of his authority; he simply allows the ordinand to share in it. This is certainly the Rabbinic model of Moses' investment of the seventy in Numbers 11: the overworked leader acted, at the time, like a candle, kindling others while in no way diminishing his own fire.[41] In this respect, the investment of Joshua as leader was more akin to a king's appointment of a successor and differed from the appointment of the seventy, which was to authorize them as Moses' assistants or representatives while he was still leader.[42]

Whether *semikhah* is literal substitution or some form of "extension," it is now clear why Jewish tradition portrays it as a chain dating back to Moses and the original Sanhedrin: anyone with ordination is, in the final analysis, standing in Moses' "sandals." A person of great erudition may be respected and even revered by some, but without ordination, he does not occupy the same *position* of authority as one who possesses *semikhah*.[43] This is why I chose to include ordination as a model of institutional authority: were it strictly an acknowledgment or formal certification of a person's expertise and skill, then the ground of authority is, in actuality, a *personal* quality, as noted earlier. In the sense I am discussing now, *semikhah* is really a classic case of ex cathedra authority, where we deem someone to be sitting in a seat of authority. The contemporary ordinand sits in his teacher's seat, but as a logical regression, the question ultimately takes us back to Moses. This forces us to address how the Jewish tradition understands the nature of Moses' authority.

The Nature of Moses' Authority

Moses' authority is a topic which deserves special attention in its own right, particularly in the way it evolves from the burning bush in Exodus 3 through the forty years in the wilderness. Nevertheless, we may briefly sketch what sort of authority Jewish tradition accords Moses.

Fundamentally, Moses is a prophet of a very unique sort. The Torah asserts that his communication with God is direct and explicit, as opposed to the indirect methods by which God addresses other prophets, requiring interpretation.[44] He is the only prophet to have reached the unparalleled level of seeing God's "back,"[45] implying that he possessed an extraordinarily intimate knowledge of God. Moses is therefore considered by tradition as the father of all prophets.[46]

This fact is the cornerstone of Moses' authority, in every respect. As lawgiver, he offers the people not his own laws but those that God has explicitly commanded. In his judicial capacity, his interpretation of the law is most valid since it emerges from a keen and unmatched awareness of the divine will and personality. Within the covenantal relationship of the Jewish people and God, such knowledge is crucial, since only proper performance of divine commandments maintains that relationship.[47] In his legislative function, Moses' status as prophet endows him with a profound understanding of what "being God's nation" entails[48] and the responsibilities that role imposes on the people. He is therefore uniquely equipped to instruct the Israelites in ways which further their religious development and deepen their commitment to God.[49]

The prophetic ground of Moses' authority may explain why the seventy who were invested as Moses' assistants approached the Tent of Communion and began to prophesy (Num. 11:25). There are several parallels between that episode and the original Sinaitic revelation recorded in Exodus 19.[50] The important thing to note is that God's visible presence was necessary to ground the seventy's authority, much as it had once authenticated Moses' authority;[51] as the representatives or assistants of so unique a leader, their authority had to be established in a similar way.[52] This may also explain why the Torah mentions no such ceremony, supernatural or otherwise, at the appointment of the judges in Exodus 18. As those who would administer justice based on the divine laws which Moses related to them, they were, in effect, Moses' agents; any matter which they found too difficult would be brought to Moses for resolution. In contrast, the seventy elders functioned as the people's *leaders* and administrators, advising the people and supervising them in ways that could not be as clearly delineated as the laws the judges implemented.[53] For this sort of authority, some ceremony was required that would put them on the same footing as Moses. In this respect, their investiture is akin to that of Joshua in Numbers 27.[54]

This prophetic or spiritual dimension of sharing in Moses' authority, at least at the time of appointment, may account for the stipulation that all ordination be performed in the Land of Israel. Given the Rabbinic doctrine that prophecy (*ruah ha-qodesh*) does not descend on individuals outside the Holy Land,[55] *se-*

mikhah had to be restricted to the boundaries of Palestine. Certification and licensing, as prima facie models of *semikhah*, do not lend themselves to geographical circumscription. But if ordination invests the ordinand with the eligibility to receive the divine spirit, evidenced in the original seventy by their ability to prophesy, then this limitation to the Land of Israel follows quite naturally.

Implications for the Sages' Authority

Furnished with this more thorough and nuanced understanding of *semikhah*, we may now apply it to our subject of Rabbinic authority.

Ordination as Substitution

First, we should be aware that by inspecting the nature of ordination, we gained an additional or alternative model for understanding the *Sanhedrin's* authority. Recall that in trying to see the Sages as the continuation of the Sanhedrin, we encountered not only historical obstacles (e.g., how long did the Sanhedrin actually exist), but conceptual ones as well, among them trying to determine the minimum criteria for the contemporary judge or court (e.g., collective body, heirs of a tradition) and the basis for the Sanhedrin's legislative authority given the juridical context of the original verses in Deuteronomy. However, we now have a model whereby the basis of the Sanhedrin's authority, at least originally, is that they shared in Moses' prophetic prowess and therefore in part of his position of leadership as well. All those who would, in the future, be ordained, would be joining the ranks of (those eligible for) this body of elders and would therefore be authorized to govern and guide the people.

If *semikhah* is the ground of Rabbinic authority, then we have freed it from any formal institutional requirements, such as constituting itself as a body or limiting its ranks to only seventy. Since the elders were chosen to assist Moses in the administration of the nation, it is reasonable that in time, as the people grew more numerous, more elders could and would be appointed, as the need arose.[56] *Semikhah* is an extremely flexible method by which the size of the governing group could be regulated. Nor must the ordained scholars act collectively, although a decision emerging from the entire group would probably carry greater weight in the people's eyes. Under this model, it is equally possible that ordination might continue even if a formal Sanhedrin ceased to exist; individual leaders could certainly delegate substitutes or replacements even though circumstances prevented them from convening regularly.

The main advantage of this approach is that it takes us further into the Rabbinic period than any other theory so far. All the Tannaim, and many of the Amoraim, particularly in Palestine, were ordained; on the view that *semikhah* rendered them substitutes for Moses (or for the original seventy), they possessed the authority to both interpret the law and legislate for the good of the people, if need be. This is the most attractive model we have examined, in that it has a built-in terminus ad quem—the early fifth century—allowing us to at once grant unique authority to many of the talmudic Rabbis and withhold it from scholars after that point.

If, however, both the Sanhedrin's and the Sages' authority is grounded in their being ordained, we must ask what is gained by having a central institution at all? What function does the Jerusalem High Court serve, if being ordained is what grounds one's authority? We noted in the previous chapter that the Sanhedrin served as the apex of the national judicature, being the final appeal in the event of any legally confusing matter (much like Moses in the wilderness).[57] Institutional frameworks allow for the orderly resolution of pressing issues, but the eligibility to register one's view on a matter derived from "licensing" by *semikhah*. Perhaps for this reason the law of the rebellious elder applied only when a Sanhedrin existed, for then he acted contrary to the ruling body, thus challenging the entire judiciary and its orderly procedures.[58] With the dissolution or exile of the Sanhedrin, then, only the formal structure disintegrated, but the "license" was still in effect (perhaps in the hope that a Sanhedrin would soon be renewed). Indeed, as it is arranged, talmudic (post-Sanhedrin?) material strikes the reader as the presentation of various opinions on a subject[59] without explicit guidelines as to how to decide between them;[60] most discussions end without a clear preference for one view over another. Ordination, therefore, enables the scholar to register a view on a particular matter; the existence of a Sanhedrin creates the institutional context in which decisions become binding law.

If this is the case, then our job is not yet complete, for if it was the Sanhedrin as a decision-making body that rendered one opinion normative for all subsequent generations of Jews, what accomplished this in its absence? The fact that the talmudic Sages were ordained only rendered their opinions as "candidates" for normative practice, and we are still left to establish what makes the decision to follow a particular talmudic view binding on all subsequent generations. The analysis so far has not answered that question.

Moreover, while the Tannaim, we may assume, were all ordained, the Babylonian Amoraim were overwhelmingly *not* so licensed. Since tradition limits ordination to Palestine, most Amoraim in Babylonia—whose views, as we might expect, make up a significant share of the Babylonian Talmud—are left out of this theory.[61] True, Babylonian scholars are portrayed, on occasion, as deferring to the authority of Palestinian scholars,[62] but in general the talmudic discussions, whether Babylonian or Palestinian, show no preference for the view of an ordained scholar over his unordained colleagues; opinions of all scholars are preserved and examined on their inherent merits. Simply being ordained never trumps an opponent in the talmudic give-and-take or in the subsequent medieval interpretation and analysis of the issue. We could create a supplementary notion whereby unordained Sages are merely interpreting the views of those Sages with *semikhah*, but this notion would likely have to be stretched beyond its tensile limits in order to encompass the vast number of legal opinions uttered by unordained Sages, many of which are not connected to statements made by ordained scholars. The appeal of grounding Rabbinic authority in ordination is considerably tempered by these facts.

One Court, Two Roles

Another way of approaching our topic is to integrate this chapter's discussion of ordination with the previous chapter's discussion on the Sanhedrin and say that the original Jerusalem Sanhedrin may indeed have embodied two functions simultaneously: a judicial role (foreshadowed in Ex. 18) and a legislative-administrative one (anticipated in Num. 11). The Torah's command to obey the High Court in Jerusalem was primarily with respect to judicial matters and as such required the presence of some institutional setting (taking over Moses' role as final arbitrator in all matters). But the legislative function may reasonably be anchored in a notion of ordained individuals who stand in Moses' place; imbued with a measure of divine spirit (such as the original seventy were), they are qualified to guide the nation in their march through history as God's chosen people.[63] While the first function may have come to an end with the Sanhedrin's dissolution, the ordained Sages, in a noninstitutional context, continued to fulfill the Sanhedrin's second role as the people's leaders all the way to the early fifth century, when *semikhah* ceased to exist.

Such a bifurcated approach (exegetical-judicial and legislative-administrative) to understanding the Sages' authority yields an important implication with respect to the force of Rabbinic pronouncements. Following this logic, we could say that while Rabbinic exegesis and interpretation fall under the commandment of the Torah to obey the High Court in Jerusalem, the Sages' legislation is binding because it originates from the ordained leadership of the nation. The ongoing authority of Rabbinic enactments and ordinances may therefore be rooted in the fact that many of the Sages were ordained; this renders the historical question of the Sanhedrin's dissolution somewhat irrelevant, since we no longer require the talmudic Sages to be constituted as a formal body in order to give them the authority of the Sanhedrin, at least with respect to legislation.

Interestingly, the resulting approach to Rabbinic authority would be a mirror image to that presented in chapter 3: when the Sages were portrayed primarily as a Sanhedrin, then we tried to broaden the category of *interpretation* (the main biblical function of the High Court) to include even preemptive legislation. Now, by focusing on the *legislative* authority implied in ordination, we are forced to view the interpretive material in the Talmud, particularly that found among the later Sages, as a type of legislation. Both these efforts to expand singular categories to encompass an admittedly broad range of activities place considerable strain on both theories.

Although viewing much of the Rabbinic enterprise as essentially legislative causes problems for this theory, its greatest difficulty lies in its inability to include all the Sages. As long as ordination is seen as the ground of Rabbinic authority, we are led to devalue in some measure the opinions and views of the Babylonian Amoraim and thus a significant portion of the Babylonian Talmud.

Summary

As a model of institutional authority, *semikhah* took us rather far in explaining the authority of the talmudic Sages. Seen more as a notion of substitution than as certification or licensing, ordination allowed us to view the Rabbis as constituting a continuous chain leading back to Moses himself and the unique authority he possessed. The following conclusions were reached:

1. Ordination confers a position of leadership on those who possess it, allowing them to stand in the place of Moses.

2. Those scholars who compose the High Court may be ordained, but their juridical authority stems more accurately from their constituting a formal institution and not from their ordination.

3. As long as the Sanhedrin functioned, the judicial decisions of the Sages possessed the authority of the High Court; thereafter, their pronouncements were uttered in the capacity of ordained Jewish leaders, not as a supreme court.

4. *Semikhah* should constitute a prima facie case for the priority of the views of those who possessed it, although that does not appear to be a consideration in either the Babylonian or the Palestinian Talmud's deliberations or in subsequent analysis.

Over the last three chapters, we have examined several institutional models for grounding the Sages' authority. All of these shared the basic strategy of describing a certain authoritative role or position—be it chief judge, Sanhedrin, or one with ordination (*semikhah*)—and then identifying the talmudic Rabbis as occupying that position. In all of these models, the authoritativeness of the Sages was grounded not in their persons but in the functions and duties they fulfilled. Their authority was thus located within a broader nexus of religious roles and institutions in Judaism. To use the terminology developed in the introduction, we may say that the Sages were *in* authority.

However, utilizing ex cathedra notions of authority necessarily places the focus on the position or role, not its occupants. As we inspected different models of institutional authority, we were required to ask whether the Sages genuinely occupied those positions and/or filled those roles, particularly those with rather specific histories. As we moved to broaden the institutional concept sufficiently so as to include the five centuries of talmudic Rabbis, we discovered that it was then *so* broad that it embraced an even wider range of Jewish scholars and functionaries. Therefore, institutional models of Rabbinic authority necessarily involve two desiderata that are in relative tension: finding a definition of the position that is wide enough to encompass five hundred years of scholars in two countries whose numerous pronouncements range from the exegetical to the legislative, yet that is also narrow enough to restrict that authority to the talmudic period, and not beyond. In general, we found that while the institutional model could be adequately expanded to include the Sages, an *additional* assumption was required to limit that model to them exclusively.

Another consequence of an institutional approach to Rabbinic authority is that the Sages' theater of operations was exclusively halakhic. Whether we saw them as the contemporary judge, an incarnation of the Sanhedrin, or a collection of ordained individuals, all these models originated in a juridical context. Of course, it is only Halakhah which claims to be normative; aggadic or homiletic statements are more aptly deemed inspirational. Nevertheless, Rabbinic nonlegal midrashim are esteemed in Jewish tradition and are studied and expounded with the same commitment and at times even rigor as the Sages' legal pronouncements.[64] It is common to encounter the attitude among traditional Jews that the Sages' views on nonhalakhic matters, including their opinions on treatments for ailments and how to interpret dreams, are binding in a religious-moral sense.[65] This issue has been debated for over a millennium, and this book makes no claims to advance the discussion further. It need only be borne in mind that juridical models of authority, while useful in grounding normative halakhic practice, are not easily extended beyond the realm of law.

The Issue of Error

Before leaving part I, I must raise an issue that does not seem to cohere with an institutional notion of Rabbinic authority: the possibility of error. As Robert Jackson, a Supreme Court justice of the United States, once argued regarding the nature of the judicial branch's authority: "We are not final because we are infallible, but we are infallible because we are final."[66] This pithy expression acknowledges that like any hierarchical system, the American judiciary has to have its person(s) at the top beyond which there is no appeal. J. L. Austin labeled this sort of authority "verdictive," where an entity's mere act of declaring something renders it valid or binding.[67] This seems to apply to all realms where institutional authority is (exclusively) operative.

Such a notion is, in fact, expressed quite vividly in the Sifre on Deut. 17:11: " '[You shall not deviate from that which they tell you] right or left': even if they show you that right is left and left is right, listen to them."[68] The import of this text is that the contemporary judge's authority is, at bottom, institutional: his decision is "infallible because it is final." An opposite approach is taken in the Palestinian Talmud,[69] but the Sifre's position captures the essence of seeing the talmudic Sages as possessing institutional authority.

However, contrary to our expectations, the halakhic system admits that the High Court *can* make a mistake: an entire tractate, Horayot, is devoted to explaining what should be done in the event the Sanhedrin commits an error and causes the entire nation to violate some aspect of Torah law. How can we possibly understand the notion of error in an institutional model of the Sages' authority?

First, it is crucial to note that there are variant forms of the notion of "error." (In all of these forms, I am assuming an error committed with a temporary or total lack of awareness of the truth. An intentional error is, more accurately, a type of deliberate neglect or offense.) In the strict sense, an "error" assumes the existence of an epistemic truth, be it a fact or a logically necessary claim. We regularly encounter these in such realms as math, the hard sciences, and logic (within a particular system). Someone who adds 2 to 3 and gets 6, someone who claims that human breathing takes place through the ears, and someone who states that A and not-A are true at the same time are all "wrong"; they have committed an error in addition, in human physiology, and in Euclidean logic. Presumably, all we would have to do is show these people some type of evidence or the correct way to do something, and they too would see what is correct.

There is a weaker sense of error that is used in those realms that are not governed entirely by strict scientific rules but that involve some sort of probability or patterns as the basis of decision making. The social sciences, where human behavior is examined and generalizations formed, share this characteristic; many of their observations may be "true," psychologists, sociologists, and political scientists would all agree that policy based on their findings is far from foolproof. Human behavior is not easily reduced to strict rules of cause and effect, and the practice of these "sciences" is inherently tentative and constantly in some state of revision, especially as research continues to reveal more to us. Scholars in these fields generally do not "show" colleagues where they may be in error; their discourse is more aptly characterized as persuasion rather than proof, using new models, studies, or data to bring about a cognitive shift in others, to "change their minds," so that they come to accept something else as the reality. Similarly, many lawmakers draft legislation or vote on a bill based on what they perceive to be the particular problem and its cause, but they may turn out to be "wrong" in the sense that their diagnosis of the problem was faulty, they were ignorant of some relevant data, or they miscalculated the impact of a known factor. Any one of these could cause a decision or evaluation to be "in error," in the weak sense.

If we seek to apply these categories of error to the Sages, we must, once again, distinguish between the various capacities in which they served. Regarding Rabbinic legislation, a weak sense of error is appropriate, since an enactment may be misguided in that it does not achieve its end or, possibly, even leads to an opposite result.[70] Indeed, Rabbinic law itself deemed decrees which could not, in practice, be observed by the majority of the populace as null and void (not "wrong" in a strict sense) and retroactively of no standing.[71]

In the realm of Rabbinic exegesis, in contrast, the notion of error presumably depends on one's prior notion of revelation and the role of the Sages in that scheme. Thus, in a maximalist view of revelation, the Rabbis merely transmitted the oral traditions which were given at Sinai. But they may have passed on the law incorrectly. Genuine error can exist on a transcendental level, from the divine perspective, if you will; God knows what was revealed, and what the Sages tell us may, in fact, be incorrect.[72] However, given that we have no way of independently corroborating the contents of the original revelation, such error remains theoretical; as far as we are concerned, whatever the talmudic Rabbis tell us is accepted as the contents of the revelation. This is essentially a faith-claim, as it is irrefutable, given the evidence we have today.

Claiming that the Sages' interpretations are theoretically irrefutable, however, does little to alleviate the genuine skepticism that might infiltrate the system were the possibility of error seriously entertained regarding all Rabbinic exegeses. It is precisely in such a situation that the strength of institutional authority becomes evident: error is admitted as ontologically possible, but the rulings of the authorized body or group of Sages establish normative law.[73] Institutional authority places greater weight on due process and the rule of law than on correctly ascertaining the legal truth.[74]

Alternatively, if we assume a more minimalist view of the Sinaitic revelation, and the Rabbis used accepted or revealed techniques to yield interpretations of the Torah, then the more apt terms for this discussion are "valid/invalid." If proper procedure was followed and the rules of exegesis were correctly applied, then the exegesis which the Sages produced, by definition, could not be in error. Of course, the more we see the application of these techniques as a hard science (in contrast to an art), then the possibility of strict error increases: someone who adds several large numbers may arrive at an incorrect answer if the rules of addition are not followed carefully. A law uttered by a talmudic Sage may be "incorrect" in the sense that either an invalid method was used or a legitimate method was applied improperly. But as long as these exegetical rules are appropriately observed, then the resultant laws cannot logically be seen as errors, certainly not in the strict sense.

Furthermore, in the absence of any divine disclosure of these indeterminate laws, it would seem that error does not even exist from the divine perspective: since the law was presumably left ambiguous deliberately, from the human perspective the divine will is indeterminate on this matter and legitimizes any law that is validly derived.[75] The famous talmudic story of "the oven of Akhnai," however, seems to suggest that at least on one occasion, God's will was, indeed, determinate regarding the law in question, siding with R. Eliezer ben Hyrcanus; nevertheless, God "deferred" to the majority of the Sages who argued against that view, since they followed proper legal procedure in reaching a decision.[76] This case is a rather bold articulation of the view that error is conceptually impossible for the talmudic Rabbis when they follow the proper rules.

There are, of course, decisions in *specific* situations rendered by the court based on either incorrect or insufficient information that later turn out to be in error; for instance, witnesses who testify to a certain fact, based on which the court renders its verdict, may later be discovered to have been false witnesses. The court would admittedly have acted in error, but as long as its procedures were properly followed, its original decision was valid. Other than in the case of an explicit law of the Torah—which are the cases deemed by Mishnah Horayot to constitute ignorance, not error—the Sages may commit an error only in the weaker sense, not in the strict sense.[77]

Thus, the notion of error committed by the Sages depends on several factors:

1. *The scope of the original revelation*: The more maximalist the domain of revelation, the more error is conceptually possible, although given our human vantage point and the absence of prophecy, any error is, in most cases, undetectable.

2. *The nature of the exegetical rules*: If the application of the rules is under-

stood to approach a science, then a particular Rabbinic view or decision may in fact violate these rules or apply them incorrectly.

3. *Specific, real cases*: The High Court or the Sages may reach a decision based on incomplete knowledge of the facts of the case.

Error in the strict sense can occur in the above cases, although in no. 1 it is unrecoverable and possibly irrelevant if proper procedure is followed in arriving at the ruling. A softer notion is possible as one moves on the spectrum of no. 2 toward greater judgment or art rather than science, but again that assumes the divulgence of the divine will. Simply put, the more institutional one's theory of authority is, where a court or judicial office is hierarchically at the top of a legal system, the more incoherent the possibility of error becomes, provided no external source is allowed to express the contents of the law.[78]

PART II

PERSONAL QUALITIES OF
THE TALMUDIC SAGES

In the introduction, we presented R. S. Peters's constructive distinction between two sorts of authority that people may possess: being *in* authority or *an* authority. The first, which involves institutional forms of authority, usually embedded in a larger social and institutional framework, was examined in part I. In the second part of the book, we will take up those theories that see the Sages as *an* authority, possessing personal qualities that render them authoritative in all matters of Jewish law.

To be sure, inspecting the characteristics of a person (or group of persons) is insufficient on its own; the study must be conducted within the context of a particular role or function. An individual's talents or skills are relevant only insofar as they meet the specifications of a job that must be done, be it mechanical, scholarly, or administrative. In other words, it is not a person's resumé that determines whether he or she is qualified or not but how closely that resumé fits the specific job description.

In the case of the talmudic Sages, what sort of job might they be seen as performing? It would be merely tautological and self-serving to offer the catalog of Rabbinic activity we reviewed in chapter 1 and then say that the Sages fit the bill perfectly. We are looking for a more *general* role filled by the Sages, a role which might conceivably entail a variety of functions. I would like to borrow E. P. Sanders's concept of "covenantal nomism" as an apt description of how Rabbinic law saw itself within Judaism.[1] The entire edifice of Halakhah stands within the context of a people who considered themselves bound in a covenantal relationship with God that could not be rescinded or revoked. The awareness of that bond permeates Rabbinic literature, as Sanders amply shows. The relationship imposes demands and responsibilities on each and every Jew and serves as the backdrop for the system of rewards and punishments outlined by the Torah and elaborated by the Rabbis. Being part of this covenant and assured of its permanence provided the religious motivation to seek atonement for transgressions, both individually and collectively; the bond with God may have been temporarily impaired due to sin, but it could readily be restored by contrition, repentance, and penitence. The covenant always remained intact.

According to Jewish tradition, then, one way of understanding Halakhah is to see it as the elaboration of the covenant, of what God demands of the people he took to be his chosen nation. Ascertaining the terms of the contract, determining what God's will truly is, clarifying how a Jew can get close to God are all legitimate ways of describing the role of Jewish law in Judaism. This multifaceted enterprise, involves explaining what was meant by specific Pentateuchal commandments; it entails reading the revealed text of the Torah as carefully as possible to see what actions are mandated by God, if only implicitly and even cryptically; it includes legislating religious laws to ensure the people's observance of the commandments and fortify their commitment to them. The "job description," then, is the ability to elaborate the terms of the covenant through both exegesis and enactments.

Appreciating this aim helps highlight the precise problematic of Rabbinic authority, indeed, of *any* human authority in Judaism: within a religious system that fundamentally sees itself as obeying God's commands, how can a human authority boldly claim that it accurately embodies, represents, or conveys the divine will?[2] Of course, this was the context for the institutional models examined in part I as well; the need to elaborate the terms of the covenant were no less urgent there. However, those theories solved this problem by essentially circumventing it: God's intention is, especially in new cases, unknown to us. However, thankfully God has *authorized* a body (a judge, a Sanhedrin, Moses, etc.) to decide these questions, bidding us to obey its rulings. We follow their decisions because that is what God has instructed us to do, whether in his covenant or through some other means.

In contrast, the models presented in part II confront the problematic head on, seeking not authorization but *identity*: they assume that Rabbinic pronouncements accurately represent God's will, which in all cases is presumed to be determinate and specific. In a word, we hear God through the Sages; Rabbinic authority is not a formal extension of divine authority but the actual embodiment of it. Error, obviously, lurks ominously beside the enterprise.

While divine commands are invoked in these two sets of strategies, the difference between them is crucial. Imagine a principal who walks in on a teacher who has just punished his class in a severe way. In front of the students, the teacher turns to the principal for endorsement of his decision, which the principal provides. In this relatively trivial situation, the principal's approval masks her true belief in the propriety of the teacher's action: she might agree with what the teacher did, or in fact she may think that the measure is too strict, but she chooses not to undermine the teacher's authority in front of the class.

The parallel is clear. In an institutional model, divine authorization of the High Court or some other entity is the only expression of divine will which is relevant, regardless of the actual convergence of the Court's decision with God's will. The story of the oven of Akhnai, where the majority of Sages overrode the divinely endorsed opinion of R. Eliezer ben Hyrcanus, exemplifies this approach most dramatically: the divine will preferred one position (expressed by the heavenly echo), but the duly authorized body, following its established procedures, decided otherwise.[3] The models examined in part II make the more daring claim that the Sages' decisions genuinely express the divine intention in *any given case*. While the institutional approach sees a general divine command attached as a "rider" to every Rabbinic law,[4] the models of personal authority effectively elevate *each* Rabbinic decision *individually* to the level of divine commandment.

In part II we will explore two models that portray the Sages as uniquely capable of performing this role. The first, treated in chapter 5, suggests that the talmudic Rabbis were the unmatched experts in inferring and ascertaining from the revealed texts what God wanted of the Jewish people. This is a rather traditional notion of epistemic authority, where the knowledge of experts is the basis of their authority. Another form of this argument, taken up in chapter 6, claims that the talmudic Sages were merely the conduit for God; like prophets, the divine will was communicated through them, through a variety of possible channels. In either case, the Sages of the first five centuries *deserve* to be authoritative, for they alone know how to fulfill that most central of concerns for every Jew: the keeping of God's covenant.

The Rabbis as Experts

Within human society, particularly industrialized democracies, one of the most pervasive manifestations of authority is that of the expert—what is called *epistemic authority*. Contemporary society has ordered itself through a highly specialized division of labor, increasing our dependence on experts of all different sorts.[1] Specialists upon whom we can rely literally grease the wheels of our daily living, from the journalists' reports we read in the morning newspaper to the instructions we follow in preparing dinner, whether found in cookbooks or on food packaging. Teachers, plumbers, lawyers, computer consultants, auto mechanics, and doctors all offer us advice or provide us with information that we use because we see them as experts, as epistemic authorities.[2]

Seeing the talmudic Sages as experts is therefore a reasonable approach to the ground of their authority, for we regularly follow the instructions or guidelines of epistemic authorities. Therefore, we will first carefully inspect what it means for experts to serve as authorities in our lives and then, equipped with a richer appreciation of this notion, examine whether and in what ways the Rabbis of the first five centuries can be seen as epistemic authorities for subsequent generations of Jews.

Epistemic Authority: An Analysis

Epistemic authority, which drives so many of our daily interactions, is inherently *relational*: it always involves two or more people. Written formally, the following is a definition of epistemic authority:

> X (the bearer of authority) is an epistemic authority for y (the subject of authority) if, because of his belief in x's superior knowledge, y holds some proposition p, which x has enunciated (or which y believes x has enunciated), to be true or more probably true than he did before x enunciated it.[3]

73

As this definition points out, epistemic authority only provides a prima facie reason for y to believe something is true; by itself, it lacks "executive authority," or the ability to demand any sort of action. Thus, an eyewitness is an epistemic authority for most legal systems; he or she provides a description of an event or set of events so that the jury or judge can assume them to have actually happened, to be true and real; the verdict or sentencing depends on the society's laws and its penal code and whether the action is both illicit and punishable under those laws.

For epistemic authority to lead to action, y must hold some *other* statement to be true or desire some end that would cause him to act based on what x told him. This is true in all cases of epistemic authority, no matter which expert we consult: our desire to improve our health motivates us to heed a doctor's advice; our wish to stop the faucet from leaking impels us to let the plumber do what must be done to fix it; and we do the homework assigned in class because we want to know the material, do well on a test, or achieve some similar academic or career goal. Y's belief in x's superior knowledge is only the ground for adopting a proposition as true (or more likely true); what y does with that information depends on the nexus of other beliefs into which the proposition enters. In the case of Rabbinic authority, the central belief is that Jews should fulfill the terms of their covenant with God. Once the Jews believe that the Sages have superior knowledge of that information, then the talmudic Rabbis would indeed function as epistemic authorities, although not executive authorities, for those Jews.

Therefore, the *relational* quality of epistemic authority means that its true ground — "y's belief in x's superior knowledge" — bears almost all the weight of the claim to authority. At first glance, this would appear an entirely subjective matter: y may hold his belief in x's competence for any number of reasons, ranging from prior personal experience to a friend's suggestion. However, it is fair to inspect these reasons and range them along a scale of rationality.

Let us take the example of a leaky faucet. If I use a plumber who has successfully solved all my plumbing problems for the last ten years, then my trust in that plumber's expertise is highly rational, because my past experience validates it. If I get my friend's son, who happens to be good with his hands, to fix the sink (although he has never fixed one before), that would be less rational, because he has not proven himself in that specific area yet, but it would not be totally irrational, because one who is mechanically inclined may be able to solve a simple mechanical problem, if that's what my leaky faucet turns out to be. Were I to consider my therapist an expert in plumbing because she has fixed so many of my other problems, that would not be rational at all, since epistemic authority does not naturally extend from one domain to an entirely unrelated one. So the "rationality of epistemic authority" depends on how the *reason* for one's trust in an individual is related to one's particular *needs*.

Furthermore, we may examine whether epistemic authority is legitimate or not, for the possession of superior knowledge is, in principle, verifiable. This concerns, not the rationality of y's belief, but whether the belief is *true*. Thus, if y believes x is an expert electrician because x is licensed by the state, then y's belief is rational and legitimate; if that certificate is in fact a forgery, the belief is still rational (based on y's limited knowledge), but it is illegitimate. Once y knows that the certificate is fraudulent, if he continues to see this person as an expert, then x's epistemic authority is irrational as well, unless prior experience has shown x's actual competence, despite the false certification.

This extensive analysis of epistemic authority dictates that we must examine the claim that the Sages are the experts in Jewish law along two axes: rationality and legitimacy. As regards rationality, we must inquire whether our belief in their competence to determine normative Jewish practice is based on reasonable grounds or whether it is merely a doctrine maintained axiomatically. With respect to legitimacy, we will inspect whether the Sages' competence is, in some way, verifiable and therefore objectively true. Yet before we set ourselves to these tasks, we must first ascertain to which aspects of the Sages' activity the notion of epistemic authority is even appropriate.

Realms of Rabbinic Activity That Relate to Expertise

Without a doubt, the talmudic Sages exhibit an extraordinary erudition in matters of Jewish law. Their extensive knowledge of the Hebrew Bible and transmitted Rabbinic sources, their ability to reason logically and exegetically,[4] and their genuine mastery of the diverse realms of Halakhah are all ample evidence why they were called *hakhamim* — scholars or sages. Their knowledge was most likely one of the sources of their authority for Jews of that time.[5] However, our inquiry is about the Rabbis' authority, not for their own generation, but for all subsequent Jews. As the expositors and developers of Jewish law, their pronouncements and decisions are deemed binding on all Jews since the Talmud was redacted. Can these Jews conceive of the talmudic Sages as epistemic authorities? Once again, we must divide our discussion according to the realms of their activity. (This parallels the treatment at the end of chapter 4, which was conducted from the other side of the coin — the commission of error.)

At first glance, Rabbinic legislation — the Sages' *gezeirot* and *taqqanot* — is the area of their activity least likely to accommodate a notion of epistemic authority. While the hard sciences have an objective truth which can be missed, the social sciences are much less predictable, involving as they do human nature in all its fickleness. Laws are not measured by truth or falsity, but by such standards as their effectiveness, their consistency with other laws, and so on. As noted earlier, the epistemological notion of "error," at least in its strict sense, is incoherent in a legislative context. Nevertheless, we are examining, not error, but whether it makes sense to rely on someone for belief in the truth of a statement. Our definition of epistemic authority is not radically altered by the following revision:

> X (the bearer of authority) is an epistemic authority for y (the subject of authority) if, because of his belief in x's superior knowledge, y holds some law *l*, which x has legislated (or which y believes x has legislated), to be reasonable or more reasonable than he did before x legislated it.

Again, within the covenantal context in which we are working, it is reasonable to say that a Jew might consider the idea of not touching animals on the Sabbath far-fetched and excessive, but after hearing that the Sages endorsed it, he might concede that the legislation is reasonable. This is perfectly consistent with the idea that epistemic authority is verifiable: had I learned all that the expert knows and had all the experience he had, I too would likely reach the same conclusion. In other words, our reliance on experts is really a shortcut to our own mastery of a discipline or field.[6] As noted in the beginning of the chapter, epistemic authority has its roots in the division of labor within society, but in principle, anyone can replace the expert by receiving the same training. The fact that the Sages could give sound reasons as the basis for their legislation, such as that these enactments and ordinances would help nurture a Jew's relationship with God or assist in the observance of the covenant, allows epistemic authority to obtain in this realm of Rabbinic activity as well.[7]

Seeing the Sages in this role of spiritual guide is certainly apt in the realm of Aggadah, the nonlegal corpus of Rabbinic statements. These homilies, parables, moral exhortations, and general pieces of advice are all within the legitimate purview of those whose religious sensibilities qualify them as appropriate guides in the pursuit of the sublime goal of living according to God's covenant. In contrast to the ex cathedra models of Rabbinic authority which were exclusively legal and juridical in nature, this emphasis on the personal qualities of the Sages allows them to function within a broader realm of activity: legal, interpretive, and homiletic. Lawmakers legislate, but leaders may also inspire.

As we enter the realm of exegesis, we may once again try and express the claim formally as follows:

X (the bearer of authority) is an epistemic authority for y (the subject of authority) if, because of his belief in x's superior knowledge, y holds verse v to meam m, which x has so interpreted (or which y believes x has so interpreted).

This formal claim depends on what is being interpreted. We are by now aware that Rabbinic interpretation of the Torah is not of one cloth. At times, they simply offered the explanation of a word or the clarification of a biblical command; for example, what exactly is "the fruit of a goodly tree" mentioned in Lev. 23:40,[8] or on what sort of garment must one put fringes, and how are they to be tied (Num. 15:38–40)? These may be termed more explicit laws which the Sages merely elaborated for us. At other times, the Rabbis used a variety of hermeneutical tools to infer laws from orthographic oddities, textual juxtapositions, or conceptual comparisons of different laws. These laws are more implicit in the text, and one could claim that the Sages were in fact deciphering the Torah's language.

Now the degree to which a notion of "truth" is relevant to exegesis depends in large measure on one's view of the scope of revelation (see chapter 1 and the last section in chapter 4). On a maximalist view where the Sages simply transmitted an extant oral tradition, there is an objective "truth" regarding these laws; Jews simply believe that the Sages, due to their upstanding character or their proven reliability, passed on the laws faithfully. If, on the other hand, the original revelation was more minimal, and the Rabbis were themselves deriving the laws from the text, then to characterize the Sages as epistemic authorities requires two assumptions: first, that they were merely uncovering the true, if hidden, meaning of the text and not *legislating* the way a commandment should be observed; and second, that their exegesis is in fact a science, employing a specific methodology and obeying strict rules of application that render their results replicable. Obviously, intermediate positions are possible, with varying amounts of Rabbinic law conveying antique traditions and the rest representing the original interpretation of the Sages.

The Rationality and Legitimacy of Seeing the Talmudic Sages as Experts

Let us now examine these claims that the Sages were indeed the unsurpassed experts in Jewish law. Again, we are discussing, not the Sages' authority during their lifetimes, but the considerably more substantial claim that their law is binding on all Jews because as people with superior knowledge, their understanding of Jewish law is closest to the truth.

Rabbinic Legislation

As regards Rabbinic legislation, we saw that the Sages could be viewed as epistemic authorities if we saw them as most qualified to decide what activities or proscriptions would promote the Jewish people's observance of the covenant. Perhaps because they were imbued with a profound spirituality, or because they were thoroughly immersed in the study of the Bible, the talmudic Rabbis were skilled at determining the best course for fulfilling the terms of the covenant with God. This is both a rational and a legitimate claim: it is rational because their competence is seen to be based on their personal erudition, and it appears to be legitimate, or at least not illegitimate, for we have no reason to doubt that these Sages were such people.

However, this version of epistemic authority is identical to one that could have been made by the Jews of Palestine in the second century or by Babylonian Jews a century or two later. The claim we are seeking to substantiate is the *ongoing* epistemic authority of the Sages. It is true that expertise of this sort does not, in any formal sense, "expire"; if these enactments and ordinances were deemed by "the experts" to nurture a Jew's life within the covenant, then in most cases, that should continue to hold true. But this overarching goal, in theory, implies that the validity of nonexegetical religious legislation rests exclusively on its ability to foster and nurture a Jew's observance of the covenant.[9]

This yields two important consequences. The first is that this type of legislation is inherently revisable, for social, economic, and political factors impact on its effectiveness as much as ideal religious ones. Legislation that was spiritually on the mark for second-century Palestinian Jewry or fifth-century Babylonian

Jewry may no longer be so. At this point, it is reasonable to distinguish between prescriptive and proscriptive legislation. Ordinances designed to distance people from sin by prohibiting other, related practices are less likely to become outdated (although not impossible); in fact, the strict observance of the protected rule may prove that the ordinance *continues* to be effective. Positive legislation, on the other hand, seems more likely to depend on contemporary social conditions, and what aided Jews two thousand years ago in their spiritual growth may or may not obtain any longer. This idea would best be inspected on a case-by-case basis.

The second consequence of this understanding is that although the Sages were no doubt qualified to legislate, their talent was not exclusive; later Jewish leaders were also endowed with spiritual sensitivity and religious insight, and their legislation should similarly be binding on all Jews. I am not suggesting that this implication is negative; it is just that in a model that vests the Sages with epistemic authority, there is no *inherent* basis for a distinction between the tal-mudic Rabbis and later Jewish scholars. Any great scholar whose character and religious astuteness led him to enact a specific practice aimed at deepening Jewish spirituality should enjoy the same authoritativeness as the Sages.

One way of reconciling the universality, at least in principle, of epistemic authority with the uniqueness of the talmudic Rabbis is to claim that although subsequent scholars were permitted to disagree with their predecessors, they sim-ply chose not to. It was merely a convention of the Jewish academic communities of the medieval and modern periods to accept the Sages of the Talmud as authoritative, even though logic did not compel such deference.[10] However, this posture, adopted rather universally, in no way implied that the later scholars were inferior to those who preceded them. We will return to this idea in part III.

It would appear that Jewish tradition has provided a theory that would accord the talmudic Sages unique status: *hidardarut ha-dorot*, or the belief that with the passage of time, the spiritual level of humanity as a whole has declined.[11] Counter to the Enlightenment view that human progress is inevitable, most traditional Jews maintain a more pessimistic posture, insisting that the march of history moves through generations of ever-diminishing religious stature, until the final redemption in Messianic times. If Sinai is the fiery source of God's reve-lation of the Torah, then those temporally further away enjoy its warmth less and less. Perhaps the most famous expression of this idea is found in the Baby-lonian Talmud itself and is attributed to the early Amoraic period:

> R. Zera said in the name of Rava bar Zimuna: If we are as human beings, then they [the Tannaim of the first two centuries] are like angels, and if they are as human beings, then we are like asses, and not even the ass of Pinḥas ben Ya'ir.[12]

This erosion, deemed inexorable by many within the tradition, could be used to claim that only the Sages of the talmudic period (and before) were endowed with the requisite qualities for genuine religious legislation, and later generations, spiritual dwarfs by comparison, cannot legislate for the entire Jewish people.

However, on closer analysis, while this theory may be necessary to secure a unique position for the talmudic Sages, it is not sufficient. Granting that the overall slope of the generational line is negative does not in itself determine *which* earlier generation is authoritative for subsequent generations. Why is the end of the talmudic period the cutoff rather than, say, the end of the Second Temple period (which was prior) or even the end of the Geonic period (which was later)? To the contrary, this theory suggests that there is *no* cutoff at all, since for *every* generation, the generation *before it* was greater, implying that one should follow the religious interpretations and enactments of *all* one's predecessors, not just those of the talmudic Sages. Some traditional Jews may indeed be prepared to accept this (and we will return to this idea in chapter 7), but the theory does not ground a *unique* authority of the talmudic Sages.

Furthermore, the traditional stance does not clearly take this decline as determinative for reaching normative conclusions. First, the decline is often perceived in spiritual terms,[13] although given the rather holistic approach the Rabbis took to the personality of the Sage,[14] one's Torah knowledge was certainly affected by one's character. Second, being late did not mean that one's views were insignificant;[15] to the contrary, every generation had to accept the level of leadership it had and could not allow this theory of decline to paralyze it.[16] Lastly, admitting one's inferior stature did not necessarily negate the fact that one was able to build on the achievements of one's predecessors; the metaphor of "dwarves on the shoulders of giants" was invoked by some,[17] and the normative notion that within a scholarly period the law should follow the opinions of more recent scholars, (*hilkhata ki-vatrai*) derives from the same idea.[18]

With respect to Rabbinic legislation, then, seeing the Sages as epistemic authorities is valid and legitimate, but the theory cannot explain why we must grant only the Sages of the Talmud this unique status. Even the additional assumption of the decline of generations cannot reserve epistemic authority *exclusively* for the talmudic Rabbis.

Rabbinic Exegesis

In a maximalist view of the original revelation, the Sages function, in essence, as a type of eyewitness, informing us of the contents of the Oral Law. As links in the chain of oral tradition all the way back to Moses, they received from their teachers the laws revealed at Sinai. Thus, in the realm of exegesis, the Sages possess an epistemic authority of a different sort, akin to the reliability of a witness testifying to what was heard rather than an expert scholar explaining the meanings of difficult words. To be believed requires competence in memorization and retrieval, which some possess to a greater degree than others.[19]

But taking the analogy of a witness further, we must distinguish between exclusive witnesses, where no one else can verify what they claim they saw (barring other related evidence), and those who testify to an event that others witnessed as well and could easily corroborate. Intuitively, the level of trust involved in the first case is greater, since there is no way to test their claims independently of their testimony; we simply take it as reasonable to trust them if their testimony has withstood the rigor of cross-examination (possibly making claims about their character relevant). However, in the case of the Sages, no method of verification exists: we have no independent record of the oral tradition against which we can check their claims, although it is possible that the challenges recorded in the Talmuds to certain oral traditions are an effort at "cross-examining" the laws to see if they stand up to other criteria of authenticity (consistency with other laws, internal coherence, etc.).[20] We are forced to say that while it is rational to see the Sages as epistemic authorities if they are transmitting the laws, there is no way to *validate* the legitimacy of that belief. It is essentially only a rational form of trust.

As we consider a more minimalist version of revelation, where the Sages actively derive talmudic laws from the text, we are faced with the question of the nature of this derivation. On one reading, exegesis is a virtual science, involving the application of accepted hermeneutical rules to yield particular, yet necessary, results. Even laws which are connected to a single word or an extra letter are, in reality, based on the unique syntax or grammar of the original Hebrew.[21] The Rabbis were experts in this hermeneutical science, and we may therefore rely on their superior knowledge to inform us what the Torah truly meant. There is a "truth" involved since the text can imply only one law based on these rules; in theory, the implicit laws are verifiable, provided one masters the accepted techniques and applies them correctly. Like mathematics, there is only one correct answer to a problem, provided the rules are applied correctly.

Such a depiction of Rabbinic exegesis is appealing and would indeed render the Sages epistemic authorities. However, epistemic authority carries with it two significant implications: verifiability (others can achieve the same results if they reach the same level of knowledge as "the experts") and revisability (given more evidence, the conclusions can be changed to accord with the new information.[22] In the case of Rabbinic hermeneutics, if we accept the challenge to learn the scientific hermeneutical rules and then apply them to the text, the Sages' conclusions may or may not be verified, but they certainly cannot be revised. If we arrive at the same results as the Sages, then we corroborate their exegeses; but if our application of the rules yields a different result, then we cannot challenge the Sages' derivation. We are immediately told that either we did something wrong or we were not aware of something in the text. In other words, Rabbinic exegesis may follow rules, but in the end, the Sages cannot be characterized as epistemic authorities, for their results are irrefutable, and any contradiction of their derivations is deemed inadmissible. If our interpretations are regarded as valid if and only if they replicate those the Sages inferred, then the Rabbis cannot legitimately be deemed epistemic authorities, for they do not offer us a shortcut to information that we could, on our own, acquire. The irrefutability of the Sages' conclusions gives their exegeses a legislative, not interpretive, character.

None of this analysis should suggest that the talmudic Rabbis are *not* epistemic authorities for traditional Jews. The fact that some Jews, as the subjects of Rabbinic authority, a priori allow no evidence that would challenge the correctness of the Sages' enactments or exegeses does not in itself invalidate their belief or disqualify it as a case of epistemic authority. All I have shown is that given our definitions of "rationality" and "legitimacy," portraying the Sages as epistemic authorities in their exegetical activity, whether on a maximalist or minimalist version of revelation, cannot truly be termed "legitimate," since it is in principle irrefutable. To state someone is right is a proposition, subject to verification; to state someone is not *and never could be* wrong is, at bottom, a faith-claim.

The problematic issue of verifiability however, may lead us to an entirely different, or significantly revised, notion of the Rabbis' epistemic authority: as experts, the Rabbis' decisions in law and interpretation are *most likely* to be true or correct.[23] Admitting that religious legislation and textual interpretation do not readily conform to the model of a hard science, it is perhaps best to adopt the model of the social sciences and insist only that as individuals spiritually and intellectually endowed, the Sages' rulings have the *greatest probability* of embodying the proper understanding of the covenant with God. All that seeing the Rabbis as experts does is to radically reduce the likelihood that their decisions are misguided.[24] We are then extremely *confident* but, in the end, not *certain* that by obeying their pronouncements, we will be properly fulfilling what God wants us to do. A strict form of epistemic authority, which we found inappropriate to legislation, may be inappropriate to all the realms of Rabbinic activity, legislative and exegetical combined.

Summary

As we sought a model of Rabbinic authority that looked to the Sages themselves rather than to the positions they held, the idea of seeing them as experts initially seemed promising. Inclined, as many of us are, to rely on experts for our daily decisions, we were amenable to a portrayal of the talmudic Rabbis as experts in elaborating the terms of the Jews' covenant with God. Epistemic authority, however, involves the constant possibility of revision of conclusions, which does not accord well with the character of Rabbinic authority as essentially unchallengeable. Regarding their legislation, a belief in the "decline of generations" might produce a humility which bars change of the Sages' laws, but it could not legitimately withhold the same authority for legislation introduced by subsequent leaders for their own periods. With respect to exegesis, if one maintains a maximalist view of the original revelation, then the Sages' authority is that of loyal transmitters, not truly of *experts* in the typical sense. And if one maintains a more minimalist view of revelation, with the Rabbis applying rules of interpretation to the Torah's text, then it is difficult to consider this as expertise when any derivation other than the ones authored by the Sages is deemed legitimate.

After the above analysis, it is not surprising to find that the model of epistemic authority is not truly suited to the religious context. The notion of relying on experts carries with it three very important implications:

1. The knowledge is, in some way, verifiable and, hence, refutable.

2. The knowledge is inherently revisable, as we learn more and know more about a subject.

3. Anyone is capable, in principle, of becoming an expert (although a group may decide, as a convention, not to dispute its predecessors).

None of these implications accords well with the aim of granting normative and irrevocable authority to a group of ancient religious scholars:

1. Challenging their exegetical conclusions is a priori inadmissible.

2. Revising or rescinding their legislation in a fundamental and self-conscious way is not permitted.[25]

3. No one could ever attain their stature.[26]

Fundamentally, granting epistemic authority is simply a shortcut to personally accepting another's evidence or argument in an area in which we are not experts, at least presently. It does not entail strict obedience to the one who utters them per se.[27] Rabbinic authority, however, is an appeal to obey the talmudic Sages in everything they said.

Epistemic Authority in the Jewish Tradition: A Postscript

Before leaving this subject, it is worth suggesting that although erudition is certainly a *necessary* condition for religious leadership, it may not be sufficient. Aside from the importance given other spiritual qualities,[28] in the actual give-and-take of talmudic discussion, a Sage's learning and wisdom are never cited as a reason to follow his opinion. Most of the rules for deciding between scholarly views are given without explanation,[29] although some medieval commentators understood them to reflect the difference in expertise among the Amoraim.[30] The famous rule that the law follows the rulings of the Hillelites over the Shammaites is defended on entirely nonepistemic grounds: either because the Hillelites accorded respect to the Shammaites' opinions in their own academy,[31] or because of the general comportment of the Hillelites, despite, the Talmud adds, the intellectual rigor the Shammaites possessed.[32] Normative law in this case is *not* based on epistemic grounds.

Indeed, within the Rabbinic tradition as found in the Babylonian Talmud, erudition alone often *fails* to trump other arguments. The Talmud at times asserts that the reason the law was explicitly stated as following the majority in a particular case (a well-known rule) is that one might have thought that the minority opinion was correct in this case because "his reason is more logical"; we therefore had to be informed to resist such temptation when ruling.[33] Even more generally, those scholars who are taken, even by their contemporaries, to be the sharpest minds and the genuine experts have their opinions rejected because they are in the minority, a strictly procedural concern.[34]

We may say, then, that while knowledge and competence are crucial to being a Sage, they are not the only attributes taken into account when reaching a normative conclusion. The institutional features of a legal system (majority rule, interpretation of prior opinions, rules for decision making), coupled with some concern for religious and ethical character, all impact on the legal outcome of an issue.

SIX

The Divinely Guided Sages

In the introduction to part II, we pointed out that no matter which model of personal qualification we might explore, the basic "job description" remained the same: the clarification, elaboration, and furtherance of God's covenant with the Jewish people. All who could, for various reasons, fulfill this critical function would be deemed authoritative in the context of Jewish law. The last chapter claimed that at least in the realm of Rabbinic exegesis, the Sages were able to "hear" what God was saying through the divinely authored text.[1] By their expert training in the use of hermeneutical tools, they were able to discern God's will because they knew how to read the text. In a figurative sense, God "continued to speak" through the words of the Torah.

In this chapter, the notion of "continuous revelation" is taken much more literally.[2] Rather than assume that God revealed the Torah once and then "left it" to the people to determine the law in more particular situations, we will examine instead several versions of the theory which posits that the talmudic Sages were, in some way, instruments for the ongoing articulation of the divine will. Much as the Pentateuch was the written record of divine speech which occurred at a specific time and place, the talmudic Rabbis were the voicebox of a divine will which continued to manifest itself.

Maximalist Revelation and Rabbinic Transmission or Recovery

To a certain degree, we have already encountered this notion, although in a slightly different form: the maximalist view of revelation, which portrays the Sages' pronouncements as constituting an oral tradition tracing itself back to Moses. God is the author of both a written and an oral law; the former had been in written form for several centuries, but the latter was inscribed only much later in the Mishnah and Talmuds of the third to seventh centuries C.E.

Actually, this theory involves *two* separate claims, one about the scope of the original revelation and the other about the Sages' role in bringing that body of traditions to us. Regarding the latter, the most basic understanding of the Rabbinic role is that of *transmission*. According to this view, the talmudic Sages were simply the last in a long chain of those charged with transmitting the Oral Law, originally revealed at Sinai, from generation to generation. The fact that the Talmud attributes a view to a particular scholar is really only a shorthand for a longer "string of attributions" which could, in theory, go back to Moses.[3] But the contents of the Talmuds in fact have the same divine origin as the Written Law.

To be sure, this theory does not include any specific assertions regarding the personal qualities of the Sages other than assuming that they were trustworthy transmitters. As such, this theory does not necessarily need to be classed in this section of the book. Nevertheless, since this theory involves investigating various models that render the Rabbis' statements as close to divine utterances as possible, part II is the most suitable place to discuss this position.

Essential to this model is the assumption that the oral tradition has been preserved intact from the time of Moses until the period of the Sages. We may be able to trust the hundreds of scholars mentioned in Rabbinic literature to have passed on without any alteration what they received from their teachers, but we have to assume that what *they* received did not suffer any serious loss or accretion in the intervening generations. Based on the history of the Jews recorded in the Bible, with lengthy periods of idolatry and sinfulness, this is far from a trivial assumption.[4] Obviously, this assumption has nothing to do with the Sages themselves; but it is necessary if we are to assume the identity of what they transmitted in the first five centuries C.E. with the Oral Law revealed at Sinai.[5]

The elegance and simplicity of this model, however, cannot mask the difficulties we encounter when we try to use this picture to describe the reality of Rabbinic literature.

As the Karaites often argued, how can there be so much debate among the talmudic Sages if the tradition was merely transmitted? Even granting that some error had naturally entered the process of transmission, it would probably still not account for the vast amount of disagreement recorded in the Talmuds. And if we assume, for the sake of argument, that error did indeed permeate the oral tradition to a great extent, this would raise the specter of doubt *with respect to virtually every law* whether the normative opinion was indeed the law which was given at Sinai to Moses. With no means of verifying the contents of the oral tradition, the identification of the Sages' views, and especially those that were accepted as normative, with a divinely revealed set of laws is, once again, strictly a faith-claim.

In an apparent effort to address this difficulty, several Rabbinic midrashim expand the scope of the original revelation (the first of the two claims cited above) to include *all conceivable legal opinions*.[6] In other words, the oral tradition revealed to Moses was, not a single set of instructions on how to act in every situation, but a comprehensive list of acceptable legal options for all cases; it was then left to the Sages to decide from among these options. The assumption that Moses transmitted an exhaustive catalog of alternatives to subsequent generations explains the presence of debate in the Rabbinic tradition, but it then introduces its own problems, one historical, one metaphysical or epistemological.

The first is the simple question of normative practice in such a scenario. If Moses was already forced to decide between these alternatives, were his decisions transmitted as well? If they were, why were they not binding on others? If they were not binding, and the other alternatives remained legitimate options for practice, then why was that diversity not preserved even after the Rabbinic period? Talmudic debates should have been left unresolved rather than decided one way or the other.

The second problem, metaphysical or epistemological in nature, is one that we have mentioned earlier: how a divine revelation could include within it multiple truths.[7] By multiple truths, we mean not indeterminate texts that may have more than one instantiation (as we argued in chapter 2 with respect to Deut. 17:9's "the judge in charge at the time") but mutually exclusive positions held by various scholars—"x" and "not-x."[8] We could, of course, retreat into claims of divine logic being incomprehensible and unmeasurable by the canons of human reason, but that is, in the end, obscurantist.

A radically maximalist view of revelation also confronts problems of scope. Were all rabbinic pronouncements included in the original revelation or only those involving exegesis of the Written Torah? How are we to understand the authority of Rabbinic enactments, customs, or new holidays? Were they too revealed to Moses at Sinai, or simply the authority to institute them? If disclosed prophetically to Moses, did he then pass them on intact, despite their contemporary nonrelevance? Why then does Rabbinic tradition present these ordinances as enacted by individuals, when in reality they had been known of for centuries?

Lastly, we must inspect the historical range of maximalist view of revelation. Is the body of inherited Oral Law exhausted by the contents of the two Talmuds? By the entire Rabbinic corpus? What about subsequent exposition of the Talmud by medieval and even modern scholars: is that considered part of the oral tradition or outside it? If it, too, is part of the Oral Law revealed at Sinai, as some Rabbinic statements suggest,[9] then there is no reason to privilege Rabbinic sources over medieval or even modern ones: all can trace their origins to the original revelation.[10]

Once again, we encounter the dilemma of widening the scope and range of a particular category sufficiently to include the talmudic Sages, yet keeping it narrow enough to exclude those beyond them. This is proving to be one of the core problems encountered in every theory of Rabbinic authority.

There exists another, slightly different, version of the Sages' role in a maximalist view of revelation: that of *recovery*. Rather than insist that everything revealed at Sinai was carefully passed on and preserved for over a millennium, this view asserts that the Rabbinic project was to transmit that which it received and to figure out the law when the oral tradition had been forgotten. Rabbinic sources cite this notion on occasion, with respect to several laws.[11] This portrayal of the Sages' activity allows us to understand the Talmud's attributions in their plain, simple sense: that the opinion recorded is indeed the view of a particular scholar and not necessarily of the last name in a long line of assumed transmission. But since the genuine origin of the legal position is, in reality, God's revelation to Moses at Sinai, it is deemed legitimate as an expression of God's will. The above discussion with respect to the scope of that original oral revelation applies here as well, mutatis mutandis. And, of course, a combination of these models—some material transmitted, some recovered through exegesis or argument—is possible.

Whether the Sages passed on an extensive legal legacy or simply sought to recover it, in the end the statement that Rabbinic opinions reflect the divine revelation is a faith-claim, for the original revelation, whatever its contents, is unrecoverable. Without the capacity for independent verification, claiming that what the talmudic Sages said ipso facto represents all or part of the original revelation disclosed to Moses by God at Sinai must be accepted on faith.

Divinely Inspired Sages

If we seek God's involvement more directly in the Rabbinic project per se rather than in its origins at Sinai, then no claim embodies this participation more than the view that the Sages were divinely inspired. Regardless of the extent of the original revelation, the talmudic Rabbis, imbued with some form of divine spirit, expressed in essence not their own opinions but those of God.[12] To be sure, the Sages believed that prophecy in its more literal sense had ceased sometime around the Jews' return from Babylonia in the 6th century B.C.E., thus closing what had previously been the most direct channel from God.[13] However, the regnant view throughout the talmudic period was that other forms of divine inspiration (such as the heavenly echo)[14] continued, although much more episodically.[15] Scholars were seen to be the heirs of the prophets, possessing some form of prophetic endowment.[16] According to some medieval scholars, this quality protected the talmudic Sages from error[17] and even granted several Rabbinic pronouncements the status of divine commandment.[18]

Dependence on the Determinacy of the Divine Will

The attractiveness of this theory lies, of course, in the consequent character of Rabbinic law. If the Sages were, in some way, divinely inspired, then the Jews who seek only to live within the covenant and to do as God desires could be assured that by following the Rabbis' rulings, they would be fulfilling God's will. This is in contrast to the anxiety implicit in both the institutional and epistemic models of the Sages' authority, for although in the end God endorses the Sages' ruling, the possibility always exists that their decision is contrary to the divine intention.[19] Granting that the Sages possessed divine inspiration would ensure that their legal pronouncements were in fact religiously desirable[20] and possibly elevate them to the level of Torah obligation.[21]

Of course, the risk that Rabbinic decisions are contrary to the divine will exists only if one assumes that on every matter God's intention is determinate. This is a reasonable assumption with respect to interpretation of the Torah, since the tradition sees the Torah as the verbatim dictation from God to Moses, and authorial intent was arguably present. Prophetically inspired, as opposed to humanly derived, elaboration would ensure that the divine will was properly articulated. However, what if we were to assume that not every word in a particular verse has a specific meaning? Take, for example, the case of the term *shofet* (judge) in Deut. 17:9. In chapter 2, I suggested that the term may be *deliberately* ambiguous in order to accommodate and legitimize any number of juridical entities that may sit at the top of the nation's judicial system. In a similar vein, other verses may have intentionally been worded by God in such a way as to allow multiple interpretations, all of which were "acceptable" to God as fulfillments of those commandments. In other words, the "risk" of failing to fulfill God's will in the performance of commandments is directly proportional to the level of the text's determinacy. But a priori, it is just as conceivable that God allowed an authorized body to determine the details of his indeterminate commandments as it is that God had a specific intention for every word in the Torah, which the prophetically endowed Sages elaborated for us.

This entire line of reasoning assumes that although the Torah's sole purpose was to reveal the set of behaviors that God requires of the Jewish people, there may be, not one particular way of doing something that God prefers, but several or even many. However, this "divinely authorized pluralism" is not the only possible reason to have preferred lexical ambiguity in the Torah. It is conceivable that one of the "behaviors" God desired was the process of studying the text, arguing the various positions which may be inferred from the verse(s), and arriving at a conclusion. In other words, Torah study and halakhic discussion are part of the *ideal*; indeed, the Rabbis portrayed Torah study for its own sake as not only an independent commandment but one that equaled all other commandments combined.[22] A straightforward, unambigious set of instructions would have reduced Torah to a mere handbook to be consulted when needed. Few would have been motivated to engage the text for the religiously positive experience involved in such engagement. Thus, the indeterminacy of the text might be deliberate in order to allow for human "participation." In this scenario, prophetic endowment is not a benefit but a handicap, for it would render the careful study and analysis of Torah unnecessary at some level.[23]

In fact, the "edge" provided by divine inspiration is blunted even further when we discuss Rabbinic legislation. In a new situation which has an impact on the social or religious condition of the Jews, seeing the Sages as prophets is valuable only if we assume that God desires a specific measure to be taken.[24] Divine omniscience, however, does not intrinsically entail the determination of his will; it is certainly possible that God may have no particular intention as to what should be done, rendering the question of Rabbinic approximation of divine will irrelevant. Let us take the holiday of Ḥanukkah, for example. The Maccabees are victorious over the Seleucid Greeks and rededicate the defiled Temple in

Jerusalem. This miraculous salvation, on many counts, deserved some acknowledgment of divine Providence and the expression of thanksgiving. Perhaps that alone was part of the divine intention; but that general goal could reasonably be achieved in any number of ways. The Rabbinic decision to institute an annual holiday that included the daily recitation of Hallel (psalms of thanksgiving) and a nightly kindling of lights was not the only conceivable way to commemorate the miraculous salvation. Granting the Sages' prophetic prowess in this regard does little for the force of their legislation unless one assumes that specifically this ritual was the way God wanted the Jews to celebrate the Hasmonean victory and the Temple's rededication.

Therefore, a Jew's anxiety about performing God's will is relieved by seeing the Sages as prophets only if we assume that in the realm of exegesis, each word of the Torah had only *one, determinate meaning*, and in the realm of legislation, God desired a *particular response* to every situation that arose. If indeterminacy is allowed, even partially, in either one of these areas (and it may even be desirable in certain cases), then the prophetic model does not necessarily provide greater confidence that Rabbinic law definitively captures the divine will.

Difficulties with Postulating the Sages' Divine Inspiration

Assuming, for the moment, that the divine will is, in fact, determinate, then we would have to conclude that for every given situation, God prefers only one type of behavior for a given individual. (Technically, the situation is different for each person, depending on age, gender, etc.) Jewish law, as articulated by the talmudic Sages, must then correspond to that list of divinely specified rules and regulations. Prima facie, if the Sages possessed some level of divine inspiration, then we could be confident that their utterances accurately reflected what God desired. Let us examine this claim more closely.

Since we are claiming that the talmudic Rabbis were, in some sense, divinely inspired, it would be instructive to substitute "prophet" for "Sage" and then see what is gained by this approach to understanding Rabbinic authority. In the simplest case, a prophet tells the Jews that God has appeared to him and told him to instruct them to perform some action at such-and-such a time and in such-and-such a way. If this prophet is an established prophet, who in the past has proven that in fact God communicates through him, and so he need not certify his prophetic status again, then it would behoove the Jews to heed his instructions. If this is the prophet's first divine communication, it would be legitimate for the Jews to insist that he validate his status before they proceed to do his bidding. Indeed, the Torah itself (Deut. 18:15–22) assumes that a prophet will need to authenticate his role by predicting something and having it come true; only then will people know that he should be obeyed (unless he instructs the people to worship idols; see Deut. 13:2–6). This is the "normal" case of the prophet.

Now let us assume that one prophet comes and tells me to do one thing, and another prophet instructs me to do otherwise. (To simplify the case, assume both prophets have established their authenticity earlier.) In assessing the situation, three possibilities exist:

1. They are both telling the truth, and God has in fact communicated these two sets of instructions.

2. Only one is telling the truth, and the other one is not.

3. Neither is telling the truth.

To a large degree, my assessment of who is telling the truth will depend on what they are telling me to do. If the two activities can both be done, then all three possibilities obtain, although the first is the most likely, given the prophets' proven authenticity. Choosing to do one of the actions would not be improper, since both probably come from God, but to be "safe," I should probably try to do both. The same is true if the two instructions are proscriptive (i.e., they prohibit me from doing something; to be cautious I should avoid both behaviors).

If, however, they are asking me to do mutually exclusive behaviors (one says to do something with my right foot; the other says to do it with my left and *not* with my right), then obviously possibility 1 cannot be true. I have two choices: (1) I can choose to do one of them, in which case there is an equal probability that I am doing the right thing as the wrong thing; or (2) I can do neither. Deciding between these two options largely depends on the nature of the instructions and how they relate to the rest of the corpus of Jewish law. Thus, if they are prescriptive but performing one entails a violation of another, different rule, then I should choose the one that will not transgress any law. If they are equally benign with respect to other laws, then I am free to choose whichever instruction I want.

The analogy to the case of the talmudic Sages is clear. As a general comment, claiming that the Rabbis were, in some sense, divinely inspired bestows on them and on their pronouncements *collectively* an aura of divinity. However, applying that notion carefully and precisely to what the Sages actually *do* in the Talmud leads to a considerable amount of confusion.

First, are all the Rabbis mentioned in the Talmud operating with a measure of divine inspiration, or only certain ones, and if so, which? The Tannaim? Those scholars with *semikhah* (ordination)?

Second, if the Sages were divinely inspired, does that apply to everything they uttered or only to certain sorts of statements? For instance, what is the status of nonhalakhic material uttered by the Rabbis, such as *aggadot*, medical cures, or historical statements? What about decision-making principles, such as "the law follows Samuel in monetary matters, but it follows Rav in ritual matters?" What about the anonymous statements in the Talmud, from unattributed tannaitic material (*mishnayyot* and *beraitot*) to the questions and answers of the *sugyot* (talmudic units of discussion), which often relate to normative matters?

Third, the ubiquity of debate must be addressed in any theory of divine inspiration.[25] If the talmudic Sages are operating with some measure of prophetic endowment, then we are forced to assert that the divine will is not monolithic in any logical sense; it may maintain mutually exclusive positions simultaneously, allowing other considerations to determine the normative law in each case.[26]

This is certainly the force of the talmudic expression "the utterances of both are the words of the living God" (*eilu ve-eilu divrei Elohim ḥayyim*), even as it is admitted that only one view can be followed practically.[27] (It should be stressed that this is not a retreat to the view, articulated earlier, that God's will is indeterminate; it is the more positive claim that *both* legal views are, at the same time, legitimate expressions of the divine intention. This notion needs more serious investigation.)[28]

The question remains, of course, *why* would God inspire scholars to maintain differing opinions on the same subject? Is God merely being playful? Is he testing us, in the manner of the false prophet (Deut. 13:2–6)? How are we to understand the Talmud's reasoned rejection of one scholar's view—did God inspire a Sage to maintain an untenable position? What could that mean logically?

If we assume that not every talmudic Rabbi was prophetically endowed, then presumably the pronouncements of only the divinely inspired Sages should be adopted as normative. Yet such a consideration is never mentioned in the course of talmudic debate; to the contrary, when R. Eliezer invokes the heavenly echo in the story of Akhnai's oven (BT Bava Meṣi'a 59b), his position is rejected nevertheless!

If we assume that the position treated as normative is the one that was expressed with the aid of divine inspiration, then how can we allow rejected opinions to retain sufficient legitimacy to be relied upon under extenuating circumstances?[29] If we are not sure which position is the result of divine inspiration, then why do we not consistently choose a behavior that will accommodate as many opinions as possible?

If, on the other hand, *all* the Sages are divinely inspired, then for practical reasons we must fall back on other criteria—institutional, procedural, or merely conventional—to establish whom the law should follow. While this seems to render the fact of divine inspiration consequentially irrelevant, there is still some meaningful benefit, for no matter which opinion is adopted normatively, Jews can be confident that it accords with the divine will. No anxiety need exist regarding fulfillment of the covenant, for all of the Sages' positions are sanctioned by God. Even rejected opinions, which, as noted, are relied upon in extraordinary situations, are similarly endorsed. To the contrary, the case may need to be made why one *must* follow the normative opinion, since as long as a Jew follows at least one of the Rabbinic positions, that person's behavior in theory reflects the divine will (unless one argues that divine endorsement of a position is conditional).[30]

The above discussion shows rather clearly that attributing some form of divine inspiration to the talmudic Rabbis is far from a simple, straightforward claim. Aside from the fact that, unlike prophets, the Sages were never asked to validate their status, trying to apply this notion to the talmudic project is fraught with both technical and substantive difficulties. As an *actual* description of what the Rabbis did, from the variety of their utterances to the prevalence of halakhic debate and the methods by which they are resolved, it is apparent that such a claim of divine inspiration will not, on its own, raise the Sages' pronouncements to the level of divine command. Assumptions regarding the determinacy of divine

THE DIVINELY GUIDED SAGES 91

intention, the scope and extent of the inspiration, and the nature of decision making in the Talmud are all needed to begin to give greater definition and substance to the claim that the talmudic Rabbis were divinely inspired.

Hashgaḥah Peratit—Divine Providence

Judaism, like several other theistic traditions, does not restrict the level of divine involvement in human affairs strictly to the realm of prophecy. There is also the cardinal belief in God's supervision of the world's events, at both the collective and the individual levels. While Jewish views on this subject are many and varied,[31] all admit that God did not simply create the world and "leave," but that the deity continued to be aware of and participate in its ongoing history.

In a similar vein, it could be argued that the revelation of the Torah, whether at Sinai or throughout the forty years of wandering in the desert, was not a one-time event, but that God has continued to supervise the history of the development of Halakhah ever since.[32] To be sure, this participation is not as explicit or direct as prophecy, but such a position ensures that although certain events appear entirely natural and ordinary, in the end they achieve God's ultimate purpose. Thus, "large" events such as the emergence of the various schools in the late Second Temple period and the acceptance of Judah the Patriarch's Mishnah,[33] as well as such "smaller" events as the decision to follow certain scholars as a general rule, can all be understood as occurring under God's watchful gaze and thus advancing the overall divine plan for the development of Jewish law.

Employing this model to account for Rabbinic authority does not entail the claim that the talmudic Sages were personally endowed with any gifts or divine qualities, such as ruaḥ ha-qodesh. Rather, the model claims that the fact that Jewish law evolved in a way which endorsed Rabbinic interpretations of the Torah indicates that God desired it to be so; it was providential that the Sages, and not other rival groups such as the Sadducees or the Essenes, achieved the authoritative status that they did. This is not a tautology but a theological affirmation of the status quo: if the Sages historically became the authorities for Jewish law, it must have been intended so by God.

At first glance, this theory constitutes an ideal intermediate position: it both affirms what we perceive phenomenologically as the human origin of much halakhic deliberation and at the same time ensures an outcome that will not contravene the divine intention. Thus, using their own rational faculties, scholars arrived at their respective legal opinions, but the view(s) which ultimately achieved normative status—be it through a formal vote,[34] an "explicit" heavenly echo,[35] or gradual acceptance[36]—were the one(s) which God had indeed desired. One advantage of this approach is that no distinction need be made between exegesis and legislation; Providence directs the outcome in either realm. We can thus be confident that by following Jewish law as explicated and developed by the Rabbis, we are acting in accordance with the divine will.

On closer inspection, however, we see that this approach requires considerable clarification. If we believe that the practice which accords with the divine will becomes normative for Jewish law, we have to assume that God's will is determinate (i.e., that God indeed prefers only one type of behavior for any particular situation). While there is nothing wrong with making this assumption, it does beget certain other difficulties.

In the standard case of various legal opinions being voiced, with a vote taken after the deliberations, there is little difficulty in applying this notion of divine Providence. But we admitted that divine Providence has at its disposal many ways by which to achieve the normativity of God's will, some of them taking several generations.[37] How are we to understand that intervening period of time? Those who follow the view that will *not* be accepted later are, in effect, not fulfilling God's commandments, since in every case God's will is determinate. We cannot suggest that God's will remains indeterminate until a decision is reached on earth, since the very basis of this theory is that God providentially directs the law to accept the position that he already desires. Of course, we could say that although God does indeed have a preference, while the "jury is still out" on a particular issue we are not held responsible for doing the "right thing" since from our perspective all positions are still valid and legitimate. However, this view implies that many Jews may be punctiliously observing laws in ways which are not acceptable to God—a rather uncomfortable position religiously for most people.

We proposed that divine Providence ensures that the position which reflects the determinate divine intention will achieve normative status. However, Providence can only work with the pool of opinions that have already been voiced. What if the view which Providence wants to endorse has not been uttered yet? Does Providence simply "wait" until that happens, or does it somehow "guide" the scholars to make sure that the divinely preferred opinion makes it to the floor for consideration? If this is the case, we are necessarily led to the subject of the extent of divine Providence.

We proposed this model as a way of reconciling the apparently human enterprise of halakhic decision making with some level of divine involvement in that process. However, we a forced to wonder why Providence controls only the later stages leading to the outcome of halakhic adjudication and not those involved in the earlier phases of the process. As mentioned, some measure of Providence may be required simply to generate the desired opinion among those raised in the course of halakhic discussion. If that is the case, then why could Providence not ensure that *only* the "correct" position will be taken from the beginning? Obviously, we have to seek some justification for the generation of "incorrect" views; perhaps they, too, are providentially desirable in extenuating circumstances (Mishnah 'Eduyot 1:5), in which case divine Providence is, in fact, orchestrating the *entire* halakhic process from beginning to end, ensuring that *all* opinions that will have any normative value will be produced. Alternatively, there is, as suggested earlier,[38] independent merit to the creation of various opinions based on intense Torah study, regardless of whether or not they approximate the divine will. Thus, Providence "allows" the ongoing generation of multiple legal opinions because, although they have little or no normative value, the enterprise itself is religiously valuable.

There is another possibility, linked to the prior discussion of the determinacy of the divine will. Up to this point, we have considered the issue rather disjunctively: either God's will is completely determinate with respect to every commandment, desiring only one specific action or behavior, or the divine will is utterly indeterminate, and any way the Sanhedrin or the Sages or the people agree to interpret the law is acceptable to God (the example we used was "the judge in charge at the time"; Deut. 17:9). However, it is equally possible to overcome the determinate/indeterminate distinction entirely by positing that while God may not have intended a single, particular interpretation of a verse, that does not imply that "anything goes." Rather, a "range" or "spectrum" of interpretations are all equally possible, and these are all acceptable in God's mind, as it were. Thus, God's will may indeed be determinate, but that determinacy encompasses an *array* of legal opinions, which Providence ensures will be voiced among the Sages. On this understanding, then, there is no religious anxiety during the time before a final halakhic position is reached; anyone who performs one of the articulated views is doing what God desires. Providence thus guides the entire halakhic process, even from its earliest phases when various opinions are initially generated, but on a rather wide road; as long as Halakhah stays within the borders of that road, it is headed in a direction that has the approbation of God.

The consequence of this view, of course, is that if and when subsequent development of Jewish law narrows the range of options (often down to one), why, if all the views had been acceptable to God originally, must all Jews now conform to the few positions that have become normative? This theory would be forced into assuming that for whatever reason, Providence did not desire the perpetuation of a pluralistic condition, but at some point preferred greater uniformity of practice among Jews. Halakhah continues to travel on the road charted by divine Providence, but at various times, the road narrows and widens, according to what God sees fit.

Uncertainty as to the extent of divine Providence leads to another serious implication regarding Rabbinic authority. Let us assume, for the moment, a more maximalist notion of Providence, whereby not only the outcome but the legal opinions themselves are overseen by God's guiding hand. Jewish law, as developed and elaborated upon by the talmudic Sages, has become the accepted form of Jewish practice. After some time, however, a schismatic group challenges the Rabbinic interpretations of the law and proposes a very different set of practices, claiming that they are in fact what the Torah commands. If we base the claim to Rabbinic authority on divine Providence, then we have no *inherent* way of limiting the application of that principle, for the emergence of this schismatic group is no less providentially determined than was the slow establishment of Rabbinic law as the normative form of Jewish practice. In other words, there seems to be an implicit quietism in the notion of Providence: God desires the state of affairs to be this way, and we are therefore enjoined not to oppose it. Of course, one could argue that a providential etiology does not grant instant legitimacy; in Deuteronomy 13, God grants the false prophet certain powers in order to test the people. This would serve as a warrant for the contemporary religious leaders to oppose the schismatic group with all the resources at their disposal. Nevertheless, it is not immediately evident or apparent when an event transpires because Providence endorses it and when it serves as a trial that we are meant to counter and resist. Is the divine echo meant to be accepted, as when it affirmed the positions of the school of Hillel, or is it meant to be opposed, as when the heavenly echo supported R. Eliezer? Is the acceptance of R. Judah's Mishnah in the third century a reflection of the ideal and to be confirmed, or is it an aberration of it, intended to be overturned?[39]

Lastly, once we raise the issue of divine Providence, there is little reason to assume that God's supervision extended over the talmudic Rabbis and their opinions but not over subsequent periods and their scholars. If after giving the Torah God oversaw its unfolding over the millennia, there is no logic to limiting that oversight to one period of Jewish history. Some scholars have seen the ongoing development of Jewish law in precisely this light: the fate of Halakhah in every generation is dictated by divine Providence.[40]

As this discussion is beginning to make clear, bringing divine Providence into a discussion of a complex and multiphasic human process means that we cannot say for certain which elements of the process are under the aegis of God's supervision and which are not. Indeed, examined independently, the notion that divine Providence guides the world even as events appear driven by human actions and decisions is not easily comprehended or explained.[41] The phenomenal world, in which all we see is what is before us, does not readily lend itself to perceiving God's noumenal Providence, as much as we may want to affirm it as a principle of faith. By grounding Rabbinic authority in divine Providence, we essentially extend the contours and features of the latter—its mysteries, paradoxes, and faith-claims—to include our subject as well.

Summary

Perhaps no theory held out as much hope for grounding the Sages' authority as that which incorporated a divine component directly into the Rabbinic project. In a system that accepts as its postulate obedience to the divine command, reducing or at least framing the Sages' authority in terms of divine authority should, in principle, succeed in establishing the basis of normative Rabbinic Halakhah. We examined three versions of this theory:

1. The Sages only transmitted a fully developed (oral) divine revelation whose origins were at Sinai.

2. The talmudic Rabbis were prophetically endowed, so that their rulings and pronouncements were really divinely inspired.

3. Divine Providence directed the development of Halakhah so that whatever was accepted as normative, or was initially uttered by the Sages, was in essence endorsed by God.

However, no matter which version of the theory we examined, we saw that three fundamental issues remained either obscure or unresolved: the ubiquity of disagreement among the Sages; the scope of Rabbinic utterances that would come under the category of divinely aided speech; and the range of rabbis to be seen as operating under divine inspiration.

In essence, then, by referring to divine authority to varying degrees, all these versions of the theory of Rabbinic authority share the theory's basic character: it boils down to a matter of faith. Just as Jews believe that the Torah was given by God at Sinai (possibly the *Grundnorm* of the halakhic system),[42] so too may that faith-claim be extended to a maximalist revelation embodied in the views of the Sages or to the divinely inspired quality of Rabbinic decisions or to the view that the history of Halakhah's development is not random but under God's careful supervision. In the final analysis, by choosing to see God as speaking and acting through the Sages and their laws, Rabbinic authority and divine command fuse to the point where both require one and the same act of faith.

The analysis in chapters 5 and 6 proved that seeing the Sages as *an* authority required inspecting two separable issues, both within the accepted context that Jewish practice is to accord with God's will: (1) an "anthropological" issue, which dealt with the qualifications required to perform the task of ascertaining the divine intention (in the absence of prophecy); and (2) a historical-biographical issue, which examined whether indeed the talmudic Sages, *to the exclusion of all others*, met those qualifications. The first issue depended directly on one's prior assumption regarding the scope of the original revelation: a maximalist conception demands trustworthy transmitters, while a more minimalist understanding requires competence and expertise in the application of hermeneutical rules, if indeed exegesis is a rule-governed enterprise (leaving aside the area of Rabbinic legislation for the moment). In either case, the accuracy of Rabbinic pronouncements cannot be tested against any corroborating data; either we have no *independent* access to the original oral tradition against which we may compare the Rabbis' statements, or our own exegeses of Scripture are deemed invalid if they do not accord with the Sages' interpretations. Epistemic authority, as it is understood in the contemporary West, is based in part on verifiability, and Rabbinic pronouncements are not, in truth, subject to verification.

Moreover, the possession of knowledge is inherently democratic and egalitarian (which also contributes to its verifiability); while it might be argued that the Sages were the only people who in fact achieved a level of epistemic mastery, such competence cannot logically be withheld from any future group of scholars. In the end, Rabbinic authority is a matter of trust; traditional Jews have faith that what the talmudic Sages said was either exactly what God told Moses orally (and in this case, the trust must extend as well to believing that the oral traditions have been transmitted in an unadulterated form) or was the precise and accurate application of valid hermeneutic principles to the divine text.

We do not fare much better when we posit that the Sages enjoyed some special status by virtue of divine involvement in their activities. Whether we claim that they were individually divinely inspired or that divine Providence governed their deliberations and decisions, we are faced with explaining why there is so much disagreement among them, whether all their pronouncements bear the same mantle of divine authorship, and whether only the talmudic Rabbis possessed this quality uniquely—all of which is hard to discuss given the inscrutability of the divine realm.

As a postscript, we might reverse the order—namely, that God subsequently endorsed what the Sages pronounced on their own initiative and using their own gifts, an idea occasionally reflected in the Aggadah.[43] This understanding is certainly conceivable, although it does involve certain assumptions regarding the mutability of the divine will.[44] At this point I can only add that the more this divine endorsement becomes automatic or routine, the closer it approximates the sort of institutional model of Rabbinic authority discussed in part I. If it is more episodic or occasional, then we would certainly want to know which Sages or opinions enjoyed divine approbation and which did not; more significantly, though, this view implies that "Rabbinic authority" does not encompass all the talmudic Sages or everything they said and did. In any event, such an approach is essentially a faith-claim, outside the realm of any sort of verification.

It must be emphasized that the aim of this analysis has not been to debunk Rabbinic authority or discredit those who follow the decisions of the talmudic Sages. The first two parts of this book have simply shown that the concept of authority is complex, involving a range of philosophical and historical claims and assumptions, some of which are, at bottom, a matter of faith. In this sense, Rabbinic authority is very similar to the divine authority upon which the entire system of Jewish law rests: for the contemporary Jew, they are both religious beliefs.

PART III

RABBINIC AUTHORITY AS AUTHORITY TRANSFORMED

Our discussion up to this point has been organized according to R. S. Peters's incisive distinction between being *in* and *an* authority. The three theories examined in part I all see authority as residing in a particular office or seat, accompanied by the historical claim that the Rabbis of the first five centuries C.E. occupied those offices or seats. It was difficult, however, to limit ex cathedra understandings of authority to the talmudic Sages alone. All these theories needed supplemental postulates, usually of a historical sort, to claim that whatever sort of authority Rabbinic authority was, it was not shared by any group or individual other than the talmudic Sages.

Since, in any event, we needed auxiliary historical claims about the Rabbis to make the arguments in part I viable, it was natural to turn in part II to theories of authority that centered on the talmudic Rabbis themselves. Chapters 5 and 6 sought to identify qualities which these Sages possessed both internally and uniquely, in order to secure for them an exclusive sort of authority. As it turned out, however, it proved difficult to see how epistemic authority could be reserved exclusively for the talmudic Sages given the inherent egalitarian nature of knowledge. Attributing certain supernatural qualities to the Rabbis, on the other hand, did indeed justify Rabbinic authority logically but on its own was seen to be a rather substantial faith-claim which itself could not be authenticated.

Nevertheless, Peters's distinction is not the only way to structure an analysis of Rabbinic authority. Other theoretical "fault lines" are equally legitimate, and no single construct is either privileged or primary. For instance, many of the theories we examined viewed authority as emanating "from the top down," whereby a prior recognized authority bestowed some measure of that authority on others. Theories such as a biblically authorized High Court or a claim of divine inspiration begin with accepting God as the supreme authority within Judaism and then seeing Rabbinic authority as derivative of it. On the other hand, portraying Rabbinic authority as an instance of epistemic authority (chapter 5) was a more subject-oriented theory in that the people's confidence in the Sages' knowledge, whether as trustworthy transmitters of a revealed tradition or as expertly trained interpreters of the Written Law, was the genuine basis for the Rabbis' authority. On this view, authority emanates "from the bottom up," not so much in the political sense of officially authorizing a designated leader but at least in the sense that it is the subjects' view of the bearers which is constitutive of the latter's authority.

Of course, these are not hermetically sealed categories; in chapter 2, I suggested that the Bible may be authorizing as the High Court any person, institution, or text that the *people* take to be the ultimate arbiter of law. This model represents an interesting mixture, for even as there is a popular "bottom-up" component in what seems to be the choice of the particular *form* of the high court, the *ground* that such an institution should have any authority at all seems to remain the "top-down" Deuteronomic command to obey the high court of the time.

This interesting combination, however, invites further reflection, for the relational nature of authority means that the people's choice of a particular organ as their divinely authorized *shofet* (judge) is more than a mere choice of "form." In accepting upon themselves a court, a king, a priest, or a group of rabbis as their *shofet*, the people grant a significant measure of de facto authority to that institution, even if the Torah must then come and accord de jure authority as well. The *ground* of such authority is less easily described as "from the top down," for the people's acceptance is a vital—indeed, definitional—component of the *shofet*'s authority. Thus, at some level, the actual bottom-up understanding of authority may be just as relevant for Rabbinic authority as it is for the case examined in chapter 2, when our gaze was focused exclusively at the "top."

The next two chapters will therefore shift their focus to the "other side" of the relational notion of authority, namely, the people. Chapter 7 will examine the view that Rabbinic authority is based on the people's acceptance of the practices instituted by the Sages, a position in fact advocated by some traditional medieval sources. The analysis will yield the possibility that what started out as the "authority of the talmudic Rabbis" eventually evolved into the "authority of Jewish tradition," even as it retained the name "Rabbinic authority."

Similarly, chapter 8 will explore the notion that the authority of the Sages, which for their contemporaries may or may not have been quite real, was ultimately invested in the tome which represented the most comprehensive collection of the Rabbis' sayings: the Babylonian Talmud. The class of post-talmudic experts who interpreted and applied Jewish law to contemporary circumstances, for a variety of historical and legal reasons, came to regard the Talmud of Babylonia as the main text of Jewish law. "Rabbinic authority" was real and palpable for the jurists who invoked the Sages' opinions in all their legal deliberations. This referencing, citation, and interpretation has continued for almost fifteen centuries, and continues apace today in traditional Jewish circles. Once transformed into the authority of a text, Rabbinic authority assumed certain features that are rather unique to legal texts, especially within Judaism.

Referring to the Sages' authority in a less "literal" sense invites reflection on the nature of the discussion of authority in any community. Inspired by Ludwig Wittgenstein's analysis of rule following in language and Stanley Fish's discussion of the role interpretive communities play in literary criticism, chapter 9 reconsiders the entire "question" of authority as it has been traditionally understood, especially in the modern West. What was described rather uncritically as the subject of our inquiry in the introduction is probed more critically in this final chapter in an effort to illuminate the more hidden dimensions of one form of religious authority in Judaism. In the end, communities, texts, interpreters, and practices are seen to be so intimately and inextricably woven together in a particular form of life as to render discussion of any single one's authority into a discussion of the authority of them all.

SEVEN

The Authority of Publicly Accepted Practice

Throughout parts I and II, I have insisted that every theory that seeks to ground the Sages' authority must make its case with respect to the various sorts of Rabbinic activity: transmission of oral traditions, biblical exegesis, and legislation. My analysis showed that in most cases, the model of Rabbinic authority under discussion was more suited to one of those activities than to others: scriptural interpretation may be a rule-governed enterprise requiring expertise or faithful transmission, whereas appropriate and effective legislation demands skills of a different sort. This circumscription of each theory to a specific domain hardly reflects its deficiency; rather, it is an indication of the rarely acknowledged multifarious nature of our subject, which may in fact force us to admit multiple, rather than single, grounds for Rabbinic authority.

Indeed, Maimonides (twelfth century) seems to have been aware of these important distinctions. Early on in his lifelong pursuit of organizing and systematizing Jewish law and thought, he distinguished between the various sorts of Rabbinic activity, noting five general areas.[1] The fourth and fifth categories, he claimed, are the province of Rabbinic "innovation," where the Sages instituted various decrees, enactments, and customs. What is interesting for our discussion is his explanation of the authority of these two types of Rabbinic activity:

> Circumstances were such that Ravina, Rav Ashi, and their colleagues were the last of the great Sages of Israel who transmitted the Oral Torah and who issued edicts, decrees, and customs which spread to all Jews, wherever they were settled. Subsequent to the compilation of the Talmud in the time of Rav Ashi and its completion by his son, Jews were further dispersed, reaching the ends of the earth and the distant islands. . . . Each regional court that was established after the Talmud['s completion] and that issued edicts, decrees, and customs for its locality or neighboring regions could not reach all Jews because of distant settlements and poor roads. . . . But all the things mentioned in the Babylonian Talmud—all Jews are obligated to follow. And we may coerce

every city and district to observe all the customs that were adopted by the
Sages of the Talmud and to follow their edicts and decrees, for all Jews have
consented to those things that are in the Talmud.[2]

In this passage, Maimonides offers a rather novel explanation of the binding
nature of Rabbinic legislation: he grounds it in the historical fact that Jews universally accepted the "edicts, decrees, and customs" of the talmudic Sages. I am
not interested in examining the historical veracity of his claim; in any event,
current scholarship with respect to that time period is considerably speculative,
given the paucity of evidence presently available to us.[3] What is relevant for our
discussion is that a historically contingent state of affairs rendered Rabbinic legislation authoritative, and the ground of that authoritativeness was the people's
acceptance.[4] Let us examine these points more closely.

An heir to Geonic views of talmudic and post-talmudic Jewish history,[5] Maimonides assumed that in the fourth to fifth centuries C.E., while the Palestinian
Jewish community was in decline, Babylonian scholars and exilarchs served as
the religious leaders for world Jewry, which was concentrated at the time in
Palestine and Persia.[6] Therefore, according to Maimonides, when these Babylonian scholars issued ordinances or decrees, they applied to virtually all of world
Jewry at the time. Toward the end of this period, however, Babylonian Jewry
also began to suffer misfortune and persecution,[7] and geographic and political
factors led to the fragmentation and further dispersion of the Jews. Consequently,
Jewish communities were no longer united under the jurisdiction of one center
or head, such that the talmudic Rabbis could no longer be seen as *universal*
authorities. Maimonides admits that this was an entirely contingent state of affairs, but it had the inevitable consequence of limiting the authority of post-
talmudic rabbinic leaders to their local regions.

To be sure, Maimonides' language suggests that he is referring only to Rabbinic legislation and *not* to the other three domains of Rabbinic activity. The
first two categories of his five-part classification—oral laws and scriptural explanations transmitted directly from Moses—derive their authority from their divine
source.[8] Maimonides' position on logical inferences and the application of her-
menutical rules (category 3) is not as clear. He claims that Abaye and Rava
(fourth-generation Babylonian Amoraim) had as much right to use these exegetical tools as Moses, and their conclusions were no less valid or legitimate. Yet
he never explains clearly whether or why this activity ceased after the Talmud
was compiled; perhaps the exegetical inferences, at least with respect to their
normative implications, had spread to the point of universal observance by that
time.[9] At any rate, according to Maimonides, the authority of Rabbinic legislation
is grounded in the broad consent it enjoyed.

Analysis of the Maimonidean Position

By basing his theory on historical realities, Maimonides goes far in accounting
for an aspect of Rabbinic authority which has proved quite vexing to all the

theories we have considered: it is broad enough to include all the talmudic Sages while at the same time sufficiently narrow to exclude post-talmudic scholars from sharing in the same authority. When we identified a category or theory that could encompass five centuries of scholars in two regions, then it seemed to include scholars of the medieval or even modern period. If it was specific enough to leave out the later scholars, it also excluded some or even many talmudic Sages, whom we wanted to keep in. Maimonides' reliance on history allows him to explain why the cutoff for Rabbinic authority (at least in the realm of legislation) is the talmudic Sages: after the Talmud's compilation, it was simply the case that no other scholar(s) enjoyed such widespread acceptance. The distinction is generated not so much by the theory as by history. Of course, *in principle* this account allows for subsequent scholars to achieve the same level of authority if their enactments are accepted universally.[10]

"Rabbinic *Authority*" or the "*Authority of* Rabbinic Practices"?

However, as we inspect Maimonides' use of public consent in this passage more closely, it appears that it is not a ground of *Rabbinic authority* at all but rather the ground of the normativity of certain *practices*. Jews of the time did not accept upon themselves to obey the Rabbis but to observe the "edicts, decrees, and customs" which the talmudic Sages had promulgated. Prima facie, this is the same ground of the general juridic principle governing all Rabbinic decrees, whether of a local court or the High Court in Jerusalem: in order to take effect, the decree must be practicable by a majority of the populace.[11] Maimonides himself, in codifying this rule, stated:

> A court that issued a decree or instituted an ordinance or initiated a practice and it spread throughout all [the people] Israel, and [subsequently] a later court desired to rescind the initial [court]'s rulings and to abrogate that ordinance or that decree or that practice—it may not, until it is greater than [its predecessor] in wisdom and numbers. . . . [12]
> Behold, if the court promulgated a decree, imagining that a majority of the populace would be able to abide by it, and after they promulgated it, the people treated it lightly and it did not spread among the majority of the populace—behold it is null, and [the court] is not permitted to coerce the people to abide by it.[13]

Maimonides continues that even if the court that issued the decree initially assumed that many Jews were able to abide by it, but another court, even many years later, investigates the matter and discovers that in fact the decree had not spread among all the Jews, then the later court, even one lacking the requisite measure of wisdom and numbers, has permission to rescind the decree.[14] This demand of broad acceptance obtains even on a local level: if the decree was originally circumscribed to a particular region, then to be binding, it still needs to become the common practice in that area.[15] From all these sources, it would seem that the normativity of a decree derives from the *actual* adoption of the practice by the majority of the people.[16]

Nevertheless, before directly linking the consent with the practice and removing the court from the equation, we must try and explain what precise role widespread assent is, in fact, playing in this case. The requirement of public approval in the form of actual performance need not imply that the people's endorsement is the *ground* of the decree's authority. We may still insist that the ground is the court's authority (whatever that may be; see next section), and that the need for popular observance is simply a condition of its *validity*: in order for the decree to be valid, it must meet several conditions, among them its practicability. Just as other areas of Rabbinic activity have certain requirements, such as the hermeneutical rules for interpreting the Pentateuch, so too does the power to legislate come with certain restrictions. This is certainly the implication of Maimonides' plea for caution in these matters:

> A court that deems it appropriate to issue a decree, to enact an enactment, or institute a practice must first seriously ponder the matter and ascertain whether the majority of the community will be able to uphold it or not, for [a court] should never issue a decree for the community unless the majority of the community is able to uphold it.[17]

Perhaps several motives underlie this constraint, including the burden on the people and concern for the court's prestige, which could suffer generally if the people perceive it as insensitive or out of touch with the people's true capabilities. In any event, the ground of the authority of a court's legislation arguably remains the fact that the court decreed it.

We might test this hypothesis by considering the contrapositive case: a custom (*minhag*) that is broadly observed in the community but that lacks any formal endorsement or formulation by a court. Jewish tradition, dating back to the Talmud itself, accorded considerable standing to these customs,[18] and two main schools of thought evolved to justify that standing. According to one group, the mere existence of a practice indicates that there must have been a prior legislative act that introduced it but that has since been forgotten. This approach, in essence, collapses the authority of a custom into the authority of other, more typical sources of law; the prevalence of the practice is a *sign*, an indication of its legitimate etiology.[19] According to this explanation, the only authorized source for normative practice is the legislative body; in our case, then, a decree's inability to take root among the people is a telltale sign that the decree had not met the formal requirement of "practicability." But the *ground* of its authority remains the court.

Another school argued that the community is indeed invested with the power to legislate for itself through custom, whether in deciding between existing legal alternatives or in actually adding to the body of law. This authority, however, is largely restricted to monetary matters; in an area where the involved parties' presumptions and intentions powerfully determine the legal outcome, it is reasonable that custom, which influences these states of mind, should play a role. In other matters, particularly in ritual law, the power of custom is severely circumscribed; some scholars accord it only the right to restrict something previously permitted (in which case, it resembles personal vows, which one is allowed to assume), while others allow custom to overrule an existing law on only the rarest of occasions.[20] In understanding the position raised by Maimonides, it seems that widespread acceptance alone is insufficient to account for the enforceability of Rabbinic legislation; we still require appeal to some formal body, such as the local court, which issued the ordinance.[21]

Rabbinic Authority as the Authority of the Local Court

As we noted, Maimonides' approach helps explain why the talmudic Rabbis alone, at least as regards their legislation, are authoritative. But what this position achieved with respect to scope, it apparently lost in force. What Maimonides is saying, in essence, is that the authority of the talmudic Sages regarding their legislation is no different *in kind* from the authority of a local court. Each has its own jurisdiction, within which it can coerce all Jewish members to comply. The only difference is in the *scope* of that jurisdiction; given the relative geographic cohesiveness of Jewish society during the talmudic period, the Sages enjoyed a de facto universal jurisdiction, while for post-talmudic scholars, the range of their authority was and continued to be more local and regional.[22] The Sages' authority, then, is no different from the authority of any other court of scholars, except that the Sages were more "fortunate" with respect to how many people followed them. While this position is logical, it seems a relatively weak basis for the extreme reverence and esteem in which the talmudic Rabbis are held in the Jewish tradition (unless we posit that attitude derives from their other functions).

Nevertheless, Maimonides frames the authority of Rabbinic legislation in terms of the more commonplace authority of a court's legislation, forcing us to investigate the latter's nature: by what authority does the court of a particular city institute a new practice which is then incumbent on all residents of that city, presently and in the future? Throughout the Middle Ages, where this method of legislation was common among Jews, this question was met with a variety of responses.[23] While the subject is complex and each of the medieval approaches certainly deserves a lengthy treatment, we can identify two main camps: those who argued "from the top down" and those who saw this authority deriving "from the bottom up." R. Jacob ben Meir (Rabbeinu Tam—twelfth century), a representative of the first group, linked the court's authority to the more general authority of the Sages as representatives of the Torah and Jewish law. Only such authority could compel the members of a community to comply. The majority of medieval scholars, however, aligned themselves with the second approach and located this authority in the notion of covenant, whereby the court acted as the representative of the community. The community, as a sovereign entity that can demand the adherence of its members, empowered its leaders— whether its scholars, its elders, or some other body—to act on its behalf. Thus, in a more striking example of this approach, R. Solomon ben Abraham Adret (Rashba—thirteenth century) writes: "The majority in every city is to the individuals within it as the High Court is to all Israel";[24] and "each community, in its own locality, can be compared to the Geonim [heads of academies] when they issued *taqqanot* which applied to all of Israel."[25] To be sure, this notion has echoes in earlier sources,[26] but it was the medieval scholars who gave it increasingly explicit formulation.

Rashba's language points to a very significant dimension of this conception of leadership. In both citations, he compares the community's authority to that of established organs of leadership: the High Court and the Geonim of Babylonia. In other words, even as the leaders represent the community, at the same time the community is expected to choose as its leaders those who are *qualified* to govern: wise men, possessing both scholarship and piety.[27] Representation does not imply strict delegation; the community is expected to have at its head individuals who realize and understand the group's "true" interests (even if certain members reject them) and who embody its ideals and can therefore not only express its will but guide it as well. Articulating a theory of authority which was grounded "from the bottom up" did not simultaneously demand drawing its leaders from that bottom. In this way, even the second, more prevalent approach among medieval scholars shared an aspect of Rabbeinu Tam's "from the top down" interpretation.[28]

While some medieval scholars of this second group did in fact invoke notions of (generally, tacit) consent in their understanding of the individual's obligation to obey the decisions of the court,[29] it seems that many of them subscribed to an organic view of the relationship of the individual and the community to undergird the latter's authority. Organic theories (as opposed to consent theories)[30] imply the submission of the individual to the general will, and if the local court is identified with the community, then each person must follow the court's legislation.[31] "Membership has its privileges"—and its responsibilities: it entails sharing in the collective goals and accepted practices of the community, and conversely, violation of these norms already implies a measure of dissociation from the group.

Returning, then, to our discussion of the ongoing authority of legislation, we can now explain how this notion of representation was relevant. After the court, *as the community's representative*, issued the legislation, and it spread among the people of that locale, the decree or enactment came to constitute the practice of that community, such that any person who was a member was obliged to observe it. The community is perceived as an organic entity, constant over time even as its membership changes from generation to generation. Therefore, claiming that either the court or the practices themselves possess authority does not capture the more nuanced and rather complex process going on, at least on the conceptual-theoretical plane, which incorporates both: the court, as the representatives and guides of the community, instituted certain practices which then became part of the particular community's way of life, committing the members of that community, presently and in the future, to upholding those practices.

The portrayal of the court's authority as that of the community also helps us to understand certain rules regarding Rabbinic legislation, particularly with respect to revocability. For instance, Nachmanides uses this notion to explain both why a communal enactment accompanied by a public ban (*herem*) applies to people not present at the time of the decree and why a communal enactment

can be revoked more easily than an ordinary vow.[32] Even the requirement examined earlier that a court's legislation must spread among the people is not
merely formal but flows directly from the identity of the court and the collective
will: if people do not observe it, then the legislation cannot be honestly seen as
a reflection of the community's will. Furthermore, the Mishnah insisted that to
overturn the decree of an earlier court, a contemporary court must be greater
than its predecessor in wisdom and numbers. One could take a cynical view of
this rule, characterizing it as an ostensibly procedural hurdle driven by deeper
conservationist motives. It may simply be the juridical expression of the concept
of the assumed spiritual decline of generations (see chapter 5). Alternatively, our
account of the court as the community's representative means that communal
legislation comes to be identified with the will of the *corporate* community,
whoever its members may be now and in the future. Subsequent generations,
then, by dint of their automatic membership in the community, are obliged to
obey these laws *as if they had willed it now*. In seeking to overturn a law, a
community is, in essence, simultaneously rejecting in the present what it has
already affirmed through "inheritance." The transhistorical, corporate view of
the community renders this tantamount to reopening the debate as to the value
or correctness of the legislation, pitting the earlier court which endorsed it against
the present court trying to overturn it. In these imaginary "face-to-face" deliberations, the latter will succeed only if their arguments are more persuasive
(greater in wisdom) and they constitute a majority (greater in number).[33]

Authority Transformed

Equipped with this understanding of the authority of a local court's legislation,
we may return to Maimonides' understanding of the authority of the "edicts,
decrees, and customs" of the talmudic Sages. According to Maimonides, initially
the authority of the Babylonian scholars was in fact that of a "local court," and
their legislation was valid because it was widely accepted among the Jews at the
time. On the conceptual-theoretical level (not necessarily historical, without solid
evidence), these scholars were at once the leaders of the various Jewish communities and its representatives; their decrees and enactments were motivated
by a genuine concern for the people's observance of God's law and for nurturing
a way of life that would embody what were taken to be the ideals of Judaism.
As scholars immersed in both the academy and the community, they were seen
by the general Jewish population to appreciate as well as to express the innermost
aspirations of "the chosen people." Their legislation, which seemed to capture
the spirit of the people's desire to fulfill their mission, was adopted by the communities they served.[34]

However, historical reality (as accepted by Maimonides) was such that the
Sages' "communities" of the third through fifth centuries included the majority
of world Jewry at the time.[35] Most Jews remained concentrated in Palestine and
Babylonia even when the Jewish Diaspora extended further; even the most far-
flung Jewish populations looked to the Fertile Crescent for religious guidance.

With few or no rivals, the talmudic Rabbis served as the de facto heads of world Jewry, an influence manifest in the widespread acceptance of their "edicts, decrees, and customs." Over time, these behaviors became embedded in the community's way of life, becoming part of the rather amorphous yet compelling notion of "the collective will," a will that the Rabbis had initially represented but that ultimately had incorporated these practices directly, given their broad adoption. As such, these legislations could no longer be said to derive their authority from their original "authors" but rather from the fact that they constituted the will of the community, demanding the loyalty and allegiance of its members. What began as the "authority of the Sages" had been transformed into the "authority of the community's accepted practice."

In a sense, then, the decision made in the introduction to exclude from our inquiry the authority of the Sages for their contemporaries was premature. Since we were interested in the authority of the talmudic Rabbis for subsequent generations of Jews, we examined theories that we thought would connect or relate those two groups *directly*. Maimonides' account, however, makes clear that we cannot "leapfrog" over that contemporary group, for in fact the Sages' authority is *mediated* precisely through those early generations' acceptance of Rabbinic legislation.

This theory which transmutes Rabbinic authority into the authority of a community's practices forces us to examine the notion of community more carefully. We cannot lose sight of the fact that Maimonides was using this rationale to ground the authority of Rabbinic legislation, which originated in the second to sixth centuries C.E., for *all* Jewish communities, wherever they exist, at least seven hundred years *after* the decrees and ordinances were instituted. How, precisely, is Maimonides employing the notion of community?

The simplest case, of course, would be a community that can trace its origins back to the times of the Babylonian Sages without interruption. For instance, a Babylonian city in late antiquity might already have had several centuries of traditions, some originating locally, others from more regional practice. Being a resident of that city (even if relocated) meant acting according to the customs of that city, or at least publicly respecting them.[36] By the late fifth century C.E., according to Maimonides' version of Jewish history, the city's practices would have included the legislations of many talmudic Sages, whether from Palestine or Babylonia. In the ensuing centuries, additional customs or observances undoubtedly would have accrued to this body of tradition, such that by the twelfth century, when Maimonides was writing, the community's practices likely included all the Rabbinic legislation recorded in the Babylonian Talmud plus many others.

Now let us consider another, slightly different community, which is, for instance, located in North Africa at the time of Maimonides but which traces its origins back only to the eighth century C.E. At that time, the Muslim conquest reached from the Arabian peninsula all the way across North Africa, and cities gained a Jewish presence which had not existed there before.[37] These Jews usually had migrated from Babylonia or at least from cities that had been under the authority of the Babylonian scholars. They may all have come from one place, such as from a city that had just expelled its Jewish inhabitants, or they may have been an enterprising clan from a region of Babylonia who had decided collectively to pursue new opportunities in North Africa. In either case, they would bring with them their local traditions, which included the Rabbinic legislation of the Tannaim and Amoraim. Even if the North African city drew its members from several Babylonian communities, Maimonides presumably informs us that all of them had, in any event, already adopted the practices of the talmudic Sages, so that the new Jewish community in North Africa would continue to observe the practices mentioned in the Babylonian Talmud. Maimonides' model still obtains.[38]

Lastly, let us consider a third type of community, one that existed far outside the Babylonian orbit and that, in fact, had originated there before the talmudic Rabbis had begun to legislate for their local Jewish communities. For instance, let us assume hypothetically that at some point in the second or third century, some Jews had settled in northern Europe, well outside the jurisdiction of Babylonian scholars, and developed its own customs and practices.[39] In such a case (and the modern migration of Ethiopian Jews to Israel is an obvious parallel), how would Maimonides explain the extension of the talmudic Sages' authority to this community? Since they have their own tradition already, what justifies our right to "coerce every city and district to observe all the customs that were adopted by the Sages of the Talmud," as Maimonides put it? Of course, Maimonides may simply have thought that all the Jewish communities of the twelfth century, or their religious leaders, had originated in Babylonia; Maimonides does continue his sentence with the historical claim that "all Jews have consented to those things that are in the Talmud." But it is unlikely that faced with historical proof to the contrary, Maimonides would have granted that a particular community was not bound by talmudic legislation.

The difficulty encountered in this situation stems from the assumption that the authority of the Babylonian Sages was originally on the local level, but given the concentration of Jews in Babylonia through the fifth century, the sum of those individual localities equaled the entirety of the Jewish people. However, it is possible that "community" here should not be construed narrowly, as in the limited jurisdiction of a town or city, but as encompassing the entire Jewish people as a whole. Recall the discussion earlier in this chapter about the medieval view of the organic relationship of the individual and the community. The force of the medieval court's legislation was not that *every* person in the community agreed with their enactment but that the *majority* of the community was represented by the court. Similarly, when judging the practicability of a decree, the court did not need to canvas every member of the community; if most of the people were deemed capable of observing it, then it was a valid decree. What Maimonides likely meant was not that the Sages' authority should be seen as an aggregate of many small local courts but that their authority over the Jewish people is in substance tantamount to "the authority of a local court" in the sense described above—namely, that they represented the entire nation. And, as Rashba pointed out with respect to any community, it is sufficient if the majority is represented.[40] Since, according to Maimonides, the majority of world

Jewry (construed collectively) actually lived under the jurisdiction of the tal-mudic Rabbis, they were, in essence, the "local court" of the Jewish people.

In this light, the medieval communities of northern Europe are bound to observe talmudic legislation not because it constitutes part of their *own* local traditions but because it represents the tradition of the Jewish people, of which they are a part. Indeed, it was the allegiance of those communities to *both* local custom and the Talmud's understanding of proper practice that drove the Franco-German tosafists to reconcile their two "traditions" exegetically.[41] As members of that large community, which is defined not in geographic terms but in ethnic and sociolegal terms, the Jews of the Rhineland had no choice but to follow the "majority," who had endorsed the legislation of the talmudic Sages. Rabbinic legislation subsequent to the talmudic period simply failed to achieve that scope of normativity.

The reader has no doubt noticed by now that this theory closely resembles the model examined in chapter 3, where we sought to portray the Sages as a Sanhedrin of sorts, classifying the bulk of Rabbinic activity, in a somewhat forced fashion, as legislation. However, the context there was to ground Rabbinic au-thority in the divine command of Deut. 17:10–11, which demands compliance with the decisions of the High Court in Jerusalem. The approach taken in this chapter is radically different: it seeks to ground the authority of both the talmudic Rabbis *and* the court in their being the people's representatives. While for most this notion is a suitable description of the Rabbinic leaders of a community, it admittedly seems less appropriate to describe the supreme court of the land (although some medieval scholars did indeed understand the Sanhedrin's au-thority this way).[42]

Furthermore, the contrast between these two theories helps highlight the real benefit which accrues from this model. We noted earlier that in contrast to the concept of Sanhedrin in chapter 3, which apparently encompassed all subse-quent rabbinic leaders along with the talmudic Rabbis, Maimonides' view builds in the "cutoff" after the Talmud's compilation, when geography and demograph-ics rendered travel much more difficult. In light of our discussion, though, this is not merely an interesting historical fact about the nature of communication at that time. Rather, this explains an important sociological and cultural fact about post-Talmud Jewry: it could no longer be seen as a unified whole. Ge-ography and other circumstances effectively divided the Jews into several smaller communities according to region, each with its own scholar or group of scholars who served as its halakhic authority. No longer could one rabbi or group of rabbis develop a sphere of influence and authority that could be said to extend to the majority of world Jewry. And as these separate communities continued their independent development, the prospects of a future reunification under one leader grew increasingly dim, even as communications improved. By the late twelfth century, there existed diverse centers of Jewry in the eastern Medi-terranean, Spain, Provence, and Franco-Germany, each with its unique (if sim-ilar) understanding of Jewish law; for Maimonides, it must have seemed alto-gether unlikely that the conditions which created the universal authority of the talmudic Rabbis would be replicated.

Thus, according to Maimonides, the legislative traditions of every Jewish community could be seen as being composed of two "layers": the shared body of practices, based on the Talmud, common to the entire Jewish people; and the customs and behaviors which originated locally. After the Talmud's compilation, every group of Jews, by virtue of their membership in the Jewish collective, was bound by the Sages' legislation, whether they were "present" to accept it or not. But each community also had a "layer" of tradition specific to it, which evolved due to its own history of leaders and circumstances and which was binding only on the inhabitants of that locale or region. Of course, another community could decide, for a variety of reasons, to accept the same practice, but then it would be binding as a constituent element of that community's own tradition, not by virtue of the authority of another community or its scholars.

Lastly, we must reiterate that Maimonides was referring *only* to the binding authority of the "edicts, decrees, and customs" of the talmudic Rabbis. According to Maimonides' five-part classification of the law, the overwhelming majority of Jewish law remained grounded in its being the firm and reliable tradition dating back to Moses or in the application of accepted hermeneutical rules. In contrast with chapter 2, where legislation sat less comfortably in the "High Court model" of Rabbinic authority, here it is precisely this area of Rabbinic activity that alone is being addressed by Maimonides regarding the ground of its normativity. All the biblical interpretations and transmitted traditions—a good part of the Rabbinic corpus of laws—are taken as binding by virtue of their divine origin.

This crucial limitation of Maimonides' theory distinguishes it most from Solomon Schechter's theory of "Catholic Israel." Schechter, a member of the Wissenschaft des Judentums (Science of Judaism) school in the late nineteenth century and later chancellor of the Jewish Theological Seminary of America in New York City, emphasized the critical role the community of Israel (the people) played in the determination of legitimate Jewish practice and thought. Thus, Schechter wrote:

> It is not the mere revealed Bible that is of first importance to the Jew, but the Bible as it repeats itself in history, in other words, as it is interpreted by Tradition. . . . Since then the interpretation of Scripture or the Secondary Meaning is mainly a product of changing historical influences, it follows that the centre of authority is actually removed from the Bible and placed in some living body, which, by reason of its being in touch with the ideal aspirations and the religious needs of the age, is best able to determine the nature of the Secondary Meaning. This living body, however, is not represented by any section of the nation, or any corporate priesthood, or Rabbihood, but by the collective conscience of Catholic Israel, as embodied in the Universal Synagogue. . . . The norm as well as the sanction of Judaism is the practice actually in vogue. Its consecration is the consecration of general use—or, in other words, of Catholic Israel.[43]

Prima facie, "the consecration of general use" echoes Maimonides' claim that once a practice spread among the Jews, it became normative for the people. Furthermore, our analysis, which understood the leadership as representatives of

the people, seems to resonate with Schechter's reference to "the collective conscience of Catholic Israel, as embodied in the Universal Synagogue."

Nevertheless, there are clear differences. By locating the ground of authority
in "the consecration of general use," Schechter's theory cannot inherently distinguish between divine law, millennia-old interpretation, and relatively recent
innovation. Maimonides' position is limited to the "edicts, decrees, and customs"
of the talmudic Sages. The bulk of Halakhah, emanating from a divine source,
remains in force for all Jews, regardless of the people's actual practice.

Schechter's notion of Catholic Israel sets in sharp relief another feature of
Maimonides' theory. For Schechter, the authority of Jewish practice was the
community, and as long as the collective continued to observe Halakhah, the
law would be authoritative. What would happen, however, if the majority of
Catholic Israel ceased to observe the full range of Jewish law and custom? Over
the course of the twentieth century, this has in fact occurred (whether out of
ignorance or genuine rejection is irrelevant), necessitating some revision of
Schechter's notion. Louis Jacobs has suggested that a "consensus of the concerned" is a more appropriate notion, essentially taking into account only those
Jews who choose to affiliate with Jewish institutions and practices at all,[44] a rather
unclear criterion, given the varying degrees of affiliation among contemporary
Jews. Despite the rather conservative spirit of Schechter's theory, Robert Gordis
invoked it in its revised form as the legitimating basis of mixed pews in Conservative synagogues in America, historically an innovation in traditional synagogue
practice.[45]

For Maimonides, however, actual communal practice is irrelevant for all
orally transmitted laws and even for a court's legislation, except in the earliest
phases of its enactment. Our analysis showed that once the people had begun
to observe the Rabbinic enactment or decree, it was the force of the court's
legislation—not the continued observance of the legislation—that bound the
Jews of that community. Rescinding the legislation would require a formal act
of a court that was greater in wisdom and number than its predecessor. Once a
custom became normative, popular desuetude was, on this account, insufficient
to annul it. As Maimonides insisted, "we may coerce every city and district to
observe all the customs that were adopted by the Sages of the Talmud and to
follow their edicts and decrees."

By way of conclusion, we must then say that Maimonides' theory of communal practice, limited as it is to Rabbinic legislation, is not simply reducible
to the authority of public norms or tradition.[46] Rather, it is a more complex
notion involving, on the one hand, seeing the rabbinical leaders or court as the
representatives of the community's will and, on the other hand, bestowing some
formal status on the enactments and decrees of this leadership such that they
cannot be summarily changed or annulled merely by alterations in the public
will.[47] In Maimonides' view, this general theoretical construct had to be informed
by concrete historical circumstances, namely, that the majority of world Jewry
accepted Rabbinic legislation, a broad acceptance no subsequent legislation enjoyed. This rendered the legislation of the talmudic Sages normative for the
entire Jewish people, then and now.[48]

Summary

In this chapter, we introduced the possibility that while the term "Rabbinic authority" may originally have referred to the (contemporary) authority of the talmudic Sages, this authority in essence transformed over time into the authority of traditional practice. Even as the adjective "Rabbinic" continued to "stick," the authority actually operating on the Jewish people was that of accepted practice. The possibility that one form of authority can evolve into another is certainly not inconceivable; given the historical contingency of authority that Maimonides admits, this possibility is reasonable and plausible. When we come to examine authority in Judaism from a philosophical perspective, we must be aware that what goes by one name may, at bottom, be a creature of a very different sort. In the next chapter we will explore the possibility that Rabbinic authority evolved, not into accepted communal practice, but into an entity that could be said to literally embody the Sages' words and that had its own distinctive sort of authority—the talmudic text.

EIGHT

The Authority of Texts

In the last chapter, we focused on Maimonides' remarks regarding the broad acceptance of the Sages' decrees and enactments as a possible basis for understanding Rabbinic authority, admittedly with respect to Rabbinic legislation only. Our analysis led us to inquire into the nature of the authority of accepted practice, forcing us to explore a more sophisticated notion, at least within the Jewish context, of the interplay and interdependence of communities and their leadership. In the context of organic theories of the community and the individual, the authority of Rabbinic legislation was seen to have evolved from an initial phase of a court representing the "true" interests and will of the collective, to the practices ultimately becoming part of a body of tradition binding on the members of that community.

Throughout chapter 7, our focus remained framed by the now familiar tripartite expression "edicts, decrees, and customs" which Maimonides had formulated and used throughout his discussion in the *Introduction to the Commentary on the Mishnah* and elsewhere.[1] These were the legislative acts of the talmudic Rabbis, instituted over the first five centuries of the common era. Reading Maimonides' treatment of these laws, one receives the general impression that each legislation was individually accepted by the people and is consequently normative for all Jews everywhere from that point on. However, in the course of his argument, Maimonides makes repeated reference to the Babylonian Talmud:

> But all the things mentioned in the Babylonian Talmud—all Jews are obligated to follow. And we may coerce every city and district to observe all the customs that were adopted by the Sages of the Talmud and to follow their edicts and decrees, for all Jews have consented to those things that are in the Talmud.[2]

The precise role played by the Babylonian Talmud in Maimonides' argument is unclear. It is possible that we have here nothing more than another expression for the Rabbinic legislation of the period we are inspecting. In other words, "all the things mentioned in the Babylonian Talmud" is not to be taken literally but is simply another way to refer to the Rabbinic legislation designated earlier by the slightly more cumbersome expression "edicts, decrees, and customs of the talmudic Sages." The phrase, however, introduces nothing new conceptually.

Nevertheless, Maimonides' final sentence—"for all Jews have consented to those things that are in the Talmud"—could be interpreted differently, namely, that the majority of Jews accepted certain practices *by virtue of their being in the Talmud*. In other words, the Jews consented to conduct themselves in accordance with the rulings of the Babylonian Talmud generally, not by consenting to each and every act of Rabbinic legislation individually. This significantly modifies the position inspected in the last chapter, and so we now turn to examine this revised model.

Before undertaking our analysis, though, I want to state clearly that I am not trying to determine what, historically, Maimonides' true position was; that is a rather extensive exercise in Maimonidean exegesis and beyond the scope of this book. Indeed, some of the conclusions of this chapter might be seen to be at odds with those of the previous chapter, although that too was inspired by the very same Maimonidean passage. What we are inspecting now is the notion, *suggested* by Maimonides' language, that what the people accepted was, not the Rabbinic "edicts, decrees, and customs" atomistically, but rather the text of the Babylonian Talmud as a whole.

Accepting a Text in Jewish Law

At the very least, this modified account dramatically redraws the "historical picture" (as understood by Maimonides) sketched in the previous chapter. In chapter 7, we were forced to reintroduce the issue of the Rabbis' contemporary authority, for the Sages' legislation could become part of the communal tradition only if accepted by those Jewish communities. The image was that of an *ongoing* process, extending over five centuries, during which the majority of Jews began to practice the decrees and enactments of the talmudic Rabbis. Thus, for instance, Jews of the second century accepted the legislation of Rabban Gamliel II and of R. Judah the Patriarch of Eretz Israel, and Jews of the fifth century accepted the enactments of the Babylonian Amoraim Ravina and Rav Ashi. Accepted legislation was added to the accumulating body of legal traditions practiced by at least a majority of world Jewry. As we noted, such a portrait requires that the Sages were authoritative for their contemporaries.

In the revised model discussed in this chapter, acceptance was not necessarily an ongoing process but more crucially occurred within a much shorter time frame, probably *after*, or at the very end of, the period of the Sages themselves. As the Babylonian Talmud was compiled and reached a greater level of textual fixity,[3] the majority of Jews at the time, concentrated as they were in the Middle East and Persia, accepted upon themselves to observe those laws contained in the massive composition called the Babylonian Talmud. (It should be noted that

according to Maimonides, the last generation of Babylonian Amoraim, specifically Rav Ashi and his academy, were in fact the authors of the Babylonian
Talmud. The consensus of modern scholarship, however, is that while some text
likely existed in embryonic form during Rav Ashi's time, the Talmud was redacted into its present form by anonymous editors known as stammaim over a
period of two centuries following the time of the Babylonian Amoraim).[4] Of
course, the Sages likely had some sort of authority within their own time period,
and many of their decisions and decrees were probably accepted. However, this
historical "fact" is, in the end, immaterial regarding the *ground* of the Sages'
ongoing authority. The critical consent occurred later (possibly fostered by the
earlier contemporary authority), and that was for the text as a whole, not the
individual rulings.

However, we cannot dispense with the question of the talmudic Rabbis' contemporary authority just yet. We noted earlier that popular assent was necessary
for a court's enactments, because that affirmation validated the legislation. Without contemporary acceptance, the Sages' decrees do not attain the status of legitimate legislation. Suggesting that the acceptance came many years after the
decrees were instituted but neglected would not help much either, for once the
decrees failed to spread among the people, they were null and void ab initio.
To gain the status of valid legislation, an enactment would presumably require
a second, formal juridical act at a time when the people's acceptance could be
anticipated. Of course, it might be the case that the people "accepted" the
Talmud as custom, without an immediately prior juridical act, but that would
mean that the bulk of Rabbinic legislation has the status of mere convention,
for which compliance generally cannot be coerced.[5]

The idea, then, found in Maimonides that "all Jews have consented to those
things that are in the Talmud" must mean an actual endorsement of each and
every enactment and ordinance of the Sages, if they are to have the full force
of coercive law. Rabbinic authority cannot be understood as the acceptance of
a text if it is to be grounded on principles of enforceability found in the halakhic
system. The phrase "found in the Talmud," at least as Maimonides seems to
employ it, is merely another way of referring to the body of legislation instituted
by the talmudic Sages, which was accepted, each decree and enactment individually, by a majority of Jews.

Understanding Textual Authority

While we cannot see the acceptance of a text as a justification of Rabbinic
authority, nevertheless the identity implied by Maimonides does invite further
reflection on the nature of textual authority in general. The most common perception of a text is that it is the voice of its author, only in written form. It
provides access to material that we might otherwise not have come to know.
Thus, a newspaper article is the written account of a reporter who "tells" us
what transpired or analyzes a current situation. A novel is the printed version of

a story the author could have told to us in person, comparable to the stories of medieval minstrels, who traveled from town to town, repeating their lengthy verses and adding to or otherwise modifying their tales with each telling. Given the limited audience allowed by face-to-face verbal communication, texts are a useful and effective alternative for reaching many people, although certain qualities are undeniably sacrificed, such as tone, inflection, and even spontaneous variation. But the text "stands for" its author's speech.

The "independence" of texts can create some anxiety in authors, in the sense that they realize that once the word is printed and out of their hands, they cannot control how it is understood by the readers. This concern may cause them to deliberate on the phrasing of a sentence for fear of being misunderstood or being unclear (of course, ambiguity may be precisely the literary technique the author is after). Of course, speech as well, to a degree, enters the public domain and can no longer be controlled; all lecturers understand that they may be misquoted later. From the listener's side, most people treat hearsay as a paraphrase of someone else's words, gauging its reliability on a variety of circumstances, such as the general character of the witness, whether the content is inconsistent or not with the speaker's character, etc. We naturally assume that the speaker's original words may have been altered in the process of transmission. In contrast, a text written by an identified author has a reasonable reliability which gives the reader confidence that these are indeed the words of the author and genuinely reflect his or her view (assuming no motive for misrepresentation).

Given that it is a text's stability or constancy that generally gives it its reliability (as the author's words), it need not be in written or printed form. Modern technology affords us an easy analogue: the tape recorder. When one listens to a recording of a lecture, one feels as if one is in the audience; whatever one takes into consideration when hearing a speech—the speaker's thoughts are impromptu, the extent to which the ideas are properly developed—also applies to listening to the tape. On the other hand, speakers who know they are being taped may be more careful in what they say for they know they could be quoted; in such a case, the lecture approaches the character of a written text. "Being a text" is measured not so much by its medium (oral, printed, etc.) as by the expectations readers or listeners have of it—that the author pondered this seriously, weighed each word, and deliberately crafted it into its present form. Indeed, we may say that the context, to a large degree, helps form our expectations, and as such determines what sort of "text" we have before us. The spelling errors in a daily newspaper are relatively ignored since we know that it was speedily put together, but in a textbook, such errors may appall us since we expect greater care to have been exercised in the production of the text. A president's speech is almost always treated like a serious text, because in our society we have come to expect presidents to articulate their policies in virtually any venue, from university graduations to Oval Office prime-time telecasts, and serious inferences will be drawn from what the president says. (The statements of the chairman of the Federal Reserve Bank in the United States have similar impact on economic markets.) Lastly, the contemporary use of electronic mail ("e-mail") offers an excellent example of a print medium whose significance in most cases lies somewhere between that of a letter and a telephone call; once again, the context will help determine how we view it.

Such was the case at the time of the talmudic Sages. Rabbinic culture was primarily oral, as indicated by the dictum that the Oral Law was not to be put in writing.[6] What this meant, presumably, was not that writing was prohibited but that the written versions of the oral traditions that did exist, whether as personal notes or otherwise,[7] were not to be taken as "a text."[8] What was privileged were the "oral texts," those traditions memorized by a person (or persons), who functioned as a "living book."[9] (The title of this functionary was a *tanna*, with a lowercase *t*.) Of course, the two methods impacted one another,[10] but the point for us is that at some point, the traditions reached a point of formulation after which they could no longer be emended from within; revisions, as it were, had to take the form of glosses or commentary.[11]

This is not to suggest that the Sages were concerned about their speech only in the academy. Whenever and wherever they spoke, they were enjoined to be careful that their words not be misconstrued.[12] Indeed, according to the Talmud, it was precisely such a case of misunderstood words that prompted the Rabbis to require that each student receive permission before being allowed to decide questions of Jewish law.[13] Nevertheless, the "publication" of a Sage's words entailed an authoritativeness which "unpublished" works apparently did not possess.

The Babylonian Talmud itself acknowledges this authority.[14] In discussing the consequences of an incorrect judgment and whether the erring judge is liable for restitution, an important distinction, attributed to R. Assi, is raised: if the error committed was with respect to a *devar mishnah* (a law cited explicitly in the Mishnah), then the prejudgment status quo is restored, the case is tried anew, and the judge pays nothing. If, however, the error was made in *shiqul ha-da'at* (reasoning among contradictory views), then the judge must pay the indemnity. The Talmud then goes on to offer an example of the latter:

> How are we to conceive *shiqul ha-da'at*? Rav Papa said: "If, for example, two Tannaim or Amoraim opposed each other's views in a certain matter and it was not clear with whom the true decision lay, but the general trend of practice followed the opinion of one of them, and yet he [the judge] decided according to the opinion of the other, that is termed *shiqul ha-da'at*."

The explanation attributed to Rav Papa underscores the difference between texts and common practice (discussed in chapter 7) with respect to authority. When the judge rules against a known law in the Mishnah, his decision is essentially null and void; to cite Rashi, "since it is explicit, his ruling is not a ruling." In contrast, common practice is able to incline the law in the direction of one opinion, but it does not render the other opinion invalid. The judge's decision therefore has standing, and he is liable for the error.

In cases of *devar mishnah* and *shiqul ha-da'at*, the two opinions start out as the views of specific scholars. However, as this passage makes clear, once the opinion of one became incorporated into the Mishnah—a *text*—something happened to it. It attained a level of authoritativeness that nullified all other opinions, invalidating them. What was it about becoming part of the Mishnah that, from the Talmud's perspective, voids all alternative positions?

To answer this question, let us digress briefly and examine how this passage developed in subsequent Jewish law. At the time the statement attributed to R. Assi was formulated (let us assume for the moment that this expression is indeed that of its author), the major "text" in the halakhic corpus was the Mishnah, compiled and edited by Rabbi Judah the Patriarch in the late second to early third centuries C.E. Was R. Assi granting unique status to the Mishnah alone, or was the reference to the Mishnah merely paradigmatic of a general principle he sought to articulate, and other "texts" could be categorized as *devar mishnah*? The answer to this question would obviously have significant ramifications for the validity of judges' rulings. In a parallel talmudic passage,[15] some further elaboration is offered:

> Ravina[16] said to Rav Ashi: "Even if [the judge] made an error in [the statements of] R. Ḥiyya and R. Oshaya [who were students of R. Judah the Patriarch but continued to compose Tannaitic sources]?"
>
> He said to him: "Yes."
>
> "Even in [the statements of] Rav and Samuel [first generation Amoraim]?"
>
> He said to him: "Yes."
>
> "Even in your [statements] and mine?"
>
> He said to him: "Are we mere reed-cutters in the bog? [i.e., our statements are also to be considered *devar mishnah*!]"

The Gemara, as the Mishnah's commentary (and which together constitute the Talmud), represents the highly redacted "discussions" of the Amoraim, who flourished in the third to fifth centuries C.E. (I put "discussions" in quotation marks, for the Gemara's back-and-forth argumentation is not always an actual conversation between Amoraim but the redactor's discursive formulation.) The amoraim spanned roughly six generations, from Rav and Samuel in the early to mid-third century, to Ravina and Rav Ashi, both of whom passed away in the fifth century.[17] The implication of this passage is that the statements of all the Amoraim, from Rav and Samuel to Ravina and Rav Ashi, have the status of *devar mishnah*. Since tradition viewed the entire Babylonian Talmud to be chiefly the work of Ravina and Rav Ashi,[18] then the work as a whole constituted a *devar mishnah*. Therefore, if the Talmud clearly reached a decision on a specific matter, no subsequent scholar was permitted to disagree, and his decisions to the contrary were null and void.

What was the status of post-talmudic scholarship? This question was debated in the Middle Ages, particularly with respect to the several centuries of Geonic scholarship in the Babylonian academies. The Geonim had clearly decided many issues based on their understanding of the Talmud; were their conclusions to be regarded as *devar mishnah*? R. Hai Gaon (939–1038 C.E.) wrote somewhat cryptically that "*kol shemuʿah shel kol ha-ḥakhamim* (every statement of each/all of the scholars) is like a *devar mishnah*."[19] Hai Gaon seems to be referring to post-talmudic Geonim by his expression *ḥakhamim*, since the Talmud itself already deemed Amoraic positions to be *devar mishnah*. What remains unclear is whether the adjective *kol* should be rendered as "each" or as "all." The difference is significant: a decision agreed upon by all the Geonim may indeed have the status of a *devar mishnah*, whereas a ruling of an individual Gaon might not be so authoritative.

Maimonides' ruling (1170s) was similarly ambiguous. In accordance with the talmudic passage above, he wrote that "if [the judge] erred in matters which are well known [*devarim ha-geluyim veha-yedu'im*], such as the laws that are explained in the Mishnah or the Gemara, the ruling is voided."[20] Maimonides' sole criterion is that the matter be "well known"; he cites the Mishnah and Gemara only as *examples* of such well-known matters, but we do not know if he viewed other rulings as similarly authoritative. In principle, at least, post-talmudic decisions could reach such a level of popular consensus and therefore be considered *devar mishnah*. In the end, the issue is historically contingent.

Subsequent medieval commentators were more explicit in their treatment of Geonic decisions. R. Zarahiah ben Isaac ha-Levi Gerondi (twelfth century), quoting an unknown predecessor, stated that if a rabbi errs in passing judgment because he was ignorant of a Geonic decision, and if, had he known of that decision, he would have altered his opinion, then it is considered as if he erred in a *devar mishnah*. R. Zerahiah's contemporary, R. Abraham ben David (Rabad) of Posquières (1125–98), concurred:

> For, at the present time, we may not differ from the statements of the Geonim because of what appears right in our opinion; we may not explain a Talmud passage in any way other than that of the Geonim with the result that the law as formulated by them would be changed, unless we have irrefutable evidence against their conception of it—which is never the case.[21]

To be sure, Rabad's deference must be measured against his actual performance; on more than one occasion, he himself disagreed with the Geonim in his interpretation of a talmudic passage, although he was extremely reluctant to alter accepted practice based on his own understanding of the Talmud.[22] Nevertheless, R. Asher, (1250–1328) while admitting that one should never rashly dissent from the opinions of the Geonim, falls short of granting their opinions the status of a *devar mishnah*, such that the rabbi's decision would be invalid.[23]

In the sixteenth-century code *Shulḥan 'Arukh*, Joseph Karo employed Maimonides' language, with a slight—but extremely significant—variation:

> Any judge who erred in adjudicating a monetary matter, if he erred in matters which are well known, such as the laws that are explained in the Mishnah or the Gemara, *or in the words of the poseqim* [decisors], the ruling is voided and it is adjudicated [again] properly.[24]

While it is not entirely clear who these *poseqim* are, from the context the term can only refer to some post-talmudic authorities. R. Karo has thus expanded Maimonides' dictum, presumably based on the "fact" that the decisions of the *poseqim* were by that time "well known."

R. Moses Isserles, a contemporary of Karo who composed glosses on the latter's *Shulḥan ʿArukh* to reflect eastern European practice, commented on the above passage:

> However, there are those who say that if it appears to the judge and to those of his generation, on the force of incontrovertible proofs, that the law is not as it is mentioned in the *poseqim*, [the judge] is permitted to disagree since [the *poseqim*'s position] does not appear in the Gemara. Nevertheless, one should not be lenient in something that the compositions [*ḥibburim*] that have spread among the majority of Jewry have been strict about, unless he has a tradition from his teachers not to abide by that stringency.[25]

R. Isserles here codified the position of R. Asher mentioned earlier, that deference to the point of invalidating a judge's decision applies only to the Babylonian Talmud. However, he added one important caveat, originally articulated by R. Israel Isserlein (1390–1460):[26] strictures contained in those books which have achieved broad acceptance are to be taken more seriously and cannot be so easily overruled, unless the judge has a specific tradition to the contrary.[27]

Maimonides' formulation, as we saw above, understood the criterion to be that which was "well known." That seems to ground the law's authority in its being a widespread practice, which we examined in the previous chapter. But R. Isserles's formulation is crucial, for he does not invoke the argument that *the particular practice* has spread among the Jewish people but rather that the *book* in which the stricture appears has achieved that widespread acceptance. What does it mean for something to be well known through its being a "text"?

Maimonides' comments elsewhere are illuminating. As we noted above, the first "text" of Rabbinic literature was the Mishnah, which is why the Gemara refers to the positions that were "well known" at that time as *devar mishnah*. Rabbinic statements were likely being preserved in some form for several generations, probably rooted in the particular academies of the various Tannaim who authored them. Then, in the early third century C.E., Judah I, patriarch of Palestinian Jewry, compiled the Mishnah.

> But all these other Tannaitic collections did not possess the Mishnah's sweet language, nor its organization and succinctness; therefore, [the Mishnah] was made primary . . . and all those other compositions subordinate to it, and it was the most important in the public's view . . . *the sole purpose of everyone who came after it and following . . . was to understand the Mishnah's contents; inspecting it and explaining it did not cease for generations.*[28]

Maimonides' point is that the Mishnah's literary excellence prompted subsequent scholars to turn their attention to it [29] and even to make it the core of the academy's curriculum.[30] Understandably, the tools of the Amoraim's reading were similar to the hermeneutical strategies that were applied to the Bible: this was the community's way of reading, and once a composition reached the level of "authoritative text" in the academy, it "deserved" to be read a certain way.[31] This is what Maimonides means by saying that everyone strove "to understand the Mishnah's contents": rather than continue producing new collections of Tannaitic statements, or revising older ones, the scholars of the academy decided to have their discussions revolve around the Mishnah. From now on, it was the starting point of all academic discourse, and every scholar was expected to be familiar with its contents. This is not to say that everyone necessarily deferred to it in every matter; Maimonides makes no mention of the normative force of the Mishnah, but only of the fact that the Mishnah became the central text of study.[32] But this unique position held by the Mishnah meant that it was the foundation for most, if not all, subsequent halakhic discussions, a relationship underscored by the arrangement of the Gemara around the contents of the Mishnah. The Mishnah's "authority," then, consisted in precisely this: that for the next several centuries, the Halakhah developed as "commentary to the Mishnah."[33]

It is not entirely accurate, however, to view every Amora as an interpreter of Mishnah, at least not in the primary sense of that term. As the body of commentary grew, scholars did not only analyze the words of the Mishnah but began to examine the words of the Amoraim who preceded them as well. This did not mean that the Mishnah was no longer authoritative, but that its authority was in a sense second-order: early Amoraim wrote commentary on the Mishnah, which then generated "supercommentaries" among the later Amoraim.[34] In other words, with the passage of time, the commentarial tradition began to build on itself, with later Amoraim studying a new, larger corpus known as "the Mishnah and its [early] commentaries." All the while, however, the structure adhered to was that created by the Mishnah.

This phenomenon points to an important feature of commentarial traditions: the authority of "early" texts is not displaced by layers of subsequent interpretation but rather is mediated through them. To be within a tradition means not only studying the original text but also studying the history of how that text was understood. Paradoxically, even as such activity renders direct engagement with the primary text increasingly rare, the latter's authority is actually deepened, for to make sense of all subsequent scholarship (indeed, of the very enterprise of interpretation), one must make appeal to the original text and why it is important to study it. In fact, to a certain degree, the interpretations begin to merge with the text, since later interpreters read the original text together with and *via* the commentaries; like an onion, each layer that accrues over the original core only merges with it to become a new whole. The clear demarcation which at one time separated text and interpretation becomes blurrier and blurrier as the tradition of commentary continues.

An interesting reciprocal relationship is thus seen to emerge: the authority of the original text initially generates the interpretive project, and the increased hermeneutic focus in turn deepens the authority of the studied text. This authority, over time, extends to the body of interpretation as well, by virtue of its attachment to the text. As the next layer of commentary incorporates elements from the new "enlarged" corpus (text plus commentary) in its discussions, the authority of the whole is strengthened, which also enhances the stature of (later) interpretation. In the case of Jewish law, the Amoraim set out to explain the Mishnah, which deepened the latter's authority as a subject worthy of scholarly attention but which also elevated the Amoraic analysis by dint of its being "Mishnah commentary." This in turn made the early Amoraic views the legitimate subject of later Amoraic study, which in turn generated new interpretations, and the cycle continued.

The metaphor of the onion does not always hold. At times, something happens that sets off the previous commentaries, forcing subsequent commentary to remain self-consciously "outside the text." At some point, the decision was made (whether by the Amoraim themselves or by subsequent scholars) to consider the Amoraic corpus closed and to self-consciously compose all interpretation outside it. This led to the redaction and codification of the Talmuds.[35] The development of Jewish law is then seen to be an ongoing process of interpretation, punctuated by "textual moments" whereby a corpus of commentary is given some formal structure that allows it to be the focal point of subsequent interpretation.[36]

Consider another helpful metaphor for this activity: Ronald Dworkin's understanding of how laws are interpreted within a legal tradition.[37] He suggests seeing the history of legal interpretation as the writing of a book, but in a very unique way. One author writes one chapter and then passes the book to the next author, who then composes his or her own chapter, only to pass it on to the next author, and so on. Each author is essentially "free" to write a chapter that he or she likes, but each author is also constrained by the chapters already written, for after all, this is a book, and the chapters need to be sufficiently integrated to ensure overall coherence. The preceding chapters constrain each author presently writing so that they cannot begin an entirely new plot, utterly ignoring the facts and characters introduced in the previous chapters. To have the book make sense, the themes introduced by the previous author(s) have to be continued or finished off; they cannot all be left hanging. Thus, within the Amoraic period and the medieval period, all were involved in composing the next "chapter," the only previous chapter being the Mishnah for the Amoraim and the Talmud for the medieval scholars. The "textual moments" discussed in the previous paragraph are, within this metaphor, the closure of a chapter and its formal inclusion in the emerging book, such that the next group of scholars, to continue writing, are forced to have their contributions "fit" with the previous chapters.

We may now finally return to our analysis of *devar mishnah*. We had set out to explain what it was about becoming part of the Mishnah that, from the Talmud's perspective, voided all positions contrary to it. In light of our discussion, the notion of *devar mishnah* is not a statement about the normative character of the Mishnah but is, in essence, another way of expressing what it means to be part of an interpretive community which sees the Mishnah as its core curriculum. The Amoraim perceived their very project to be the explication and analysis of the Mishnah; the daily activity in the academy was premised on that text. A decision rendered by someone in that community that ran counter to something explicit in the Mishnah had no standing because it went against the text that gave the Amoraic enterprise coherence. Within the community, therefore, such a ruling was null and void ab initio.

Similarly, decisions that are clear in the Talmud have the status of *devar mishnah*, not because everybody actually accepted them, but because the universe in which post-talmudic commentaries functioned was that of the Talmud. Scholarly discourse could not be understood without appeal to that tome; all legal analysis and academic discussion were conducted in terms set largely by the Babylonian Talmud. "Matters which are well known," as Maimonides and Karo put it, refer not simply to decisions or halakhic positions with which many people are familiar but rather to the texts or decisions which serve as the bedrock for future halakhic deliberation and decision making, for the continued writing of the book. The medieval debate about the status of Geonic pronouncements was not directly about the authority of the Geonim; throughout the discussion, the Geonim's authority, whether institutional or personal, is rarely invoked. What was truly at issue was whether the decisions of the Geonim had achieved the level of bedrock such that all subsequent halakhic discourse was to be conducted on their basis: had the Geonim's decisions closed off further discussion on certain matters to the point that they could now function as the accepted foundation for subsequent analysis, or did these matters remain open? Bedrock hardens slowly, and the medieval debate on the status of Geonic views affords us a rare window on this gradual process and how it evolves. Depending on how they saw their *own* activity in relation to the Geonim, various medieval scholars came down on different sides of the issue.

Admittedly, the above discussion has been rather extensive, but now we are in a position to shed considerable light on our original subject. It turns out that the notion of Rabbinic authority is really a claim, not about the authority of a specific group of individuals, but about a particular form of life, about a particular legal tradition that takes as its foundation the Babylonian Talmud. For over fifteen centuries, Jewish law developed with constant reference to talmudic sources, which served as the basis of virtually all halakhic decisions. Many of these citations include attributions to named Sages; indeed, much medieval talmudic analysis was couched in terms of explicating or elaborating the view of this or that Rabbi. The natural tendency, cited earlier in this chapter, to see written statements as the expression of a person's view frequently allowed the discourse's evident allegiance to the Talmud to be understood as loyalty to the persons mentioned in its pages. For instance, the early medieval debates between the Rabbanites and the Karaites were often about the authority of the talmudic Sages, when what really was at stake was whether the Talmud would be the new basis for determining the Halakhah or whether legal discourse would remain directly linked to the Bible.[38] In the terms we used above, the argument was whether the Talmud would be the next chapter in the growing "book" of Jewish law.

"Rabbinic authority" then describes, from a different perspective, what those within the community living by talmudic norms feel: that their legal deliberations, their normative lifestyle, their way of ordering the world, are all based on the words of the talmudic Sages. Most often, in explaining this attitude, the stress has been on the word "Sages"; what this chapter has tried to show is that from another perspective, the stress must be placed equally on the word "talmudic."

Implications of Textual Authority

Articulating Rabbinic authority in terms of the text that grounds future discourse bears certain implications, to which we now turn.

Historical Contingency

First and foremost, this analysis underscores the historical contingency of the process. Focusing on the Sages themselves in order to justify Rabbinic authority held out the hope that some theory could compel *all* Jews who came after the Talmud to defer to the Sages of the talmudic period. This hope grew out of a certain picture of that authority, namely, that deferring to it was immediate and ongoing. However, the approach sketched in this chapter is very different: it portrays that authority as evolving over time, deepening with each generation of scholars who viewed the Talmud as the basis for their legal deliberations and the foundation of their entire worldview. And as in all cases of textual authority, we must be candid and admit that the position a text achieves in a particular tradition is historically contingent.

This feature characterizes the Halakhah's development since the Rabbinic period, starting with the choice of the Babylonian Talmud as its foundation and centerpiece.[39] In late antiquity and the early Middle Ages, the Palestinian Talmud was a readily available alternative,[40] forcing one medieval scholar to justify the Babylonian Talmud's superiority simply on the basis of its later composition.[41] Certainly, internal reasons had much to do with preferring the Babylonian Talmud over its Palestinian counterpart, including the former's impressively rich discussions, exhaustive analyses, and comprehensiveness. Nevertheless, historical forces were also at work. The ascendancy of the Babylonian academies at this time, coupled with the decline of Palestinian academies under Christian persecution, no doubt had a significant impact on this development. The Muslim conquest of the seventh century advanced this process further, uniting most of the areas in which Jews resided under one polity with Baghdad as its capital. With the political and cultural epicenter of the empire located between the Tigris and the Euphrates, the stature and influence of the academies located there were understandably strengthened. New Jewish communities developing in North Africa in the post-talmudic period thus looked to the Babylonian academies for religious guidance, for as long as the Muslim empire looked to Baghdad, so did its Jews.[42] Moreover, these new commercial centers were settled by Jewish merchant families or communities who, in the absence of a native Jewish tradition, brought with them the practices and customs of Babylonian Jewry. It is therefore not surprising that the text which embodied these traditions would become the main legal text of most Jews.

Nor should we discount the role played by individual polemics, such as that of Pirqoi ben Boboi, who defended the Babylonian Talmud's superiority against the traditions of the Palestinians, which apparently survived into the eighth century. Even the opening of talmudic academies in the Andalusian peninsula did not attenuate the Babylonian Talmud's centrality, since most scholars called to head the new institutions were, by and large, trained in the East and carried with them the traditions of the Babylonian academies (although like their Muslim hosts, they sought in various ways to express their independence).[43] Therefore, by the eleventh century, when Spanish, Provencal, and Franco-German academies began to flourish (those who were to write the next "chapter" in Jewish law), the Babylonian Talmud was assured its position of primacy in all future legal analysis.[44]

The extensive legal literature of the Middle Ages, in all its various forms, helped to deepen the Halakhah's dependence on the Talmud even further. This is not to say that the medieval scholars were necessarily bound by the conclusions of their predecessors, or by their methodology; at some level, they were free to develop their own, distinctive approaches to the text, which they did. Indeed, the historical vicissitudes experienced by Jewish communities at this time forced Jewish law to respond to the needs of its adherents, often in regionally distinctive ways.[45] Dispersed among Christians and Muslims, prospering or suffering in the unstable conditions created by their hosts, settling and resettling in the seemingly incessant peregrinations of the Middle Ages, Jews and their law continued to be exposed to different situations and different societies, each with its own particular cultural and legal nuances. This post-talmudic millennium (sixth to sixteenth centuries) saw Jewish scholars produce an immensely rich and exceedingly diverse legal literature, including talmudic commentaries, responsa, and legal codes. But as free as these medieval scholars were to develop their own methods, all ultimately based their decisions and interpretations on the Babylonian Talmud, which supplied the vocabulary for the discussion and the terms for evaluating the various arguments which were advanced. Each of these medieval works contributed chapters to the burgeoning "book of Halakhah" (à la Dworkin); some had a greater impact on the "plot" than others, and some were all but forgotten. But all were compelled to "fit" with the previous ones in such a way that the book remained coherent, and invariably, the Babylonian Talmud served as their mooring.

Community of Scholars

It is clear that on this understanding of halakhic development, the relevant community is that of the scholars and jurists, who are constantly involved in analysis of the sources to arrive at normative conclusions. We noted in the last chapter that if the community is the ground of the law's authority, a notion summed up in Schechter's term "Catholic Israel," then we should always examine those practices which are broadly observed among Jews. As the twentieth century witnessed widespread erosion of the traditional lifestyle, proponents of this view (such as Louis Jacobs)[46] were forced to qualify it to "the consensus of the concerned." Our present analysis, however, implies that our focus should properly be on those who were interpreting the law, and not the general public, for it was the jurists who were linked to the halakhic tradition through their examination and application of the sources. Their authoritativeness derives, in large part, from their ability to interpret the traditional texts, showing how their decisions are based on the accepted "cumulative canon," whatever that may be at the time. This does not mean that all scholars will necessarily arrive at the same conclusion, but their discourse, to varying degrees, is built on the contemporary "bedrock."[47]

Attitude toward Historical-Critical Study

The "special status" of the foundational text similarly bears implications for the inspection of the text's accuracy and the history of its development, the main program of Talmud criticism as it is practiced in the academy.

This criticism takes place at several levels. The first, a type of lower criticism, is simply ascertaining the correct talmudic text. That is, does our contemporary printed text reflect the authentic words of the Talmud redacted in the fifth to seventh centuries, or have variants slipped in through scribal error or deliberate emendation? This is not merely an academic question. Normative conclusions derive from the talmudic text, and if it is inaccurate, then the inferred practice would be "wrong" at some level. To be sure, traditional scholars had for centuries engaged in this sort of inquiry, comparing manuscripts in order to ascertain the most "reliable" text of the Talmud. For these scholars, though, it was no more than an episodic or occasional observation; the overwhelming portion of the Babylonian Talmud remained, in their opinion, a correct record of Rabbinic deliberations. However, since the nineteenth century, the examination of manuscripts has become a discipline unto itself, and studies abound as to the ongoing development of the talmudic text, even after printing began. Moreover, comparison with other Rabbinic texts, as well as internal evidence, has produced a rather radical skepticism in contemporary scholarship with respect to the reliability of attributions in the Talmud.[48] Indeed, a consensus has emerged, at least in American Talmud scholarship, that most of the talmudic text as we have it is likely *not* the actual words of the talmudic Sages themselves.

While there is no reason to impugn such a conclusion within the academy, such a view can seriously affect those who see their religious practices as rooted in the words of the Rabbis. If the talmudic text is not the genuine words of those Sages, then the project of teasing thousands and thousands of laws out of that text over the last fifteen centuries was essentially conducted on a false premise. Seeing one's behavior as connected, even derivatively, to the utterances of ancient scholars supplies meaning to the practice; claiming that the language was a later accretion or a scribal error threatens to drain the practice of religious significance. Moreover, the concern that critically examining the text would undermine one's observance seems to be corroborated by the personal practices of at least some of the members of the historical school.

In other words, one cannot simply assess the historical-critical enterprise as such; it is always practiced within a particular context, from which it is perceived as either acceptable or religiously perilous, if not downright harmful. Thus, in the mid–twentieth century, R. Abraham Isaiah Karelitz (1878–1953), known as the Ḥazon Ish, was led to write about the study of manuscripts:

I see little value in arriving at truth through variations culled from the [different] *genizot* [storage rooms or libraries which contain centuries-old manuscripts and early printed editions]. They only succeed in perverting judgment and distorting truth, and they ought to be buried [lit., "stored away"], for the cost outweighs the benefit.[49]

To learn that the way one had learned a talmudic passage, including all the commentary on that section and the legal inferences drawn from it, was in fact a scribal error is religiously very unsettling.[50] The inviolability of the present text is thus desirable, if only to ground the enterprise of traditional learning, regardless of whether it has normative implications or not.

The second type of Talmud criticism, a form of source or redaction criticism, seeks to ascertain the sources that contributed to the final version of the talmudic passage and whether what the text attributes to a particular talmudic Sage is in fact what he said. To be sure, this project is threatening only as long as the authoritativeness of the statement derives from its authorship, which is how Rabbinic authority has traditionally been understood. In this context, the work of David Weiss Halivni is relevant. As an observant Jew, he is committed to the authoritativeness of the Rabbis, yet as an academic scholar, he actively pursues the historical investigation of the talmudic Sages' original statements (as they were made in a certain time and place) and the alterations of the tradents and redactors. Indeed, he views this scholarly enterprise of "excavating the text" as a religious imperative, precisely because we are committed to the words (i.e., the actual *utterances*) of the Tannaim and Amoraim. Thus, he rejects the analogy of the Talmud to art or law, where the artistic or legal product may be detached from the author's intent:

> Not so in a religious statement. There the author is inexorably connected with the authority of the statement. It is he who lends validity to the statement, he who makes it worthwhile to study in the first place. Remove the author and the statement loses all its efficacy and the weight of its authority. In such a context, history and exegesis converge. . . . To *usurp*, therefore, a person's name, a person's authority for an interpretation which that person did not intend, or, what is worse, outrightly rejected, smacks of historical distortion.[51]

Halivni's subscription to the traditional notion of Rabbinic authority forces him into a tension between his historical studies and his practical observance, a tension which animates his philosophical and theological writings.[51] Although he tries to harmonize the two, it is interesting that the more basic implication—that historically excavating may *negatively* affect one's religious practice—goes unaddressed. Denying the authenticity of the statement from which laws may be derived eviscerates the inferences and, at some level, deprives them of their religious significance. Of course, new legal inferences from the "corrected" text may be seen as religiously positive; one regrets that an unfortunate error had been made and moves on in light of the new evidence. But for someone committed to the centuries of existing halakhic development with little change, that is a difficult thing to do.[53]

The model proposed in this chapter partially alleviates this anxiety and tension, in that it is more concerned with how the final redacted product of the Talmud, however it came to be that way, functioned as the basis for subsequent halakhic deliberation. The interpretive community which received the text and turned its attention to it is determinative in this regard. Nevertheless, even this approach admits that the original text derived its status, at least in part, from the fact that the great scholars in the history of the academy contributed to these discussions, therefore warranting our academic attention. One cannot entirely sever the connection of author and utterance without affecting how one understands one's personal practical commitments.

"Authority Spreads to Fill Its Container"

At the beginning of this chapter, I cited Maimonides' expression regarding the continuing authority of Rabbinic legislation and used it as a springboard for the analysis of textual authority. I should emphasize that my analysis means that it is no longer appropriate to distinguish between Rabbinic legislation and the other components of Rabbinic law. Recall that this distinction arose in the previous chapter, in the context of analyzing Maimonides' explanation for the authority of Rabbinic legislation. While popular assent was critical in establishing the Sages' decrees and edicts as normative, for Maimonides the bulk of Jewish law remained authoritative by virtue of its divine origin, whether directly as the word of God revealed to Moses and transmitted down to the Rabbis or indirectly through the proper application of authorized hermeneutical rules. In these two categories, popular acceptance played no role whatsoever.

At first glance, we could view the authority of the Babylonian Talmud as an aggregate of the authority of its constituent parts, and hence essentially derivative. Like an anthology or encyclopedia, the various components of Jewish tradition — revealed laws, derived laws, rabbinically instituted laws — could each be justified separately. But, also like an encyclopedia, we are aware that something happens to the text as a whole when a group of people comes to regard it in a certain way. Encyclopedias, course textbooks, and physicians' desk references are all classic examples of texts which are not entirely reducible to the authority of their individual authors, editors, or contributors but for which, in a real sense, "the whole is greater than the sum of its parts."[54] Indeed, the Babylonian Talmud's impressive comprehensiveness — incorporating Halakhah and Aggadah, ancient laws and Rabbinic innovation, scriptural exegesis and transmitted traditions, extensive discourse and popular adages, technical legal minutiae and general religious advice — contributed greatly to its unique status within the Jewish community. A mere digest of the Sages' legislation would likely not have achieved similar standing.

The incorporation of all this material into a single entity (in this case, a text), and particularly in one that evolved into the foundation of an entire discourse, helps explain how authority extends to so many different elements in it. Even though many, and possibly most, of the separate components of the Talmud can be grounded individually in independent sources of authority, many elements of the text cannot be so grounded. For instance, certain scholars are mentioned only very rarely, their lives and opinions fairly obscure. Now we could say, as a matter of faith, that the fact that they are mentioned in the Talmud even once definitionally denotes their membership in the august company of "the Sages." (This is equivalent to our analysis in chapter 5 that if Rabbinic authority is essentially epistemic, then we must posit that every Sage was an expert.) More likely, however, the Talmud's inclusion of so many great scholars whose names were quite "familiar" and whose scholarship and erudition were well known elevated the stature of the work *as a whole*, helping it become the focus of commentarial attention. That, in turn, helped to distinguish other, less renowned scholars whose names appeared in the Talmud, a sort of "fame-by-association." Indeed, even opinions which are rejected in the course of a talmudic discussion nevertheless retain some measure of authoritativeness.[55] This is the nature of all "collective authority," whether of persons (organizations, committees, etc.) or of texts (encyclopedias, digests, etc.): the group derives its authority from some or even many of its constituent elements, then reciprocally bestows authority, whether equally or unequally, on all its members. Like the behavior of a gas, authority spreads to fill its container: in this case, the Rabbinic text of the Babylonian Talmud.

Similarly, this observation that authority spreads "laterally" once several diverse elements are clustered or arranged together is detectable in the centuries-old question concerning how much authority to accord Rabbinic statements of a nonlegal nature.[56] Of course, this phenomenon is not unique to texts or other collections; authority grounded on personal qualities also shares this tendency (although not necessarily institutional grounds of authority, since they are, by definition, situationally specific). Thus, as noted in the chapter on epistemic authority, it is natural, although not necessarily rational or justified, to take seriously the opinions of experts even in areas where they are not experts. This trust may be proved wrong, and I might from then on restrict my faith in a person's opinions to his or her recognized areas of expertise alone. On this model, there would be little trouble admitting that the Sages erred in biology or history even as one continued to maintain their unimpeachable authority in legal matters. But texts generally "present themselves," as it were, as all of one piece (more akin to one prophetically endowed), rendering it more difficult (or less reasonable) to make these distinctions. This is not to say that it is impossible, especially if one regards a text as the written voice of its human author(s); I might argue that only certain sections of the text are authoritative, while others are not. But to preserve the authority of a text generally inclines one to preserve the authority of everything in it, because its integrity, its wholeness, is bound up in its character as a text. Thus, a textbook or encyclopedia which is shown to be wrong in certain facts has its general trustworthiness compromised; even if different scholars contributed the various entries, readers tend to treat the text as a single entity.[57] Their experiences with each part necessarily erode or reinforce their confidence in the whole. This tendency is amplified with respect to a text which becomes the basis of a realm of discourse: if error is admitted in part of it, then the whole enterprise can be destabilized.[58]

Finally, the fact that authority spreads to fill its container allows us to reflect briefly on the nature of Rabbinic texts other than the Babylonian Talmud. If authority is borne by the Sages themselves, then it is logical to elevate the status of every collection of their sayings: the books of *midrash halakhah* (Mekhilta, Sifra, Sifre), the Tosefta, and the Palestinian Talmud, not to mention the non-halakhic compendia of Aggadah. As noted throughout this book, the Babylonian Talmud has pride of place in the Rabbinic corpus, a fact best accounted for by the model we are proposing. Nevertheless, authoritativeness is not all or nothing; it is subject to varying degrees. Even as the status of the Babylonian Talmud is secured by virtue of its function in academic discourse, it cannot be denied that the same Sages who appear in the Talmud appear as well in these other Rabbinic works. Through this shared feature, other texts are also deemed authoritative, even if at a lower level. Thus, authority is seen to spread even "beyond its container," through the vehicle of Rabbinic authority.

Summary

This last point regarding the spread of authority raises a crucial issue about the nature of authority when it comes to texts and interpreters. The above discussion may leave the reader with the impression that this is always a clear, historical process with distinct or discrete phases: for example, the Rabbis were authoritative, which then gave the Talmudic text its authority; or the Talmud became authoritative and then its authority "spread" to other Rabbinic works. This is not really the case, however. Particularly, in the presumedly oral culture of the Rabbinic academy, the text was not "produced" in the way we imagine an author writing a book today. Rather, scholars' statements were memorized and transmitted over several centuries, each generation building on the cumulative body of tradition through interpretation and innovation. The relationship of scholar, text, and interpreter is a complex one, each member contributing at all times, through a variety of activities and roles, to the overall authority of the tradition in the academy. We will likely never be able to pull these apart entirely and isolate each one to determine its precise role at a particular moment in the evolution of an academic tradition. I only wish to point out that certain things "happen" to oral statements when they are treated as a text. More than merely making accessible, in written form, a particular person's mind or ideas, a text elicits or creates certain expectations in the community receiving it. In the next chapter, we will explore the nature of interpretive communities and the implications they bear for understanding this authority.

NINE

Rethinking Authority

Interpretive Communities and Forms of Life

Texts and the Authority of Interpretive Communities

The image most people have of textual interpretation is similar to observing a painting: there is an object outside us with a clearly independent existence (i.e., if we walk away from it, it presumably remains hanging on the wall), whose meaning we, the observers, try to understand. We are all aware that not everyone will appreciate the painting or articulate its meaning in the same way; we admit that in most cases, to be able to "see" the significance of various motifs in the work of art requires training or at least exposure to certain cultural artifacts. If the artist intended to evoke specific themes by incorporating into the painting salient elements associated with earlier works of art, then viewers unacquainted with those other paintings would fail to "see" these allusions; they would be "missing" something that is "there" for those trained to notice it. Of course, this is not a permanent handicap; viewers can be instructed to see things they did not "see" before. Just think of the recorded tours a person may listen to while touring an exhibit: the oral tour guide "points things out" that one may not have known before, after which one "sees" the work of art in a new light.

The reason I put so many words and expressions in quotation marks in the last paragraph is that the image we have in our mind is that the painting has a meaning which is "out there," in some sense, possessing its own reality, waiting for people to come along and notice it. We think of interpretation like excavation: we can recover what is buried there, if only we have the proper tools. Our inability to reach it does not alter the fact that it really is "there"; we just have to work harder to get it. Similarly, interpreting texts is the act of uncovering what is there; the text (whatever that may mean) exists independently, and it is our job, as excavators, to reveal it.

In the last few decades, this "picture" of interpretation has been seriously challenged in several fields. Whether in the realm of texts, art, or really any phenomenon that we set out to understand, such as a foreign culture or religious practice not our own,[1] we have become increasingly aware of the active role the interpreter's assumptions play in this effort to understand. Seeing and describing are no longer taken to be entirely passive, or neutral, activities; in profound yet often undetected ways (only because they are not rendered explicit), our perceptions are shaped by our conceptions so that the "simple" act of observing already involves a significant amount of processing. We take things to be poems or abstract paintings or religious rituals, not because they possess specific essences according to each type, but because our society has certain conventions and norms that we, as members of that society, "naturally" employ in our very act of perceiving.

It must be stressed that this is not merely a modification of the earlier model, such that the presence of a noumenal object "out there" is still admitted, but that now we acknowledge that we lack access to it, save through the lenses which we inherit from our culture (Kant's noumenal-phenomenal distinction). To say we are ontologically stuck behind a veil created by our present circumstances (broadly construed) is still to remain fixed in this "picture" created by the sharp distinction between subject and object; instead of trying to cross the divide, we just admit our fate that we are rooted in our subjectivity and accept it. It is this view of the "shift to the subject" that makes it seem so anarchic, that in the absence of any determinate meaning, people will do as they please without any constraints or controls. This shift is genuinely problematic only if the subject-object distinction is maintained, the two seen as independent entities situated in an adversarial relationship, where one exerts control over the other.

What I am arguing for, in contrast, is the obliteration of that distinction entirely; that interpreters and the objects they interpret are not really independent, but both are constituted by the ways of thinking and seeing which inhere in social organizations. Every act of perception and interpretation is never acontextual but occurs in a specific situation, in a setting which necessarily entails its own practices, norms, values, and interests. Interpreters always "see" with the eyes of their context because no other way is possible. The dichotomy of subject and object is thus not a problem to be solved but is not a problem at all.

This way of looking at interpretation was first proposed by Ludwig Wittgenstein, a philosopher of the first half of the twentieth century who was deeply interested in understanding how language conveys meaning. Western philosophers had been oriented to see mental states or acts as sources for our action: meaning derives from the intention of the speaker when forming the sounds. Ideas form in my mind in some real sense; trying to remember something is seen as "searching my memory" in the same way that I may look in the park for my friend. In his later thought, represented primarily in his *Philosophical Investigations*, Wittgenstein proposed instead looking at language as related to particular "forms of life," where the meaning of a sentence is its use, or application — the "language-game" in which it plays a part. In other words, expressions have circumstances in which they make sense; certain behaviors or circumstances "go" with the sentence. For instance, depending on the particular situation, we would be able to understand the same sentence as a question, an assertion, or simply as the repetition of what someone else said. In Wittgenstein's view, the problem of meaning that philosophy has analyzed for so long is a false one, rooted in a picture of the world that separates meaning from a person's perception of it. That picture, Wittgenstein argued, was the wrong one.

> Here we come up against a remarkable and characteristic phenomenon in philosophical investigation: the difficulty—I might say—is not that of finding the solution but rather that of recognizing as the solution something that looks as if it were only preliminary to it. "We have already said everything.—Not anything that follows from this, no, *this* itself is the solution!"
> That is connected, I believe, with our wrongly expecting an explanation, whereas the solution of the difficulty is a description, if we give it the right place in our considerations. If we dwell upon it, and do not try to get beyond it.
> The difficulty here is: to stop.[2]

Wittgenstein was saying, in his typical elliptical style, that our way of looking at language, meaning, and people is what created the problem of meaning in the first place. If we describe differently the way language functions, then we will see that no problem exists at all.

In the realm of literary criticism, Stanley Fish has been one of the most articulate exponents of this Wittgensteinian orientation (although he does not cite the philosopher directly).[3] For Fish, interpretation is never the result of the exclusive and private interaction of text and reader but is always an activity that goes on within a specific community, which determines, at any given time, which strategies of interpretation are acceptable. Claiming that the text does not have a stable, determinate meaning constitutes a danger of utter relativism only if one sees the interpreter as an independent self acting entirely alone, arbitrarily substituting whatever meaning he or she desires.

> However, if the self is conceived of not as an independent entity but as a social construct whose operations are delimited by the systems of intelligibility that inform it, then the meanings it confers on texts are not its own, but have their source in the interpretive community (or communities) of which it is a function.

The fact that many people agree to an interpretation is evidence, not of that interpretation's "truth," but of the power and force of the interpretive standards of the community.

Insisting that all interpretation goes on in the context of interpretive communities does *not* mean that all members are merely passive recipients of the collectively endorsed interpretation, powerless to disagree. Referring to his disagreement with another literary critic, Fish claims that discourse is still possible because

> I speak to him *from within* a set of interests and concerns, and it is in relation to those interests and concerns that I assume he will hear my words. If what follows is communication or understanding, it will not be because he and I share a language, in the sense of knowing the meanings of individual words

and the rules for combining them, but because a way of thinking, a form of life, shares us, and implicates us in a world of already-in-place objects, purposes, goals, procedures, values, and so on.[4]

Fish insists, however, that the authority of interpretive communities should not be misunderstood as providing, at least for a particular point in time, accepted standards by which the correctness of one specific interpretation can be "demonstrated." That is still to perceive the text as being the source of "facts out there," even if we know that the facts may change in a few months or years. Fish objects to seeing literary criticism as a field where the word "demonstration" is an apt description of the activity being performed. Rather,

> we try to persuade others to our beliefs because if they believe what we believe, they will, as a consequence of those beliefs, see what we see; and the facts to which we point in order to support our interpretations will be as obvious to them as they are to us. Indeed, this is the whole of critical activity, an attempt on the part of one party to alter the beliefs of another so that the evidence cited by the first will be seen *as* evidence by the second.[5]

The notion that an interpretation can be "demonstrated" is, in Fish's view, a consequence of operating under a model of logic and scientific inquiry, whereby theories are confirmed or disproven by facts.[6] But in Fish's model, where a critic's aim is to have another "see a fact as a fact," literary criticism is "constitutive of its object,"[7] creating the entities it wishes to analyze.

Fish's approach would be incomplete if he did not, in some way, account for the "spell" which the other model has cast on our culture for the last several centuries. Why, indeed, do literary critics "feel" like they are "demonstrating" the correctness of their interpretation, that the "facts" of the poem or novel "prove" a particular reading? In Fish's view, "it is a testimony to the power of social and institutional circumstances to establish norms of behavior not despite, but because of, the absence of transcendental norms."[8] Since all interpretation goes on in the context of a particular community, that "form of life," as Wittgenstein put it, enables its members to construct reality according to the categories which it has rendered normative. According to Fish, that is why the field of literary criticism "feels" like it is "progressing"; whatever interpretation is currently being preferred is embedded in the contemporary interpretive community and hence feels like it is the "correct," indeed the "most correct," interpretation ever given of a particular work.

Fish-ing for a Model of Legal Interpretation

It will be recalled that our discussion of Rabbinic authority in the previous chapter employed Dworkin's model of the development of legal traditions. We portrayed the last two thousand years as adding several chapters to the "open-ended book" of Jewish law, each one constrained, to varying degrees, by the preceding chapters of the book. For the new chapter, using the terminology of the previous chapters accomplished two things. Most basically, it established a coherent link between the new chapter and the rest of the book, allowing it to be incorporated into the evolving book. Moreover, its inclusion in the book meant that whatever status the book previously had now extended to the latest addition. But the new chapter also had a reciprocal impact on the existing book, for by employing the terms of the earlier chapters, the most recent installment further deepened their presence in the "plot" of the book. As the authors wrote each chapter, they felt compelled to use this terminology and rendered it increasingly indispensable for the next writer(s).

Dworkin's portrayal of legal interpretation was presented during a symposium entitled "The Politics of Interpretation," held at the University of Chicago's Center for Continuing Education in the fall of 1981 and sponsored by the journal *Critical Inquiry*. Stanley Fish was invited to critique Dworkin's paper at the symposium, and the two essays—Dworkin's "Law as Interpretation" and Fish's "Working on the Chain Gang: Interpretation in Law and in Literary Criticism"—appeared together in several different places.[9] The two thinkers exchanged one more volley of articles on the subject, which were regrettably printed separately.[10] With Dworkin, we noted in chapter 8 that in a book written serially by several authors, those writing the later chapters would presumably be more constrained in terms of creative latitude than those writing the earlier ones. Asking us to imagine Dickens's *A Christmas Carol* written by chain novelists, Dworkin claims that "a novelist at the end of the *Christmas Carol* chain will have more difficulty seeing Scrooge as inherently evil than a novelist second in line."[11] In both his essays, Fish criticized this notion of constraint rather severely,[12] reminding us that whether one is reading the book up to that point or writing the next chapter, both activities are performed within a specific social organization which helps determine how the book will be understood and what will count as a coherent continuation.[13] Chapters 1, 2, and 3 constrain the writing of chapter 4 only to the extent that the most recent author's *context*—the way of thinking, the form of life in which he or she writes and thinks—has institutionalized certain modes of interpretation and standards of coherence. Since reading is always a matter of interpretation, each novelist, whether reading seven pages or seven chapters, is constrained only by what her or his interpretive community "sees" in what was already written and what would constitute a proper fit. Thus, for instance, we could imagine a plot in which Scrooge wakes up the next morning, sees an empty jar of painkillers next to his bed and concludes in an instant that his nocturnal visitors were in fact hallucinations. This may not be a satisfying ending, nor one that Dickens would have imagined, but it is not *incoherent*; all writers are constrained only by what their interpretive communities would accept as reasonable.

Another way of seeing this is to imagine a series of beads that I am stringing together to make a necklace. While I might have some latitude in the bead I choose to put on next, I realize that it has to match the beads that are already on the string. As more beads are added, the choices for the next bead "seem" to become more limited; for example, if a 3-bead pattern is repeated twice, then I might insist that the seventh bead be the same as the first and fourth. It is not the necklace itself which constrains my choice but what I conceive as a "pattern" (and if I want to sell the necklace, then I am concerned as well with what others take to be an aesthetically pleasing pattern). I could just as easily imagine a pattern where different 3-bead sequences repeat twice (ABC-ABC-DEF-DEF); or where a 6-bead sequence (made up of two 3-bead sequences) is followed by a single large bead of a different color before it repeats again (ABC-ABC-D-ABC-ABC); or where two 3-bead sequences are followed by two 4-bead sequences (ABC-ABC-DEFG-DEFG). The community of which I am a member is what allows me to "see" this as a pattern (indeed, as a necklace) and constrains how I will be able to imagine the pattern continuing. If I feel more constrained after six beads than after two, it is because the form of life in which I live and which understands necklace patterns has not yet come up with more patterns that would "fit" six beads so strung. And if I imagine a pattern which is nothing more than the random choice of beads, and I can persuade others to see this as a "pattern" (or, at least, as aesthetically pleasing), then the range of what is deemed acceptable in the interpretive community will have been enlarged. But it is never the length of the necklace itself that limits my choices.

Returning to the realm of literature, Fish's point forces us to acknowledge that Dworkin's model functions within a specific social organization, with its institutionalized form of reading and writing. The constraints we undeniably feel in writing the next chapter, which seem, under Dworkin's model, like the "authority of the text up to that point," are seen in reality to be the authority of the form of life in which we both read the first few chapters and begin to compose the next one. Neither activity can be done "outside" a situation.

Legal interpretation, for Fish, is no different. The judge who comes upon a hard case of law may write an opinion which seems to either fall back on a well-established precedent or strike out in a new direction, shunning precedent entirely. But, according to Fish, "the point made in relation to the novelists applies *mutatis mutandis* to the judge: the question of whether legal history is being ignored or consulted depends upon a prior decision as to what the legal history is, and that decision will be an interpretive one."[14] No matter what the judge does, he or she is constrained to the same degree by the chain to the extent that the decision involves interpreting the chain. Relying on precedent is as much an interpretation of the legal tradition as showing that the precedent is irrelevant in the present case (or simply mistaken). Those who come at the end of a "long chain" of a legal tradition are not constrained by the tradition itself but by the interpretive community's understanding of what it means to be part of (or even loyal to) that tradition.

Nevertheless, Fish notes that "there is, at the level of practice, a distinction between continuing the legal history and striking out in a new direction," although "it is a distinction *between methods of justifying arguments* and not between actions whose difference is perspicuous apart from any argument whatsoever."[15] Indeed, it is from this descriptive level of practice where Dworkin may have derived his perception of "constraint" in legal interpretation. As Fish observes, even as "the space in which a critic works has been marked out for him by his predecessors," he "is obliged to dislodge" those earlier interpretations, for "the unwritten requirement" of literary criticism is "that an interpretation present itself as remedying a deficiency in the interpretations that have come before it."[16] Judges and lawyers, in contrast, especially when faced with a "hard case," examine their predecessors, not in search of a weakness, but to see where *connections* could be made to the present situation. Fish admits as much when he writes, "Rhetorically the new position [in literary criticism] announces itself as a break from the old,"[17] an announcement that is relatively rare in judicial reasoning. If the two activities are so similar, why is the "posturing" of each interpretive enterprise so different?

I believe that this rhetorical difference stems from the respective forms of life in which each enterprise is situated. At the level of the interpretive act alone, literary critics and judges appear almost identical: each examines a text and offers some reading meant to accurately capture its "meaning." But as Wittgenstein pointed out, we cannot separate the search for meaning from the circumstances in which that search takes place.[18] Thus, when we consider Fish's notion of a form of life as he fleshes it out with respect to literary criticism, we are apt to imagine a group of scholars at a conference debating the interpretation of a piece of literature or professors with their students discussing the meaning of a poem. Their discourse is no doubt governed by rules and norms, but overall, we see their enterprise as a relatively self-contained discipline; few people change their behavior based on the way a Shakespearean sonnet is interpreted or the way a novel by Faulkner is understood (although some readers may be profoundly affected).

But in legal interpretation, the stakes are much higher, for in our society, the way a statute is interpreted often has immediate normative consequences. Not only does the case at hand reach a conclusion, but in some decisions, especially those by the Supreme Court, the entire legal system of the country can be affected. For example, if an election district that was gerrymandered by one state to give a particular ethnic group a majority is deemed unconstitutional by the Supreme Court, then all states will need to redraw the boundaries of their districts, even without separate lawsuits for each district.[19] How a statute is understood often affects many people, and in many aspects of their lives. Given the wide applicability of most laws and the ways they are interpreted, when judges or lawyers analyze a particular statute, they must take into account the whole society's form of life, which in many ways is shaped by that statute. This may be the "constraint" Dworkin correctly described but diagnosed differently: while small, self-contained groups or disciplines may more easily undergo rapid and significant change regarding acceptable procedures and practices, broader societies in general tend to evolve more gradually. Since the form of life in which legal interpretation takes place includes or impacts so many people, the changes the interpretive community may undergo are often, although certainly not always, at a slower pace.

Of course, one could say that this is merely one of the many norms by which the community of legal interpreters operates: they must be cognizant of consequences that might follow from their pronouncements, akin to the principle of Jewish law we examined in chapter 7 which required the court to evaluate the practicability of their ordinances before pronouncing them. In contrast, no such rule of caution exists in literary criticism. But this would trivialize the distinction, for while both interpretive communities may be narrowly construed, legal interpretation is embedded in a form of life that may encompass an extremely wide circle of people, whose values and practices are equally important components in the calculus of what counts as a valid interpretation. In many cases, these considerations impel judges to articulate their opinions that seem to "strike out in new directions" in terms of continuity with *other* values of the society still in place: while gerrymandering achieves the respectable aim of giving minorities a voice in government, it simultaneously tramples on the equally important principle that voting in the United States ought to be entirely blind to race, religion, and gender.

It should be noted that the continuity often sought in legal interpretation is, in part, determined by the given structure of a legal system. A situation could readily be imagined where the interpretive community sees it as its duty not to interpret but to modify the laws it has received; indeed, Thomas Jefferson viewed this as the ideal, assuming that every generation must choose the form of government most appropriate to its interests, concerns, and historical realities.[20] But what Jefferson's position failed to appreciate was that a constitution, while certainly a document in need of interpretation, does not remain a mere document. Rather, it becomes embedded in a form of life which makes it seem both "obvious" to the members of that community and also an embodiment of its values. In the United States, certain rights were created in (or interpreted out of) the amendments to the Constitution, which in turn shaped the character of much of contemporary American life, whether it be in what we perceive to be the government's role in our lives or how we expect to be treated by law enforcement officers. We would find it hard to imagine life without them not because it is "inconceivable" in some logical sense but because no interpretive procedures have yet been elaborated which would make such a form of life conceivable for most Americans.[21] Even were a new constitution drawn up every thirty years, it is reasonable to assume that a majority of each new one would be similar to the one preceding it. And this similarity would be due not to the "authority of the (first) Constitution" but to the authority of the form of life in which legal interpretation—and constitution writing—occurs.[22]

Another feature of legal interpretation which is absent in most literary criticism, admittedly at the level of method, is highlighted by Dworkin's model of a chain novel. We mentioned that although literary criticism builds on earlier interpretations of a work, it is, for the most part, in order to unseat them and offer a new reading. The subject of analysis, however, is always the primary text. But in much legal interpretation, with the writing of each "chapter," the *primary* text grows: each new chapter interprets not only the original text but the *accumulated* tradition. Thus, using Dworkin's metaphor, the second chapter is an interpretation of the first chapter (usually the primary text), but then chapter 3 may subject the first *two* chapters, or even only chapter 2, to rigorous analysis. Chapter 4 may deem only chapter 3 worthy of interpretation or only chapters 2 and 3 or perhaps all three chapters. Literary critics certainly have to read all the chapters that came before them, but whatever chapter they write—whether the second, fifth, or ninth—they are essentially engaged, at the most basic level, in interpreting chapter 1.

This difference is significant in several respects. First, since study of the previous layers of legal interpretation is to interpret them further, and not to show where one parts company with them, the student is inclined to accept the claims of the ealier material as "a given," not to be challenged or doubted. (Of course, this is, in the end, a function of the interpretive community's accepted norms.) Second, by studying the earlier chapters, students are "inducted" into the ranks of interpreters; they begin to "see" with the eyes of their interpretive community, and those eyes are continuous with the eyes of earlier interpreters. This reinforces the community's patterns of thinking, although by no means does it prevent modification. Third, and perhaps most important, this prima facie acceptance of "chapters 2, 3, and 4" and the subsequent interpretation of them in later chapters raise the stakes even further for asserting some interpretation which would leap-frog over them back to chapter 1. Again, as Fish repeatedly censured Dworkin, this is far from impossible; an interpretive community could create an environment or a way of reading which would render such a strategy not only legitimate but the norm. But as for what that might look like, it would presumably entail debunking the intervening chapters, or asserting their irrelevance in some way.

It is tempting to reduce Fish's model (and Wittgenstein's) to a certain sort of intellectual communism whereby the individual is able to think only as the group does. On this reading, divergence from the community's way of thinking is seen to be logically impossible, since each person's total conceptual apparatus derives exclusively from the interpretive community, and independent thinking is therefore inconceivable. However, this is a serious misreading of Fish's (and Wittgenstein's) argument. The point these writers were making is not that the way we construe language and the meanings we attach to words or rules are socially determined but that they are public. Society is not the *source* of intelligibility but its *arena*. What someone says "counts" as an interpretation not because something in the text makes it so or because the community hegemonically declares it so but because it fulfills the role of an interpretation in practice— a role which is possible only in a community.[23] It is the linkage between meaning and practice which is critical for these thinkers; without a form of life with which to connect a particular interpretation, meaning is impossible. And the more prevalent a form of life becomes, the more "obvious" the meaning becomes, for more and more people relate their practice to that particular interpretation.

As a final point in this section, it should be noted that this analysis implies that the word "authority" in Fish's subtitle—*The Authority of Interpretive Communities*—must be clarified. Recall Wittgenstein's comment that in some cases, the role of philosophy is not to solve a philosophical problem but to *dissolve* it by showing that the "picture" which created the problem is incorrect. In his book, Fish sought to show that the question consuming literary criticism— whether the text has a determinate meaning or whether the meaning is entirely the reader's construction—is based on the objective-subjective distinction and the view of the text and reading that flows from it. It is this "picture" which creates the difficulty. Since the distinction is false, but instead both text and reading are "produced" by the interpretive community within which all reading (and interpreting) occurs, the difficulty is "*dis*solved." If we understand Fish's subtitle to mean that we are under the power of an interpretive community, unable to resist complying with its conventions, then we miss the point entirely. There is no "authority" here in the sense of an external force exerting control over us; Fish has *described* how a particular activity is situated in a particular setting and how much the former depends on the latter. He then showed how that picture explains much of what is "felt" by those who engage in literary criticism, and why the problems of modern literary criticism stem from seeing or describing this activity from the perspective of a misleading distinction. If, after reading Fish's book, some people were to ask him, "But why should I listen to or obey the interpretive community?" we would know that they had missed the point. There is no answer to their question; it shows that they have either not grasped or not been persuaded by the new picture, and they are still in the grips of the old one. All one can do is to pause, take a deep breath, and try explaining it once again.

Reading Rabbinic Texts

Dworkin's model of writing within a legal tradition, which had served heuristically in chapter 8, has given way in our discussion to a model closer to Fish's understanding of literary criticism. Analyzing these two models, which stand, to a degree, in a complementary relationship with one another, has yielded a rather rich and textured exposition of the interpretive community within a legal tradition. Our discussion of this more particular type of "reading and writing" puts us in a better position to reexamine the question of Rabbinic authority, the subject of this book.

In chapter 8, we explored the authority of texts and noted that in the history of Jewish law, different "texts" (broadly construed) served as the center of academic attention over the centuries. Thus, the Mishnah was the "core curriculum" of the Amoraim in the land of Israel, and in Babylonia, the Babylonian Talmud was the main text studied by the medieval Geonim and Rishonim (scholars of Jewish law after the Geonic period up until 1564–65), and since the mid–sixteenth century, traditional scholars continue to analyze the Talmud primarily through the insights and commentaries of the Rishonim. Fish's discussion of interpretive communities further illuminates this notion of being "the center of academic attention," showing that it involves not merely the choice of what to study but how the community construes the material "as a text" in the first place. In the 1,500-year Jewish academic tradition, to be a (certain kind of) text meant to be read in specific ways: for example, scholars view every word as deliberately chosen and therefore significant; the sequence of sentences bears implications for the determination of law; internal contradictions (even of implications) must be resolved; and normative conclusions may legitimately be drawn from the arrangement of subjects. In this environment of presumptive meaning, even *ex silentio* arguments are valid, for the commentators perceive the author(s) as having chosen one specific sentence or argument out of all other possible formulations. In a word, the text is seen to be literally "dripping" with meaning.

This unique way of reading is evident at virtually every recorded phase of the development of Jewish law. The *soferim* (scribes) and *ḥakhamim* (scholars, sages), as they were known in the Second Temple period (and later), looked to the Pentateuch to discern the contents of the divine will. With the proper tools of reading, the Torah, as the revealed word of God, could yield all the details of how Jews are to lead a life in accordance with God's covenant. The hermeneutical rules recorded in Tannaitic sources were the keys to unlocking all the halakhic details implicit in the words and letters of the revealed text. The sources collected in midrashic literature, whether of a legal or a homiletic nature, demonstrate quite clearly the unwavering belief that every aspect of the Torah text— its every word and letter, the sequence of its verses and paragraphs—bears some significance.[24] Similarly, the Sages felt obliged to reconcile verses that stood in opposition or whose implications were in tension, for the Torah was the voice of a single Perfect Author. For centuries, these were the accepted hermeneutics of the rabbinic academies.

With the emergence of R. Judah the Patriarch's Mishnah in the early third century C.E. as the next "text" of Rabbinic Judaism, scholars began to "read" it with the same lenses as the Torah had been read for centuries. The Mishnah's words were examined for the precision and omnisignificance previously attributed to the Torah alone. Furthermore, *mishnayyot* that conflicted with one another or even with other Tannaitic sources, whether explicitly or implicitly, had to be rendered consistent, for a unitary text could brook no contradictions. As R. Isaiah ben Mali di-Trani astutely observed, "the Mishnah is to the Amoraim as the Torah [was] to the Tannaim."[25] To be sure, this attitude was not necessarily universal, monolithic, or instantaneous; it may have evolved over the Amoraic period, and the degree of significance attributed to the Mishnah's language and syntax likely varied among Amoraim.[26] Furthermore, such an attitude is occasionally in evidence between the generations of the Tannaim or Amoraim themselves, such that later scholars drew hermeneutic inferences from the pronouncements of those who preceded them,[27] reinforcing what we noted in the previous chapter that many oral traditions constituted a "text" as well. This last point underscores Fish's insight about interpretive communities: whatever the text, how one "reads"—the assumptions, values, and strategies that are unavoidably part of every act of reading—is determined by the community of readers in which one finds oneself.

The tenacity of this way of reading is particularly evident in the medieval scholars' interpretations of the Babylonian Talmud. Continuing di-Trani's metaphor, the Talmud was to the Geonim and Rishonim as the Mishnah was to the Amoraim. While it is not surprising to see inferences drawn from every word and sentence of the Talmud, one feature of this exegetical enterprise is rather striking: the effort of medieval scholars, especially the Franco-German tosafists, to systematically reconcile all portions of the Babylonian Talmud. Contemporary historians see the Talmud as the work of generations of redactors who compiled, edited, and stylized the material they inherited into its present literary form.

Seeking consistency in such a work is like trying to insist that every entry in an encyclopedia or anthology be perfectly consistent one with the other. (In fact, depending on the subject of the work, we expect [Fish again] that contrary views will be presented.) The medieval project, in contrast, was to reconcile every line of the Talmud as much as possible, for it was *taken to be* a unitary text; utter consistency could therefore be reasonably demanded of it. Of course, many medieval scholars thought Rav Ashi was solely responsible for putting the Babylonian Talmud into its present form, perhaps making such an expectation of consistency unremarkable. However, it is more likely that this historical claim of authorship went *hand in hand* with the practice of reconciling the various portions of the Talmud; they were mutually reinforcing and exemplify the assumptions of this interpretive community. This is possibly another source of the traditional community's antagonism to the historical-critical method of studying Talmud: to see the Talmud as an evolving piece of literature is not just an alternative view of the text; it renders much of the thousand years of commentarial tradition irrelevant and even mistaken. It is not primitive narrow-mindedness but understandable self-preservation for an interpretive community to defensively reject a premise that threatens to undermine a large portion of its revered canon—and form of life. Few communities would act differently.

In Jewish law, the attribution of omnisignificance persists into the modern period. Commentators to such codes as Maimonides' *Mishneh Torah* (twelfth century) or Joseph Karo's *Shulḥan ʿArukh* (sixteenth century), and even the Aharonim's (legal scholars of the late medieval period) analysis of the Rishonim's talmudic interpretations, all apply the same hermeneutics as the Amoraim did to the Mishnah: for example, every word and expression is seen to possess significance, and each element must be interpreted in a way consistent with every other part. The endurance of these principles is at least partially explained by what was noted above: concern for the normativity of the law naturally (and implicitly) disinclines one to substitute other forms of reading that might delegitimate the earlier expositions of the law, and phenomenologically, immersion in the centuries of texts that employ these forms of reading helps train students to "read" this way themselves. Interestingly, this conservatism is not seen as a constraint, for the conviction expressed by Ben Bag Bag regarding the Torah— "turn it over repeatedly, for everything is in it"[28]—is extended to these texts as well, motivating the student to delve ever more deeply in search of the meanings "hidden" within the fecund text. Fish's observation that the enterprise is "constitutive of its object" is certainly apt.

The close reading of the Torah was not merely a model for the techniques of this interpretive community for the next two thousand years; it became paradigmatic of its underlying rationale as well. Grounded in the theological claim of God's perfection, the premise that the Pentateuch was a divinely revealed text did more than just explain why the Torah was sacred; it justified, indeed impelled, the Sages' search for significance in every aspect of the text. As Jewish tradition saw it, in personally composing the Torah, God had chosen each word to convey some message to the Jewish people, and it was the Sages' role to discover as many of those messages as possible.[29] Indeed, given God's infinite creative capacity, the Torah's significance could not, in principle, be exhausted—another aspect of Ben Bag Bag's assertion—thus providing space and motive for future generations to find something new in the Torah's words whenever they examined it.[30]

Understanding the Rabbinic project in terms of the Torah's *authorship* became paradigmatic for this interpretive community. On the model of a God who embedded infinite meaning in what was, after all, a finite text, the "reading" of the academy was understood as uncovering the myriad meanings which the divine author had deliberately, if somewhat cryptically, encoded in the text. Thus, the Amoraim saw their focus on Tannaitic literature as justified by reflecting on the Tannaim's greatness. For the scholars of the Gemara, the Tannaim, whose transmitted statements they studied, stood out as towering figures, both religiously and intellectually.[31] Reverence and awe, to the point of hyperbole, characterize most Amoraic talk of the Tannaim:

> R. Zeira said in the name of Rava Bar Zimuna: "If the earlier scholars were sons of angels, we are sons of men; and if the earlier scholars were sons of men, then we are like asses, and not even like the asses of R. Ḥanina ben Dosa and of R. Pinḥas ben Ya'ir, but rather like ordinary asses."[32]

The metaphors chosen to describe the current generation in comparison to those which preceded it is extremely telling. And if the precise referent of "earlier scholars" is unclear, a statement attributed to R. Yoḥanan, R. Zeira's teacher, provides the details:

> R. Yoḥanan said: "The heart of the earlier ones was as wide as the antechamber [of the Temple]; that of the later ones, [as wide as] the sanctuary; and ours [as wide as] the eye of a needle. The earlier ones—R. Akiva; the later ones—R. Elazar ben Shamu'a."[33]

R. Yoḥanan, a second-generation Palestinian Amora of the mid–third century, refers to Tannaim from the mid– to late second century C.E.—a span of only one hundred years. In both these remarks, the feeling of inferiority is palpable.

At this point, I must emphasize that I am not suggesting that the Amoraim's apotheosis of the Tannaim *prompted* the careful study of Tannaitic statements, or that the academic attention paid Tannaitic utterances was justified *post factum* by seeing their authors as extraordinary human beings. Not only is this question unanswerable given the available evidence, it is beside the point: either portrayal is in the grip of seeing the authority of the text and/or the Sages in some cause-and-effect relationship. In the Jewish tradition of text and commentary which began with the exposition of a divinely revealed Torah, the authority of text and author cannot be separated. Using Fish's language, in this interpretive community, constituting a work as a particular sort of text involves unique strategies of reading *as well as* theories of justifying it in terms of authorship; they both grow out of this unique form of life.

A brief survey of several medieval views as to how Maimonides' *Mishneh Torah* should be read offers a unique glimpse at the evolution of such an attitude, providing further proof how characteristic this is of traditional Judaism's form of life, especially within the talmudic academy. Maimonides' legal magnum opus, completed in the 1170s, represented the most comprehensive and systematic summary of Jewish law since the Mishnah's codification almost one thousand years earlier.[34] Writing in thirteenth-century Spain, R. Solomon ben Abraham Adret (Rashba) responded to a person who inferred a certain halakhic conclusion from Maimonides' wording. Rashba reacts:

> You arrived at this inference from what Maimonides of blessed memory wrote . . . [but] you are inferring from his language as if you were inferring from the language of the Mishnah.[35]

For Rashba's interlocutor, Maimonides' code was to be treated as the same sort of "text" as the Mishnah, thereby legitimating all the hermeneutic strategies reserved for texts such as the Mishnah and Talmud. Apparently, such an attitude startled Rashba.

Nevertheless, only one generation later, Rashba's student, R. Shem Tov Gaon, wrote:

> The words of Maimonides of blessed memory are received from his teachers of blessed memory [who received them] from the Geonim of blessed memory. They are [exactly] like the Talmud's language, no more nor less; infer from his language, as you would from the Talmud's language.[36]

Clearly, some scholars were treating Maimondes' code as generations of scholars had treated the words of the Babylonian Talmud: one could legitimately draw inferences from its language, because Maimonides was perceived as having written his code with utter editorial precision, carefully choosing each word and phrase out of all other possible formulations.

The fifteenth-century R. Solomon ben Simeon Duran (Rashbash), in observing the unique hermeneutical posture taken with respect to the *Mishneh Torah*, speculatively grounds it in a special divine endowment granted its author:

> [Maimonides] divided [the *Mishneh Torah*] into books, and each book into sections of law, and each section of law into chapters, and each chapter into smaller laws, with a clear and pure language as if *ruaḥ ha-qodesh* had rested on him.[37]

What was mere speculation (if not metaphor) for Rashbash was now an unchallenged premise for the sixteenth-century R. Isaac Eizik Safrin of Komarno:

> Know, my brother, that all who strive to thoroughly understand the opinion of [Maimonides] our Master, his intention and his position, which is sweeter than honey and the drippings of the honeycomb, will be overwhelmed except for someone upon whom the Divine Presence dwells and who speaks with prophetic inspiration, which is our Master's uniqueness, for he composed a work such as the *Mishneh Torah* with prophetic inspiration and the [Divine] Presence dwelling on him.[38]

These citations, which are not exhaustive,[39] point to the evolving status of Maimonides' code. Initially, it was taken as an impressively written articulation of a great scholar's halakhic views, which was to be read as any other medieval text.

Over time, however, traditional scholars came to regard it as a special "text" that approached the character (although not the authority) of the Mishnah or Talmud and upon which one could apply the hermeneutical methods appropriate for such a precisely formulated text. And hand in hand with this developing attitude came the view that Maimonides was in some sense divinely inspired when he wrote his great code of Jewish law. Again, it must be emphasized that I am not saying that the academic attitude emerged and was justified *ex post facto* by appeal to Maimonides' divine assistance, or that people began to regard Maimonides as an inspired scholar and consequently began to read his *Mishneh Torah* a certain way. That is still to perceive authority as a "result" of some specific "cause." Rather, both the implications of authoritativeness and the way it is justified are embedded in the interpretive community's unique form of life and its actual practices.

Similar language attends discussion of R. Joseph Karo's *Shulḥan 'Arukh*, the sixteenth-century code of Jewish law which, together with R. Moses Isserles's glosses, became the accepted guide for Jewish practice among traditional Jews.[40] For traditional Jewish scholars, the universal acceptance of this code constituted unambiguous evidence of its inspired nature:

> In writing which indicated that the hand of God was on it in the composition of the *Shulḥan 'Arukh* and its glosses which were accepted by all Jews in our generations as their legal code in all the laws of the Torah and in a person's conduct according to the Torah, without doubt their words were not arbitrary; [rather] God sent his spirit on them so that all their words are deliberate.[41]

And if the *Shulḥan 'Arukh* is an inspired text, then one is certainly permitted, and perhaps even obliged, to read it with the same hermeneutical lenses that one uses when reading the Torah and the Talmud.

It is noteworthy that although both Maimonides' and Karo's codes are considered divinely inspired, and scholars "read" them with the same level of care and precision, nevertheless, only Karo's *Shulḥan 'Arukh* has normative status in Jewish law (disregarding, for the moment, the Yemenite community, which abides by Maimonides' *Mishneh Torah*). This striking fact underscores how "authority," far from being a monolithic notion, must be understood in relation to particular contexts. The interpretive community of the academy, which engages in the ongoing exposition of the Talmud and Jewish law, deems both codes as "texts" that may, indeed should, be read using specific hermeneutic tools. The world of practical Jewish law, however, looks to those texts that were widely accepted among the Jewish people and grants them the status of normative law (see chapter 7). Both codes may be "inspired," but ultimately, the form of life in which their inspired status is relevant determines the impact they have on actual Jewish practice.

This emphasis on the form of life in which these texts abide and "act" forces us to consider not only the community's explicit hermeneutical strategies but also its values. I noted above the Amoraim's esteem for their predecessors and offered some examples. This reverence, perhaps prompted or intensified by the publication of the Mishnah, actually characterizes many other periods of Jewish history as well, where the current generation often views its predecessors as superior, whether intellectually or spiritually. The theory of "the decline of generations," known alliteratively as *hidardarut ha-dorot*, has been a pervasive belief among traditional Jewish scholars.[42] Contrary to the Enlightenment's optimistic notion of progress, many Jews saw and continue to see the line of history as possessing a negative slope; the spiritual and intellectual level of earlier generations surpasses that of later ones. Such an attitude reinforces the conservative nature of Jewish law, for the foundations of Halakhah as formulated by the talmudic Sages, the medieval commentators, and the more recent codes cannot presently be replaced, given the relative inferiority of contemporary jurists. Once again, we return to the same point: to see the theory of *hidardarut ha-dorot* as evolving *post factum* to justify the unchanging character of Jewish law is to seek to pin down every belief and practice in some cause-and-effect relation. Rather, the theory of the decline of generations reflects the deep-seated attitude of the interpretive community that the words of those who preceded them deserve to be studied and rigorously examined; the words were, after all, uttered or composed by minds and souls greater than our own. This belief, and in some cases, conviction, that the contemporary generation is inferior is embedded in the form of life which sees the exposition of earlier scholars' works as its primary task. In this unique interpretive community, the day-to-day activity deepens this general attitude, and the general attitude inspires the community to continue to engage in the activity. The religious value and academic activity are mutually enforcing and are thus inseparable.[43]

Interpretive Communities and Jewish Denominations

Situating the analysis of Rabbinic authority within the interpretive community allows us to reflect on the historical circumstances which in fact evoked discussion of the topic in the modern period. As we noted in the introduction, the liberal forms of Judaism which began to emerge in the early nineteenth century concurrent with the political and social emancipation of western and central European Jews challenged the continued validity of much of Jewish law. As Jews sought to integrate into the newly welcoming Christian culture, many found the continued observance of traditional practices troublesome. For some Jews, particularly those who had absorbed Enlightenment values and contemporary attitudes toward religion, many rituals (particularly in the synagogue) seemed to be irrelevant or even primitive. Others, who were perhaps chiefly concerned with being accepted by their non-Jewish countrymen and with assimilating into the general culture, found the many halakhic restrictions with respect to food, the Sabbath, and holidays to be a severe impediment to their integration. Since virtually all these laws traced their origins to the talmudic Sages, whether as interpretations of biblical commands or as Rabbinic legislation, the debate over the validity of Jewish law largely revolved around the authority of the talmudic Rabbis.

To be sure, sociologists may claim that in light of European Jewry's intense desire to end their social segregation and legal persecution, such theological and religious debates were really beside the point. Nevertheless, it is important to note that such debates did occur and that they centered on the authority of "authors," reinforcing our earlier observation that the Jewish "form of life," at least until the mid-1900s, involved portraying or understanding authority in terms of the people who issued the commands. Both those who challenged traditional law and those who sought to defend it formulated their arguments by appeal to the authority of the scholars who had articulated it. Thus, many early reformers who felt bound by the law of the Torah because of their belief in its divine authorship did not feel similarly obliged by the Rabbinic interpretations of the Torah, especially when many of those interpretations seemed to violate the simple, plain meaning of the text.[44] Many defenders of the tradition sought to show that Rabbinic exegesis was in truth quite loyal to the plain sense of the divine Torah[45] or that the talmudic Sages did not innovate, or recklessly interpret, but merely transmitted an oral tradition that was similarly authored by God.[46] In either case, Rabbinic authority was in essence being "reduced" to or conflated with divine authority, which presumably the reformers accepted. By the mid-1800s, Protestant biblical criticism had begun to challenge the divine authorship of the Pentateuch as well, and the reformers' ideological acceptance of this theory in many cases forced traditionalists to either "prove" the Torah was divine or seek other strategies to defend the authority of Halakhah.[47]

In reality, however, what was transpiring at a more fundamental level during this debate was not the exchange of specific arguments but the frontal clash of interpretive communities (or, if you will, the cleavage of a new interpretive community from an older one). While the language being used suggested that the debate was genuinely about the authority of the talmudic Sages, the real controversy was about the role of traditional Jewish law, which grew out of the Talmud and centuries of commentaries, in contemporary life. When the two groups cited talmudic passages, although they may have been quoting the same words, they were not quoting the same "text," for each interpretive community "constituted its object" very differently. For traditional Jewish scholars, who saw themselves as the next link in a two-thousand-year-old chain of ongoing halakhic discourse, the Babylonian Talmud and the words of the talmudic Sages continued to serve as the ground for their entire *Weltanschauung*. Emancipation brought changes in circumstances, not substance; the commitment to halakhic observance was to continue as it always had, now thankfully under more tolerant conditions. In contrast, for those who had absorbed, to varying degrees, the values and attitudes of the Enlightenment and rationalism, the Talmud was no longer the same "text"; it was now an extremely lengthy record of a rather "peculiar" sort of discourse, one that had no complement in the world of Western law or literature. Its methods of "reading" the Torah appeared at times rather odd; words of the Hebrew Bible did not mean what they seemed to mean (which the field of biblical studies had helped ascertain), and immense significance was attached to what seemed to be irrelevant syntactical features. Precisely because some people had begun to construe texts as certain types of cultural entities, with particular characteristics and qualities they began to "notice" that the Talmud was not what a text "should be." Those who had been trained initially within the traditional Jewish academy and then been exposed to Western scholarship may have experienced a measure of dissonance when trying to understand the Talmud as a "text." Their assimilation into nineteenth-century Western culture meant, in reality, that they were moving from one interpretive community into another, their assumptions and values changing so that it no longer "made sense" to read the Talmud in the way they had originally been taught. Talmudic ways of reading no longer connected with any aspect of their current literary or cultural practices. By the second generation, Jews who had had no formal religious training could only view the Talmud as "bizarre"; the interpretive community of which they were members could simply not accommodate the unique structure and content of talmudic discourse.

This is not to suggest that in understanding the Talmud, either "you're in or you're out." Interpretive communities are not insulated institutions; as Stanley Fish has emphasized, they (or, more correctly, their assumptions, values, methods, etc.) are constantly in flux. As the nineteenth century progressed, there were those who sought to identify or even construct bridges between these seemingly polarized worlds, creating as a result a "new" interpretive community, one with a rather unique set of premises and practices when reading the Talmud. For this group, characterized as the members of the *Wissenschaft des Judentums* (Science of Judaism) school, the Talmud was a text of yet another sort. As these scholars and the methodology they developed found their way to American shores, they founded the Conservative movement, which sought at the same time loyalty to the tradition and an openness to change based on the insights of contemporary understandings of humankind and the world.

As a result, when members of the various Jewish denominations meet today to discuss issues related to Jewish law, while they may ostensibly be reading— and citing—the same talmudic passages, these are far from the same "texts" for all of them. The difference of views between these religious streams is almost always a manifestation of their respective notions of what it means to be a "text" in the Jewish legal tradition: how to read it, what weight to give it, and how it fits into the overall argument one is constructing.[48] Of course, there may be overlap, with some strategies shared by more than one scholar or group. But like the Tower of Babel, the denominations are in reality speaking different languages, for even if many of the words are similar, the interpretive communities in which those languages function and develop are significantly different. And in settings where normative claims are being made, interpretive communities embody much more than mere strategies of reading; the act of construing texts and interpreting them involves an entire range of tacit assumptions. I mentioned earlier that in the case of the Jewish tradition, whether humanity as a whole is in decline or is seen to be progressing inexorably forward affects the weight one gives to earlier sources.[49] Similarly, views on what Judaism demands of its members, the relationship of human beings to God, and even the relationship of Jews to non-Jews are just a few of the many issues which impact, to varying degrees, on the ways one "reads" the texts of Jewish law. Authority cannot be understood independently of these interconnected issues.

Summary

In this chapter, we have seen that authority, on the model of literary criticism, is really embedded in a form of life that has its own set of beliefs, assumptions, convictions, values, and practices. Rabbinic authority—or any authority of this sort—cannot exist outside this context; the effort to analyze "authority" in some disembodied form is, in a serious sense, an ill-fated enterprise. Several important consequences follow from this approach.

First, this discussion suggests that it may not be helpful to view the issue of Rabbinic authority in some cause-and-effect relationship with other principles or beliefs. The urge to offer justifications comes from a certain "picture" of seeing each human action on the model of a mathematical or scientific proof: it is the result of reasoned deliberation, of a decision to act in accord with a certain rule or directive which the subject takes as compelling. On this view, "Rabbinic authority" is taken to be a *reason* one may offer to explain why one has chosen to perform a particular practice that originated, whether through interpretation or legislation, with the talmudic Sages. And as such, it invites critical inspection whether such a *reason* is either rational, coherent, or sufficient.

However, I have tried to show in this chapter (and, to a degree, throughout part III) that this approach to understanding Rabbinic authority is not necessarily the "right picture." As Wittgenstein noted, sometimes the role of philosophy is to know when to stop, when not to answer a specific philosophical question but to get "behind" it and realize the picture out of which it emerges, and then to suggest a different picture which simply dissolves the problem. Thus, authority is not always an external reason operating on a subject and compelling him or her to act a certain way but is often a notion embedded in a particular form of life that has its own set of values and norms. Therefore, since the notion of "Rabbinic authority" cannot be separated from the form of life in which it is seen to have meaning and significance, it is most apt to try and *describe* that form of life. Among traditional Jewish scholars, academic attention is still centered on talmudic opinions and their subsequent exposition and interpretation, and all legal reasoning is formally built, at least initially, on the Sages' words. Speakers and writers in that community lend weight to their arguments by invoking and interpreting the Sages' insights and biblical exegeses. For the average person, not only is daily language sprinkled with Rabbinic expressions or sayings, but the categories by which events are ordered are those which originated with the talmudic Rabbis. For those in this culture, the world of the Sages is vibrantly alive; in a real sense, these ancient Rabbis still walk among them.[50]

It is therefore not surprising that for this form of life, the Babylonian Talmud occupies such a central place in so many facets. Educationally, it is the core curriculum during one's school years,[51] to the point that schools compete to

begin instruction in Talmud at the earliest possible age—this despite the Talmud's own recommendation of beginning Gemara study at age fifteen.[52] Socially,
status in the community is in many cases achieved in terms of talmudic knowledge: how many tractates has one studied, how many subjects has one mastered,
how many talmudic passages has one committed to memory, and so on. Adult
males are expected to continue studying the Talmud for the rest of their lives;
at present, tens of thousands are committed to studying a folio of the Talmud
daily (*daf yomi*), many aided by modern technology (recorded instruction available on tapes, over the phone, or through the internet), and many others at-
tending regular classes either in Talmud or in related subjects that are often
based on Rabbinic sources. All this both boldly reflects and deeply reinforces
the form of life in which the talmudic Sages figure so prominently.

   Second, situating Rabbinic authority in a form of life bears implications for
understanding the relationship of such authority and the individual. The traditional Enlightenment model saw action as the result of a person's internal deliberation, a rather insulated process that ends in an intention to perform some
activity. We now recognize, however, that no mental process is so insulated;
instead, each involves a host of unstated assumptions and values that are so
prevalent that they are taken to be "intuitive" or "natural." As Fish argued with
respect to the field of literary criticism, communities not only are the arena in
which conversation takes place but also literally enable all discourse to occur,
in that the categories and concepts by which we perceive and order our experiences and process them "have a life" within those communities.[53] Similarly,
communities provide the context for the practices which express and embody
Rabbinic authority. Therefore, Rabbinic authority may mean very different things
for different communities, in the sense that regular behaviors will make sense
in some societies but not in others. And it is always with respect to these societies
and their practices that individuals must gauge to what degree the talmudic Sages
are authorities in their lives.

   Thus, for some, "Rabbinic authority" is seen in having every aspect of one's life
guided, even determined, by Halakhah; it implies that with respect to a wide range
of issues, it would be appropriate to consult a rabbi or halakhic expert on the relevant halakhic issues; it means that various proportions of one's spare time are devoted to studying Rabbinic texts, in general, for nothing other than their own sake.
For these Jews, their daily practices render "public" the language and terminology
of the Sages; Rabbinic authority is visible and palpable everywhere they turn.[54] For
other Jews, Rabbinic authority may be embodied largely in the conversations and
sermons of the scholarly echelons and does not always filter down to their own
practices or perceptions of the world. For these Jews, relatively little in their form
of life, whether in observances or study, can be connected to the notion of Rabbinic authority. And for others, Rabbinic authority may be the fact that Jewish tradition has a very strong voice within their form of life, but it is one authority among
many—science, literature, psychology, or sociology being others—such that their
practices will bear out and instantiate these multiple allegiances.[55]

   Not surprisingly, one's form of life furthermore determines the perspective
through which *other* forms of life are viewed. Thus, persons whose lifestyle in-

cludes relatively few Jewish ritual observances may have actively chosen that path as connected to the form of life that they prefer, or they may have simply "backed into" this level of observance passively, due to lack of education or other reasons. Nevertheless, in the eyes of those who adhere more strictly to halakhic norms, these people will probably be seen as having rejected Rabbinic authority on principle. Alternatively, Jews who think of themselves as guided by talmudic law and its subsequent interpretations by traditional scholars might be seen by those reared in environments far less attuned to this "language" as practicing either a quaint form of atavism or a primitive, fundamentalist rejection of modern society. In both cases, the others' motives are understood only superficially or not at all. The proper nexus in which to understand the question of one's allegiance to the talmudic Sages is the complex of one's form of life.

Although seeking justifications of the Sages' authority is, as I have tried to show in this chapter, in the "grip" of a misguided view of how authority and action are related, one *can* give reasons *why* one has chosen to live a life where such authority is operative: it can provide a sense of overall purpose to one's activities; it can create or deepen feelings of community with other Jews; it can offer guidelines for behavior and a relative certitude with respect to moral and other sorts of dilemmas; and it can supply a person with a connection to or a rootedness in a millennia-long tradition. This is not to say that all these are necessarily universal desiderata; for some, the material, social, or ideological costs (to name a few) of living in accordance with such strict rules may be too great. Nor is the issue all-or-nothing; in an open, free, and individualistic society such as the contemporary West, different people choose different levels of commitment to Jewish law, enjoying and sacrificing various benefits commensurately. In this sense, reasons can be "justifications," in the sense of justifying a particular choice as to how to lead one's life. But all such "justifications" are impossible without appeal to a form of life—a public community—which gives substance and body to these very reasons.

Indeed, the answer to the question "why should we listen/obey the talmudic Sages?" is rarely a function of a particular ideology. Many factors contribute to the average person's decisions on how to lead one's life, and those choices are "public" in the sense that they appeal to practices which others are doing and arguments they are making at the time. It is this public character of one's choices in observance that forces the question of Rabbinic authority to the level of communities rather than merely the individual.

Rabbinic authority, then, describes a form of life that seeks to understand all human activity and choices through the prism of a lengthy tradition in which the talmudic Sages loom very large. The Rabbis of the first five centuries left a legacy that, to varying degrees for various interpretive communities, serves as the foundation for an ongoing project of study and interpretation which helps define one's role and purpose in life. In the final analysis, the "authority of the talmudic Rabbis" is a notion that rather accurately reflects the practices and values of living communities, communities by which we understand and measure ourselves.

Conclusion

After nine chapters of lengthy discussion and analysis, what may we say about Rabbinic authority? In many ways, the most significant outcome of our study is the acknowledgment that the concept of Rabbinic authority is rather complex. What appeared, at first glance, to be a relatively straightforward question—why should one obey the talmudic Sages?—was shown to be a considerably complex and sophisticated issue. In chapter 1, we saw that the Rabbinic project was in reality diverse and multifarious, including transmission of oral traditions, both legal and homiletic biblical hermeneutics, as well as social and religious legislation. Furthermore, our ongoing analysis suggested that these spheres were not always separated by hard-and-fast boundaries but were often blended in ways suggesting that certain Rabbinic rulings were really mergers or fusions of multiple Rabbinic roles. After recognizing the complex and composite nature of Rabbinic activity, it is clear that simple, one-dimensional explanations of the Sages' authority are hard to defend and are best avoided.

The appreciation of this complexity, however, had its consequences when, in parts I and II, we examined various theories, in their archetypal forms, that may be proffered to justify Rabbinic authority. Using Peters's categories of *in* authority and *an* authority, I offered a typology of models of Rabbinic authority that portrayed the talmudic Sages either as occupying preestablished seats of authority or as being inherently endowed with certain skills or gifts which rendered them deserving of obedience. The discussions were revealing in several respects. First, most theories of Rabbinic authority seem to be insufficiently nuanced to ground the admittedly diverse realm of Rabbinic activity. To be sure, this is not necessarily a handicap; our understanding of the Sages' authority may need precisely such fine-tuning and variety to match the diversity of the Rabbis' pronouncements. The Sages' authority to interpret the Torah may be based on a theory regarding their personal endowment, and their authority to legislate may be grounded in a more "institutional" view.

Second, the analysis highlighted the temporal, geographical, and historically differentiated scope of our subject: as a group, the talmudic Sages spanned five centuries and had two centers (Palestine and Babylonia), and only some were ordained while likely many others were not. This forced all theories to balance two conflicting desiderata: to be inclusive enough to encompass this large and diverse domain of scholars but at the same time to be sufficiently defined as to limit this authority to the talmudic Rabbis alone. In all cases, such a balance was extremely hard to strike and generally required the importation of other historical or theological assumptions which had to be taken almost entirely on faith. The purpose of this observation was not to show that some theories of Rabbinic authority are merely faith-claims but to lay bare the extent to which these theories do not stand alone or independent of other assumptions but instead are interwoven and integrated with them in crucial, if not always explicit, ways.

Rather than locate the ground of the Sages' authority in the Sages themselves, as the theories in parts I and II did, part III explored the possibility that the notion of Rabbinic authority really stood for some other religious value in Judaism. Chapter 7 sought to frame Rabbinic authority in terms of the authority of the accepted practices of the Jewish people. This suggests that authority, or more accurately its ground, can evolve from one form into another; what can be called "the authority of the talmudic Sages" for one generation is transformed generations later into "the authority of Jewish tradition." Such an understanding of authority implies that it is both historically contingent and, to some degree, mutable.

Continuing to explore models of "transformed authority," chapter 8 examined the notion that Rabbinic authority was, in reality, another name for the authority of the talmudic *text*, which is, after all, the record of the Sages' interpretations of the law. This allowed us to discuss the authority of a text within a legal tradition, for which Ronald Dworkin's model of a serially written "chain novel" was rather helpful. "Rabbinic authority" became the name for the sense of writing within a particular tradition that analyzes all matters using the categories and principles established in the foundational text of the Babylonian Talmud. While there is always some independence in interpretation, there are also the constraints imposed by a lengthy legal tradition that has chosen to follow certain paths and reject others.

Interpreting legal texts led us in chapter 9 to introduce Stanley Fish's analysis of literary criticism, which situates all interpretation within the context of interpretive communities. Indeed, a "text" has no existence independent of such a community, for only a community, with its values, assumptions, principles, etc., may construe a text as a "text" in the first place. We teased out the implications of such a model for interpretation in legal traditions in general and in the Jewish legal tradition in particular, showing how the ways the Sages read the Torah became characteristic of that community and were subsequently (consequently?) applied to the Mishnah, the Talmud, and even medieval codes.

All three chapters of part III offered alternative understandings of authority that, to varying degrees, rejected the Enlightenment assessment of authority. The

Enlightenment model demands that some justification be provided for forgoing one's own independent judgments and decisions in order to defer to another's view. But in part III I tried to show that authority is embedded in a form of life which, in the end, renders such rational justification beside the point. Applying a Wittgensteinian approach to the issue of Rabbinic authority, we saw that the issue could not truly be understood outside a set of circumstances that already situates it—and those subject to it—in a particular context. Description, rather than justification, was seen to be a helpful and productive way of analyzing authority. The question that came up in the nineteenth century and that continues to the present is not really about the authority of the talmudic Sages but is about the contemporary relevance or appropriateness of a form of life that makes the Sages of late antiquity central to one's entire outlook and set of concerns. Various interpretive communities, represented in part by the range of Jewish denominations today, have resolved this issue in a variety of ways, and each, in the end, construes the "text of the Talmud" and "Rabbinic authority" quite differently. The choices made by each community naturally bear consequences for its members, but it is only in terms of these interpretive communities that we can properly discuss the issue of the Talmud's, or Rabbinic, authority.

No simple solutions, therefore, await us as we inquire into the nature of Rabbinic authority. Sages, texts, and interpretive communities and forms of life mix inextricably in complex and subtle ways such that the effort to separate them and view one as antecedent or primary to the others fails to capture how authority is to be understood in Judaism. Rabbinic authority is necessarily conceived in the intricate interface of community and text, a fitting condition for "the people of the Book."

Notes

PREFACE

1. Antony Flew and Alasdair MacIntyre, eds., *New Essays in Philosophical Theology* (New York: Macmillan, 1955), p. x.

2. See, for example, ibid.; H. H. Price, *Essays in the Philosophy of Religion* (London: Oxford University Press, 1972) David Shatz, ed., *Contemporary Philosophy of Religion* (New York: Oxford University Press, 1982); Baruch A. Brody, ed., *Readings in the Philosophy of Religion: An Analytic Approach* 2nd edition (Englewood Cliffs, N.J.: Prentice-Hall, 1992. Many individual philosophers have also written their own introductions to the subject.

3. On atonement, see Richard P. Swinburne, *Responsibility and Atonement* (New York: Oxford University Press, 1989). On prayer, see D. Z. Phillips, *The Concept of Prayer* (London: Routledge & Kegan Paul, 1965), and P. Geach, "Praying for Things to Happen," in his *God and the Soul* (London: Routledge & Kegan Paul, 1969). On life after death, see C. J. Ducasse, *A Critical Examination of the Belief in Life after Death* (Springfield, Ill.: Charles C. Thomas, 1961); Terence Penelhum, *Survival and Disembodied Existence* (London: Routledge & Kegan Paul, 1970); and some of the contributions in Price, *Essays in the Philosophy of Religion*.

4. A telling example is the journal *Faith and Philosophy*, begun in 1984. Despite the generic title, the subtitle is "Journal of the Society of Christian Philosophers."

INTRODUCTION

1. This is not to say that the issue of *emunat ḥakhamim* (faith in the Sages) was never challenged before the end of the eighteenth century. Karaism, for instance, drew the most attention in the early Middle Ages, with scholars such as Saadia Gaon (10th c. Babylonia) and Maimonides (12th c. Egypt) composing tracts against the Karaite challenge. See Gerald Blidstein, *Masoret ve-samkhut mosdit le-raʿayon torah she-be-ʿal peh bi-mishnat ha-rambam*, *Daʿat* 16 (1986): 11–27. A number of apologetic works were also produced in the seventeenth century, particularly in Amsterdam,

justifying Rabbinic authority. These challenges, however, emerged almost exclusively from the intellectual classes, who absorbed from the general culture either philosophical and deistic rationalism or a form of Christian fideism. In both cases, it was exposure to one's surroundings that prompted the skepticism regarding Rabbinic authority. See Shalom Rosenberg, "Emunat Hakhamim," in *Jewish Thought in the Seventeenth Century,* ed. Isadore Twersky and Bernard Septimus (Cambridge: Harvard University Press, 1987), pp. 285–341.

2. For examples of laxity in medieval times, see Ephraim Kanarfogel, "Rabbinic Attitudes toward Nonobservance in the Medieval Period," in *Jewish Tradition and the Nontraditional Jew,* ed. Jacob J. Schacter (Northvale, N.J.: Jason Aronson, 1992), pp. 3–35.

3. It is therefore appropriate to characterize premodern Jewish societies as "traditional," where practices were simply accepted without question. This is in contrast to "Orthodoxy," where observance of Halakhah, in the face of other options, is embraced by choice. See Jacob Katz, "Orthodoxy in Historical Perspective," *Studies in Contemporary Jewry* 2 (1986): 3–17; Michael K. Silber, "The Emergence of Ultra-Orthodoxy: The Invention of a Tradition," in *The Uses of Tradition: Jewish Continuity in the Modern Era,* ed. Jack Wertheimer (New York: Jewish Theological Seminary of America, 1994), pp. 23–84, p. 26, n. 4; Haym Soloveitchik, "Rupture and Reconstruction: The Transformation of Contemporary Orthodoxy," *Tradition* 28, no. 4 (1994): 64–130. See also n. 10.

4. For a comparison of Jews under Islam and those under Christianity, see Mark R. Cohen, *Under Crescent and Cross: Jews in the Medieval Period* (Princeton, N.J.: Princeton University Press, 1994).

5. I refer here to those who, for a variety of reasons, chose to convert to Islam or Christianity. The extenuating circumstances that accompanied large-scale conversions, such as those that preceded the expulsion from Spain in 1492, obviously do not fall under this generalization. See Yitzhak Baer, *A History of the Jews in Christian Spain* (Philadelphia: Jewish Publication Society of America, 1966), vol. 2, pp. 244–99, 424–39.

6. Jacob Katz has paved the trail for our contemporary understanding of this critical period. Emancipation did not topple a solidly intact society; rather, traditional society and its institutions had already begun to erode steadily in the eighteenth century, so that political emancipation, when it finally arrived, dealt the final blow to a social structure already in decline. See his *Tradition and Crisis: Jewish Society at the End of the Middle Ages,* trans. and with an afterword and bibliography by Bernard Dov Cooperman (New York: New York University Press, 1993); *Out of the Ghetto: The Social Background of Jewish Emancipation, 1770–1870* (Cambridge: Harvard University Press, 1973); *Emancipation and Assimilation: Studies in Modern Jewish History* (Farnborough: Gregg, 1972); and *Jewish Emancipation and Self-Emancipation* (Philadelphia: Jewish Publication Society, 1986).

7. Michael A. Meyer offers several detailed portraits of Jews who responded to the nascent integration of Jews into German culture in different ways. See his *The Origins of the Modern Jew: Jewish Identity and European Culture in Germany, 1749–1824* (Detroit: Wayne State University Press, 1967).

8. That Reform Judaism must be seen against the backdrop of emancipation is established by Michael A. Meyer in his *Response to Modernity: A History of the Reform Movement in Judaism* (New York: Oxford University Press, 1988).

9. In the relatively open society of Spain, Jews who embraced their surrounding culture also dropped many practices. This was, however, perceived as religious laxity,

both by the moralists and pietists and by the transgressors themselves. See Baer, *History of the Jews in Spain*, vol. 2. What is new in nineteenth-century Germany is the effort to legitimize these changes by revising the standards themselves to accord with common practice.

10. The response of traditionalists was not limited to the realm of polemics, with Jewish practice merely maintained as it had been for centuries. Orthodoxy itself must be seen as a response both to the Reform challenge specifically and to modernity in general. See Katz, "Orthodoxy in Historical Perspective"; and Silber, "Emergence of Ultra-Orthodoxy." Obviously, that confrontation was not momentary or universal but must be viewed locally, as each community encountered modern culture. Some more isolated communities thus remained "traditional" up to their destruction in World War II; see Ben Zion Pinchuk, *Shtetl Jews under Soviet Rule: Eastern Poland on the Eve of the Holocaust* (Oxford: Blackwell, 1990).

11. Joseph H. Hertz, chief rabbi of the British Empire in the early part of the twentieth century, composed an English translation of the Pentateuch along with a commentary intended to counter the claims of biblical critics. In the words of the preface to the first edition (London: Oxford University Press, 1929–36): "My conviction that the criticism of the Pentateuch associated with the name of Wellhausen is a perversion of history and a desecration of religion, is unshaken." The commentary cites Jewish and Christian Bible scholars (some of whom Hertz admittedly characterizes as "iconoclastic") who support the idea that the text is of single authorship.

12. The work of the Italian Bible scholar Umberto Cassuto is exemplary of this approach. See his various works on the books of Genesis and Exodus, and his *Torat ha-teʿudot vi-siduram shel sifrei ha-Torah* (Jerusalem: Magnes Press, 1941), which was translated by Israel Abrahams as *The Documentary Hypothesis and the Composition of the Pentateuch: Eight Lectures* (Jerusalem: Magnes Press, 1961).

13. For instance, "an eye for an eye," the *lex talionis* clause of the Torah (Ex. 21:24; Lev. 24:20) is understood as monetary compensation, as are other cases where capital punishment is mentioned (e.g., Ex. 21:29). Another interesting case is Lev. 19:14, "do not put a stumbling block before the blind," which is taken to mean offering bad advice to those likely to sin, rather than its simple meaning. See Maimonides, *Mishneh Torah*, Hilkhot Roṣeaḥ u-Shemirat Nefesh 12:14–15.

14. The expression is found in the Babylonian Talmud (hereafter abbreviated BT) tractate ʿEruvin 21b. Cf. Menaḥot 29b.

15. Some scholars have suggested, however, that this awareness did not obtain throughout the entire Rabbinic period but evolved only in its later phases, among the Amoraim. Thus, Gedaliah Alon, in *Meḥqarim be-toledot Yisrael* (Tel Aviv: Kibbutz ha-Meʾuḥad, 1958), vol. 2, p. 239, argues that the effort to find exegetical basis for Rabbinic authority is the activity only of later Amoraim. Similarly, Yitzhak D. Gilat, in "Bet Din matnin laʿaqor davar min ha-Torah," *Bar Ilan* 7–8 (1970): 117–32, notes that the Amoraim were troubled by the use of the expression "who sanctified us with his commandments and commanded us to . . ." in the blessings recited before fulfilling certain Rabbinic laws, such as kindling the Ḥanukkah lights. Gilat suggests that the early Sages saw no problem in extending this liturgical formula to laws that they instituted because the demarcation between biblical and Rabbinic law had not yet been clearly made. In a similar vein, Jacob Neusner and others have argued that the notion of the "dual Torah" appears only among the Amoraim, implying the absence of such a doctrine prior to the third century. See Neusner's *Torah: From Scroll to Symbol in Formative Judaism* (Philadelphia: Fortress Press, 1985), pp. 53–56, 145; Martin Jaffee, "Oral Torah in Theory and Practice: Aspects of Mishnah-Exegesis

in the Palestinian Talmud," *Religion* 15 (1985): 390; David Kraemer, *The Mind of the Talmud: An Intellectual History of the Bavli* (New York: Oxford University Press, 1990), pp. 117–18.

16. See Maimonides' nuanced discussion of the five categories of Oral Law in his *Haqdamah le-perush ha-Mishnah* (Introduction to the Commentary on the Mishnah), ed. Y. Kapaḥ (Jerusalem: Mossad Havav Kook, 1963), vol. 1, pp. 19–22.

17. Paradigmatic of a maximalist understanding of this concept is the talmudic statement explicating Ex. 24:12: "Rabbi Levi bar Ḥama said in the name of Rabbi Shimon ben Laqish: What is the meaning of the verse, 'I have given you the tablets of stone and the Torah and the commandment that I wrote to instruct them'? 'Tablets' refers to the Decalogue; 'Torah' refers to the Pentateuch; 'and the commandment' refers to Mishnah; 'that I wrote' refers to the Prophets and Writings [the other two parts of the Hebrew Bible]; 'to instruct them' refers to Talmud. This teaches that they were all given to Moses at Sinai" (BT Berakhot 5a). The same idea is found in the Palestinian Talmud (hereafter abbreviated PT) tractates Pe'ah 2:4, Megillah 4:1, and Ḥagigah 1:8. See the discussion in ch. 1.

18. There is a genuine naiveté on the part of the traditional scholars of this period, who perceived the reformers to be motivated by strictly intellectual concerns. If these concerns could be countered, then presumably the attrition would be curbed, if not cease. The real motives of the majority of those who adopted these reforms were, of course, of a social and cultural nature, not ideological.

19. See BT Beṣah 4b.

20. Mishnah Rosh Hashanah 4:3, Sukkah 3:12. For the biblical requirement, see Lev. 23:40.

21. See Silber, "Emergence of Ultra-Orthodoxy," pp. 50–59.

22. This claim was actually advanced almost a thousand years earlier by some of the Geonim in their early attempts to counter the Karaite challenge. See Blidstein, Masoret ve-samkhut mosdit pp. 11–27. The fact that polemicists often referred to contemporary reformers as Karaites reflects that the nineteenth-century challenge to Rabbinic authority was perceived by traditionalists as merely a reincarnation of earlier challenges to the Oral Law. See Meyer, *Response to Modernity*, p. 112.

23. See Silber, "Emergence of Ultra-Orthodoxy," p. 57.

24. This, of course, is the crucial tension within the Conservative movement of Judaism, which grew out of the Historical School. In the nineteenth century, the scientific study of Judaism (*Wissenschaft des Judentums*) demonstrated the evolutionary nature of Jewish tradition and that careful, reasoned change was legitimate. The Conservative movement, particularly in the last half century, has therefore implemented certain significant modifications to marriage law, Sabbath observance, and women's participation in synagogue services. However, the movement has found it difficult to articulate the precise parameters of legitimate and illegitimate change. For a recent effort, see Joel Roth, *The Halakhic Process: A Systemic Analysis* (New York: Jewish Theological Seminary of America, 1986).

25. This is not the only way to view the problematic of Halakhah's authority in the modern world. The Enlightenment commitment to the exercise of personal autonomy in human behavior necessitates the justification of *all* normative authority, halakhic or otherwise. For a discussion of Rabbinic authority from this angle, see ch. 1 and Moshe Z. Sokol, ed., *Rabbinic Authority and Personal Autonomy* (Northvale, N.J.: Jason Aronson, 1992).

26. Thomas D. Weldon, *The Vocabulary of Politics* (Baltimore: Penguin Books, 1953).

27. See the preface to this book.

28. For an excellent example of the scholarly determination of a particular thinker's view of Rabbinic authority, see Menachem Kellner, *Maimonides on the "Decline of the Generations" and the Nature of Rabbinic Authority* (Albany: State University of New York Press, 1996).

29. For Sabbath observance, see Shimon D. Eider, *Halachos of Shabbos*, 4 vols. (Lakewood, N.J.: S. D. Eider, 1970); Y. Y. Neuwirth, *Shemirat Shabbat ke-hilkhatah* (Jerusalem: F. Feldheim, 1964 or 1965). For the laws of mourning, see Maurice Lamm, *The Jewish Way in Death and Mourning* (New York: Jonathan David, 1969); Y. Y. Greenwald, *Kol Bo ʿal Aveilut* (New York: Feldheim Publishers, 1973); and most recently, Chaim B. Goldberg, *Mourning in Halakhah* (New York: Mesorah Publications, 1991).

30. Many of the arguments can, of course, apply to a justification of the Sages' *contemporary* authority, whether in Palestine or Babylonia, although that historical dimension is hard to gauge accurately in the absence of diverse sources (see ch. 7). Our interest, however, remains on the Sages' ongoing authority.

31. His remarks can be found in the symposium on authority in the *Aristotelian Society Supplement* 32 (1958), pp. 204–24.

32. This is why a medical professional can be revered by some patients and reviled by others; the assessment often depends on the patient's personal experience.

33. The scientific community has recently come under serious scrutiny for the hegemonic institutional structure of research, which often leaves innovative ideas or nonmainstream theoreticians out of the conversation. The problem stems in large part from situating the evaluators of quality and value within the institutional framework itself rather than outside it. Those who challenge the norms of the system are thus excluded from the entire enterprise. See Deborah Shapley and Rustum Roy, *Lost at the Frontier: U.S. Science and Technology Policy Adrift* (Philadelphia: ISI Press, 1985); and Michael T. Ghiselin's more recent but bitter treatment of the subject in *Intellectual Compromise: The Bottom Line* (New York: Paragon House, 1989). Harry Redner's *The Ends of Science: An Essay in Scientific Authority* (Boulder: Westview Press, 1987) is likely the sharpest attack of this nature.

34. Lenin's case is studied from the perspective of authority by Robert C. Tucker, "The Theory of Charismatic Leadership," *Daedalus* 97 (fall 1968); 731–56.

35. This is the apparent case with revolutionary theories that, once verified and accepted by the professional community, possess an authority independent of their original exponents. This topic will be discussed at length in ch. 5.

36. Kim Lane Scheppele and Karol Edward Soltan argue that the notion of authority must be rethought, focusing on the subject and what he or she accepts rather than on rulers and their will. This renders discussion of the authority of texts and other nonpersonal entities meaningful. See their "The Authority of Alternatives" in *Authority Revisited*, ed. J. Roland Pennock and John W. Chapman, NOMOS, vol. 29 (New York: New York University Press, 1987), pp. 169ff. Hannah Arendt, in a provocative essay entitled "What Is Authority?" (*Between Past and Future: Six Exercises in Political Thought* [New York: Viking Press, 1968]), argued that authority in the West was traditionally connected to religion and tradition. With the latter two now effectively gone from the West, authority no longer existed. William E. Connolly agrees with Arendt that authority as traditionally conceived no longer exists, but this does not imply that authority exists no more. He admits that authority cannot be grounded in anything outside the range of human deeds and presents a subject-oriented account of authority which allows authority its moral footing. See his "Mod-

ern Authority and Ambiguity," in Pennock and Chapman, *Authority Revisited*, pp. 9–27.

37. *Leviathan*, pt. 1, ch. 16 (Penguin ed., 1968, p. 218).

38. The view that a law derives its validity from the *procedure* by which it is rendered into law is articulated most clearly by H. L. A. Hart, *The Concept of Law* (New York: Oxford University Press, 1961). The rules for this process must, of course, be laid out in some primary text which governs all these procedures. The natural implication of Hart's theory is that even Nazi law was valid law, for it followed the proper procedure of lawmaking in the Third Reich. Hart's position generated considerable reaction from those who wanted to deny that immoral laws could be valid.

39. See Martin Golding, "Sacred Texts and Constitutional Interpretation," in Pennock and Chapman, *Authority Revisited*, pp. 267–286. See also the final chapter of Joseph Vining's *The Authoritative and the Authoritarian* (Chicago: University of Chicago Press, 1986).

40. See the relevant contributions in Pennock and Chapman, *Authority Revisited*.

41. Frank Kermode has written on the subject of how texts become classics, and his focus is on the community as well as on the text itself. Just as no work can become a classic without a community of readers, not every popular book becomes a classic. There must be some elements in the work itself which enable later generations and cultures to see themselves as continuations of the life represented in the classic. See his *The Classic* (London: Faber & Faber, 1975) and *Forms of Attention* (Chicago: University of Chicago Press, 1985). In a similar vein, E. D. Hirsch sought to identify those literary classics which he deemed indispensable to understanding Western, and especially American, culture. His *Dictionary of Cultural Literacy* (Boston: Houghton Mifflin, 1988) sparked intense debate because of the hegemonic claims it made concerning the content of the American cultural heritage. Using Kermode's insight, recent immigrants and non-Western Americans cannot see these works as classics when their lives either do not resemble the lives portrayed in the classics or in fact resemble a way of life embodied in an *alternative* set of classics.

42. Collaborative works, which dictionaries and encyclopedias almost always are, present a special case of personal authority. It is possible that a text which emerges as the articulation of a *collective* group cannot be reduced to the simple sum of these persons' individual authority. Joseph Vining takes this approach in understanding the authority of Supreme Court decisions before the bureaucracy of law turned the making of those decisions into a more atomistic and disjointed affair. See his *The Authoritative and the Authoritarian*.

43. The centrality of the community for all interpretive activity will be taken up in the last two chapters.

44. As will be discussed in ch. 6 this strategy may also partake of several other models, such as constituting a form of prophecy (an institutional approach) or giving the Sages a metaphysically unique form of expertise (a personal approach).

CHAPTER 1

1. For a thorough review of the literature on this issue, see David Goodblatt, "The Babylonian Talmud," in *Aufstieg und Niedergang der römischen Welt II* (Berlin and New York: de Gruyter, 1972), vol. 19.2, pp. 304–18. See also Richard Kalmin, *The Redaction of the Babylonian Talmud: Amoraic or Saboraic?* (Cincinnati: Hebrew Union College Press, 1989).

2. Maimonides offers a succinct formulation of the classic position in his introduction to the *Mishneh Torah*. After a list of forty names which represent the chain of tradition from Moses to Rav Ashi, Maimonides writes: "All these aforementioned Sages were the great men of the generations, some of them [serving as] heads of academies, exilarchs, or members of the Great Sanhedrin. In every generation, tens of thousands of scholars were with them who had heard from them [various traditions], including Ravina and Rav Ashi, who are the last of the talmudic scholars. And Rav Ashi is the one who composed the Babylonian Talmud in the land of Shinar." See also B. M. Lewin, ed., *Iggeret Rav Sherira Gaon* (Berlin, 1921; reprint, Jerusalem, Makor 1972), pp. 66ff. (An uncritical English translation of Sherira Gaon's epistle was recently published by Nosson Rabinowich under the title *The Iggeres of Rav Sherira Gaon* [Brooklyn: Moznaim, 1988].) Goodblatt, "The Babylonian Talmud," pp. 307–312, summarizes how the traditional view evolved.

3. For an excellent historical survey of the evolving role of the Sages in the Land of Israel during this period, see Gedaliah Alon, *Toledot ha-Yehudim be-Erets-Yisrael bi-tequfat ha-Mishnah veha-Talmud*, 2 vols. (Jerusalem: Magnes Press, 1954–55); translated and edited by Gershon Levi under the title *The Jews in Their Land in the Talmudic Age (70–640 C.E.)* (Jerusalem: Magnes Press, 1980–84). As for the evolution of Rabbinic institutions and roles in Babylonia at this time, see Isaiah M. Gafni, *Yehudei Bavel be-tequfat ha-Talmud* (Jerusalem: Zalman Shazar Center for Jewish History, 1990).

4. See, e.g., BT Sanhedrin 5a–b, where authorization to adjudicate cases is limited to specific realms or time periods.

5. The first effort to classify the variety of Rabbinic activity was by the great medieval codifier Maimonides in his *Haqdamah le-perush ha-Mishnah* (Introduction to the Commentary on the Mishnah), ed. Y. Kapah (Jerusalem: Mossad Harav Kook, 1963), vol. 1, pp. 19–22. His five-part classification, which is also an effort to explain how and where disagreement entered the oral tradition, bears some similarity to the one presented here. See Y. Shilat, *Haqdamot ha-Rambam la-Mishnah* (Jerusalem, Ma'aliyot 1992), pp. 88–101.

6. Maimonides gives this example in his *Haqdamah le-perush ha-Mishnah* (Kapah ed., p. 3.)

7. It is unclear within the tradition whether the Rabbinic appeal to common practice points to an *independent* source of authority (i.e., the people) or whether it indicates that the Sages' approved of the practice and for whatever reason gave it their imprimatur. This question obviously has a bearing on whether these arguments should be seen as falling under the rubric of the Sages' authority or not. It may, however, be unanswerable, since very often the only evidence of a common practice *is* the passage in Rabbinic literature.

8. See David Weiss Halivni, *Peshat and Derash: Plain and Applied Meaning in Rabbinic Exegesis* (New York: Oxford University Press, 1991), esp. chs. 2–3.

9. See, however, Isaak Heinemann, *Darkei ha-Aggadah* (Jerusalem: Hebrew University 1970); Joseph Heinemann, *Aggadot ve-toledoteihen* (Jerusalem: Keter, 1974). For more recent discussion, see James Kugel, "Two Introductions to Midrash," in *Midrash and Literature*, ed. Geoffrey H. Hartman and Sanford Budick (New Haven: Yale University Press, 1986); James Kugel, *In Potiphar's House* (San Francisco: Harpers, 1990); and Daniel Boyarin, *Intertextuality and the Reading of Midrash* (Bloomington: Indiana University Press, 1990).

10. See C. G. Montefiore and H. Loewe, *A Rabbinic Anthology* (Philadelphia: Jewish Publication Society of America, 1960), chs. 17–20.

11. Some remedies are collected by Fred Rosner in his *Medicine in the Bible and the Talmud: Selections from Classical Jewish Sources* (New York: Ktav, 1977).

12. The history of this question is a long one, extending from the Geonic period to the present. Hai Gaon (*Oṣar ha-Geonim*, ed. B. M. Lewin [n.p.: 1931], Ḥagigah, pp. 59–60) and Samuel ha-Naggid (*Mevo ha-Talmud*) both emphasize that aggadic interpretations reflect the personal opinion of the utterer and are in no way binding, a view shared by Maimonides (*Commentary to the Mishnah* on Sotah 3:3, Sanhedrin 10:3, Shevuʿot 1:4) with respect to Rabbinic debates that have no practical outcome. Samuel ben Ḥofni (*Oṣar ha-Geonim*, Ḥagigah, pp. 2–5) even claims that if an *aggadah* contradicts reason, then we are not obliged to accept it. Nevertheless, throughout Jewish history there have always been scholars who found it more appropriate to take the *aggadot* literally, particularly those recounting historical events. See the *Ketav Tamim* of Moses Taku (thirteenth century) (R. Kirchheim, ed., *Oṣar Neḥmad* 3 [1860]: 63–64) and the response of Judah Loew ben Bezalel (Maharal) of Prague (seventeenth century) to Azariah de Rossi's *Meʾor ʿEynayim*, in the former's *Beʾer ha-Golah* (Jerusalem, s.n., 1970 or 1971), the sixth *beʾer*, pp. 105–41. The presumed excommunication of de Rossi's book by R. Yosef Karo shows the intensity which the debate sometimes reached; see Meir Benayahu, "Ha-pulmus ʿal sefer Meʾor ʿEynayim le-rabi ʿAzariah min ha-adumim," *Asufot* 5 (1991): 213–66. For a brief overview of attitudes to Rabbinic *aggadot*, at least through the thirteenth century, see Marc Saperstein, *Decoding the Rabbis: A Thirteenth-Century Commentary on the Aggadah* (Cambridge: Harvard University Press, 1980), ch. 1.

13. On this, see Yitzhak D. Gilat, "Bet Din matnin la ʿaqor davar min ha-Torah," *Bar Ilan* 7–8 (1970): 117–32. Gilat contends that, in fact, the clear distinction between *de-oraita* (Torah or divine) and *de-rabbanan* (rabbinic) began to develop only after the earliest generations of Amoraim, after well over two centuries of Rabbinic activity. In a similar vein, David Kraemer suggests that the Rabbis were aware that the *written* canon was closed but made room for their contribution by reopening the *conceptual* notion of "Torah." See his "The Formation of Rabbinic Canon: Authority and Boundaries," *Journal of Biblical Literature* 110, no. 4 (1991): 613–30.

14. See Yohanan Silman, "Torat Yisrael le-or ḥidusheha—beirur fenominologi," *Proceedings of the American Academy for Jewish Research* 57 (1990–91): 49–67.

15. For centuries, scholars have sought to examine and systematize the hermeneutical principles employed in the Talmud and Rabbinic literature. One of the earliest is the *Sefer Keritot* of R. Samson ben Isaac of Chinon (fourteenth century), the most recent edition of which is by Simḥah Bunim, David Sofer, and Yosef Moshe Sofer (Jerusalem: Divrei Soferim, 1982); in the eighteenth century, Malakhi Coen composed *Yad Malʾakhi* (New York: Keter, 1945). A book collecting several medieval works on Rabbinic hermeneutics appeared in 1925 under the title *Baraita de-shelosh ʿesreh midot* (Vilna: Rom). In English, Louis Jacobs has written the popular *Studies in Talmudic Logic and Methodology* (London: Vallentine, Mitchell, 1961). Modern scholarship has noted that these heremeneutical tools were not employed in the same way over the entire Rabbinic period but evolved from the Tannaitic, Amoraic, and late Amoraic-Saboraic periods. See, e.g., Michael Chernick, *Le-heqer ha-midot "kelal u-ferat u-kelal" ve-"ribui ve-miʿut" be-midrashim uve-talmudim* (Lod: Makhon Haberman le-Meḥqarei Sifrut, 1984); Michael Chernick, *Midat "gezeirah shavah": suroteha bi-midrashim uve-talmudim* (Lod: Makhon Haberman le-Meḥqarei Sifrut, 1994). See also Yitzḥak D. Gilat, "Le-hishtalshelutah shel ha-gezeirah shavah" (On the Development of the *gezeirah shavah*), in his *Peraqim bi-hishtalshelut ha-*

Halakhah (Studies in the Development of the Halakha) (Ramat Gan: Bar Ilan University Press, 1992), pp. 365–73.

16. Scholars continue to debate the *historical* question of when these hermeneutic methods were adopted by the Sages, and whether they developed internally among the Jews or were more the result of outside influences, such as that of Greek grammar and rhetoric. On this issue, see Saul Lieberman, "Rabbinic Interpretation of Scripture," in his *Hellenism in Jewish Palestine* (New York: Jewish Theological Seminary of America, 1950), pp. 47–82; reprinted in Michael Chernick, ed., *Essential Papers on the Talmud* (New York: New York University Press, 1994), pp. 429–60.

17. Thus, Joseph Albo, a fifteenth-century Spanish Jewish philosopher, writes: "For it is impossible that the divine Torah be complete in a manner which would be sufficient for all times, for the circumstances which emerge constantly in human life, in legal matters or in any form of activity, are too numerous to be included in a book. Therefore, general rules, only suggested in the text, were given orally to Moses at Sinai, through which the scholars of each generation could extract the new rules" (*Sefer 'Iqqarim*, third treatise, ch. 23).

18. The *gezeirah shavah* is the best example of this model, although in the Rabbinic tradition, its validity depended entirely on receiving that particular interpretation from one's teacher. Others who did not have that transmitted tradition were free not to accept the resultant law. See PT Pesahim 6:1 (33a) and parallels; Lieberman, "Rabbinic Interpretation," pp. 58–62; Menachem Elon, *Ha-mishpat ha-'ivri* (Jerusalem: Magnes Press, 1973), vol. 2, pp. 295–98 (subsequently published as *Jewish Law: History, Sources, Principles*, trans. Bernard Auerbach and Melvin J. Sykes [Philadelphia: Jewish Publication Society of America, 1994], vol. 1, pp. 351–55). Cf. Gilat, "Le-hishtalshelutah shel ha-gezeirah shavah"; Chernick, *Le-heqer ha-midot "kelal u-ferat u-kelal"*; Chernick, *Midat "gezeirah shavah."*

19. Similarly, BT Megillah 7a struggles with the divine (or Pentateuchal) source for the Rabbinic holiday of Purim.

PREFACE TO PART I

1. E.g., Mishnah Yadayim 4:1,3; BT Shabbat 81a, 'Eruvin 13b, Yevamot 92b, Sanhedrin 74a.

2. Gafni portrays the Rabbinic courts as fully integrated into the academy's structure. See his "Ma'asei beit din bi-Talmud ha-Bavli: surot sifrutiyot vi-hashlakhot historiyot," *Proceedings of the American Academy for Jewish Research* 49 (1982): 23–40; I. Gafni, *Yehudei Bavel be-tequfat ha-Talmud* (Jerusalem: Zalman Shazar Center for Jewish History, 1990), pp. 226–32.

3. Following a simple majority appears primarily within the juridical context of the courts, which according to Rabbinic law necessarily maintained odd numbers of judges to ensure a majority (Mishnah Sanhedrin 1:6). Talmudic discussions often invoke the principle of *yahid ve-rabbim halakhah ke-rabbim* (the law follows the opinion of the many against the opinion of the individual); this may be another instance of the same juridical principle (cf. the story of Akhnai's oven, BT Bava Mesi'a 59b, which uses the same prooftext, Ex. 23:2, as that of the majority rule in court), or it may apply only to negotiating among Rabbinic views, some of which are portrayed as the opinion of individuals, and some as that of the many (see Mishnah 'Eduyot 1:5; cf. Tosefta 'Eduyot 1:4).

4. See Mishnah Avot 1:1.

CHAPTER 2

1. E.g., to Adam and Eve (Gen. 2–3, passim), to Cain (4:9–15), to Noah (6:13–21, 7:1–4), and to Abraham (12:1–3, 13:14–17).

2. E.g., to Abraham (15:1) and perhaps to Jacob (46:2–4). See Moses Maimonides, *The Guide of the Perplexed* 2:46, trans. Shlomo Pines (Chicago: University of Chicago Press, 1963), p. 404.

3. E.g., to Abimelekh (20:3), to Jacob (28:12–15, 31:11–13), and to Laban (31:24). The dreams of Joseph (ch. 37), Pharaoh (ch. 41), and Pharaoh's servants (ch. 40) are understood as means of divine communication (see 40:8; 41:25, 28, 32), although God does not address the dreamers directly.

4. In Judaism, the distinction is drawn between *bein adam la-haveiro* (between a person and his neighbor) and *bein adam la-Maqom* (between a person and God).

5. See Lev. 24:10–23 (the case of the blasphemer), Num. 9:1–14 (the second opportunity for the Paschal sacrifice), 15:32–36 (the stick gatherer on the Sabbath), and 27:1–11 (the daughters of Selofhad).

6. Num. 27:15–23.

7. Deut. 18:15–19.

8. Deut. 13:2–6, 18:20–22.

9. Ex. 18:26; see also Deut. 1:17.

10. The text is from the Jewish Publication Society translation of the Hebrew Bible (Philadelphia, 1985). I have chosen to deviate and translate the Hebrew *shofet* as "judge" rather than "magistrate" since the latter term, as defined in Black's Law Dictionary (6th ed.), refers to a public civil officer, usually of an inferior level.

11. Most medieval scholars see this passage as containing *two* commandments on following the decisions of the Sages. Based on a talmudic observation (BT Makkot 23b) that the Torah contains a total of 613 commandments—248 positive commandments and 365 negative ones—a genre developed in the early Middle Ages to specify each of them individually. Not all scholars arrived at the same list, and each list was organized along different classificatory lines. In all of these compendia, however, two commandments—one positive, one negative—are derived from the passage in Deuteronomy dealing with obedience to the High Court. The following is from Maimonides' *Sefer ha-Misvot (Book of Commandments)* (ca. 1165): "[Positive] commandment 174 is that we were commanded to obey the High Court and to do all that they might command with regard to that which is prohibited and permitted. And there is no difference in this regard whether they arrived at the conclusion through their own reasoning or through one of the exegetical devices used to expound the Torah or something which they agree is a secret of the Torah, or some other issue which in their view is proper and which strengthens the Torah. All these we are obliged to obey and do them and to stand behind their pronouncements and not to cease from following [them]. . . .

[Negative] commandment 314 is that we were forbidden to disagree with the transmitters of tradition, peace be on them, and to deviate from that which they say in the practices of Torah, and that is what [the Torah] says "You must not deviate from the verdict that they announce to you either to the right or to the left." It should be noted here that the negative and positive precepts are not merely two sides of the same coin. A careful reading of Maimonides' text shows that the prohibition against deviating applies specifically to that which "transmitters of the tradition" instruct Jews to do. The positive precept, however, explicitly refers to the High Court. To be sure, in Maimonides' *Mishneh Torah* (Hilkhot Mamrim 1:2), the language suggests that both the negative and positive precepts do indeed refer to the High Court. But in reviewing the verses in Deuteronomy clause by clause, he limits the proscriptive portions of the verses to that material which "they received one man from the mouth of another"—in other words, transmitted traditions stemming from Moses. This seems consistent with the distinction observed in *Sefer ha-Misvot*. See n. 22. See also Gerald Blidstein, "Maimonidean Structures of Institutional Authority: Sefer Ha-mitzvot Aseh 172–177," *Dine Yisrael* 17 (1993–1994): 103–26.

12. Quite a few medieval scholars felt that the verse "You must not deviate from the verdict that they announce to you either to the right or to the left" specifically applied to the Sages. See Nachmanides' commentary to Deut. 17:11, and Judah Halevi's *Kuzari* 3:39. The application of the doctrine of *lo' tasur* (you must not deviate) to Rabbinic activity appears already in BT Shabbat 23a (and parallels) in connection with using the formula "who sanctified us with his commandments and commanded us to . . ." in the blessing recited for a rabbinically instituted practice. Nevertheless, it would be illegitimate to infer from the somewhat technical issue of a benediction's formula a broad justification of all Rabbinic activity. See n. 21.

13. Tannaitic sources outline the procedure whereby the matter was brought before a series of successive courts of greater and greater erudition. The matter was taken up by the High Court only if the lower courts could not reach a conclusion. See Mishnah Sanhedrin 11:2; cf. Tosefta Sanhedrin 7:1, and Maimonides, *Mishneh Torah*, Hilkhot Mamrim 1:4.

14. Mishnah Sanhedrin 1:5, *Mishneh Torah*, Hilkhot Sanhedrin 5:1.

15. Tosefta Sanhedrin 7:1 explicitly refers to the debates between the academies in its discussion of the High Court's role.

16. Maimonides gives this impression in his *Haqdamah le-Perush ha-Mishnah* (Introduction to the Commentary on the Mishnah), ed. Y. Kapah (Jerusalem: Mossad ha-Rav Kuk, 1963), p. 2, where he portrays Moses descending from the mountain with the written Torah and immediately explicating all the details for the proper performance of the commandments. In *Derashot ha-Ran*, attributed to the fourteenth-century R. Nissim of Gerondi, ed. Leon A. Feldman (Jerusalem: Makhon Shalem, 1973), several of the "discourses" deal with this issue of the relationship of divine will and human exposition of the law. He posits that it might very well be that God desires one action, yet the Sages, using their innate intellectual talents and skills, may arrive at a different conclusion. See esp. discourses 7 and 11.

17. This dual role of the court is underscored by Rabbeinu Asher (Rosh), a thirteenth-century Franco-German scholar, in a responsum he composed. He sees the initial function of a court as ascertaining the truth of the matter, but in the event that this is impossible, then the court has the obligation to see to it that the matter is at least resolved peacefully: "Once the case comes before the judge and he cannot clarify the matter, he is not permitted to withdraw from the case and let the litigants battle with each other. It is written 'Truth and justice [and] peace, etc.,' for through judgment there is peace in the world. Therefore, the power was granted to the judge to rule and do as he sees fit even without reason and proof, in order to achieve peace in the world." See *She'elot u-teshuvot ha-Rosh* (Vilna, 1885), no. 107 (p. 196), s.v. 'od.

18. This case is discussed in BT Bava Meṣi'a 47b and parallels.

19. See Mishnah Gittin 4:2–7, 9; 5:2–3, 5–6, 8–9.

20. Perhaps this is the reason that these legislative acts were, in many cases, subsumed not under the clause "all their instructions to you" (Deut. 17:10) but under a second and quite different biblical verse: "And you shall guard my law" (Lev. 18:30). The talmudic exegesis on this verse is "And you should make a protective law

around my law" (BT Mo'ed Qatan 5a, Yevamot 21a, although in both contexts the exegesis seems limited to a specific range of Rabbinic ordinances). In truth, however, the conclusion of the discussion in Yevamot is that this verse is not a ground for rabbinic enactments but merely an *asmakhta*, a loose form of literary linkage (see responsa of R. Isaac ben Sheshet, no. 294). In spite of the Talmud's conclusion (at least in Yevamot), Maimonides, in several places, cites this verse from Leviticus as proof of the rabbinic prerogative to create a fence around the Torah. (See his *Haqdamah le–perush ha-Mishnah* [Introduction to the Commentary on the Mishnah] p. 12, his comments to Mishnah Avot 1:1, and the introduction to the *Mishneh Torah*; See also Rashi, BT Beṣah 2b, s.v. *veha-tanya*; Nachmanides' commentary to Deut. 4:2.) *Megillat Ester*, Isaac de Leon's commentary to Maimonides' *Sefer ha-Miṣvot* (Book of Commandments), argues (at principle I) that the Talmud's conclusion was that although the resultant decree remains at the level of a Rabbinic commandment, the directive to issue such decrees is indeed biblical (i.e., divine).

21. The Babylonian Talmud struggles with the notion that the Sages could invent new holidays; it uses a verse from the Scroll of Esther (9:27) to justify the institution of Purim (see BT Shevu'ot 39a) and sees Hanukkah as deriving its validity either from our passage in Deuteronomy or from the verse "Ask your father and he will tell you, your elders and they will say" (Deut. 32:7). It should be noted that the Talmud's concern is not in the institution of an annual commemoration per se but in the formula of the blessing; see n. 12. Apparently, the Talmud does not find the phenomenon of Rabbinic innovation itself extraordinary. Maimonides, it should be noted, viewed prayer as a biblical command (Ex. 23:25), thus rendering the entire Rabbinic enterprise of standardizing prayer an extensive elaboration on the divine command; see *Mishneh Torah*, Hilkhot Tefillah 1:1ff.

22. Maimonides' version of the negative commandment as derived from Deut. 17:11 (see n. 11) specifically mentions those who transmit the oral tradition, and not a particular authoritative institution. This is an example where a verse can be seen as authorizing a functional, rather than a formal, office. Of course, such a function is not inherently limited to the talmudic Sages; any post-talmudic scholar who continues to transmit oral traditions would have to be obeyed based on this verse. On the possibility of seeing the Talmud as a textual embodiment of the Oral Law, see chapter 8.

23. A word on my treatment of the subject of divine revelation is appropriate. While I assume any Rabbinic interpretation of the biblical verse to be inadmissible for a theory of the Sages' authority, one should appreciate that according to the traditional Jewish view, an Oral tradition is deemed to be as "revealed" as a written one; the fact that the Sages transmitted an oral tradition is by no means grounds for disqualifying it. In fact, the interpretation is considered to be the plain and simple meaning of the text, not an interpretation external to it. See David Weiss Halivni, *Peshat and Derash: Plain and Applied Meaning in Rabbinic Exegesis* (New York: Oxford University Press, 1991), on the evolving distinction of the plain and applied meanings of the biblical text. Much of what he says there informs this caveat.

24. See *Derashot ha-Ran*.

25. The language of Judah Halevi in the *Kuzari* (3:39) echoes a similar notion: "And we are commanded to obey the judge who is appointed in every generation, as [the Torah] says, 'or to the judge in charge at that time.'" Halevi's work refers to other grounds of Rabbinic authority, as well; see, e.g., ch. 6, n. 18.

26. BT Rosh Hashanah 25b.

27. On the three main institutions of Jewish political leadership before and during

the Rabbinic period, see Stuart A. Cohen, *The Three Crowns: Structures of Communal Politics in Early Rabbinic Jewry* (Cambridge: Cambridge University Press, 1990).

28. On this reading, the text leaves open the possibility that a judicial system imposed by an external power, such as in many cases in the Diaspora, may be authoritative. This authority may depend in large measure on the degree to which the people recognize this appointment and utilize its offices. Solomon Zeitlin contrasts the Spanish and Franco-German medieval experience, citing several contemporary sources, in "The Opposition to the Spiritual Leaders Appointed by the Government," *Jewish Quarterly Review* 31 (1940): 287–300.

29. Apparently, Thomas Jefferson felt that to be the most democratic route and hence desired that a constitutional convention be held every twenty years in order to reaffirm or revise the 1789 constitution. See his letter to James Madison of September 6, 1789, in *The Writings of Thomas Jefferson*, collected and ed. by Paul Leicester Ford (New York: G. P. Putnam's Sons, 1892–99), vol. 5, p. 121.

30. See n. 26. R. Eliyahu Mizraḥi, in his responsum no. 57 (Jerusalem: Darom, 1937), p. 188a, considers the *official* rabbinic authority of a community (*he-ḥakham ha-manhig*) as possessing *political status* that gives him the same authority (locally) as the High Court in Jerusalem.

31. See, e.g., *Oṣar ha-geonim le-masekhet Sanhedrin*, ed. Ḥayyim Ṣvi Taubes (Jerusalem: Mossad Harav Kook, 1967), p. 44, s.v. *hakhin ḥazina*, and p. 45, s.v. *teshuvah*.

32. One area which seemed somewhat more flexible was that of custom, even when it conflicted with an explicit statement in the Talmud. Thus, tosafists (BT Megillah 31a, s.v. *le-maḥar*) remark regarding a custom to read a prophetic portion on the holiday of Simḥat Torah: "Certain locales have the custom to read 'And it was after the death of Moses' (Joshua, ch. 1) as the prophetic portion, and it is an error, for the Talmud does not say so; yet there are those who say that R. Hai Gaon established this . . . but we do not know the reason why he altered the talmudic guidelines [regarding what to read]." Similarly, custom governed large areas of marriage, inheritance, and monetary matters, even in contravention of talmudic law. See Menachem Elon, *Ha-mishpat ha-ʿivri*, (Jerusalem: Magnes Press, 1973), ch. 22.

CHAPTER 3

1. S. Schreier was the first to raise the question of the reliability of the Jewish sources with respect to the Sanhedrin. See his "Le-toledot ha-sanhedriyah ha-gedolah biyrushalayim," *Ha-Shiloaḥ* 31 (1914–15): 404–15. Hugo Mantel, *Studies in the History of the Sanhedrin*, Harvard Semitic Series, no. 17 (Cambridge: Harvard University Press, 1961), pp. 303–6, finds Schreier's pervasive doubts, which are based on Josephus's testimony in particular, unjustified. The rules and practices of the Sanhedrin may admittedly have been different during the period of Roman occupation, but that is not grounds for totally disregarding the Rabbinic pronouncements as to what the proper procedures indeed were. In politically unsettled times, the law and actual practice often do not coincide.

2. For a summary of some of the diverse opinions regarding the Sanhedrin, see the article "Sanhedrin" in the *Encyclopaedia Judaica*, vol. 14 (Keter Pub., 1971), pp. 836–39, and the bibliography at the end. Of note are Sidney B. Hoenig's *The Great Sanhedrin* (New York: Dropsie College, 1953) and Mantel's *Studies in the History of the Sanhedrin*. One of the most comprehensive treatments of the original Sanhedrin and of the one that existed *after* the destruction of the Temple in 70 C.E.

is Gedaliah Alon, *The Jews in Their Land in the Talmudic Age (70–640 C.E.)*, 2 vols., trans. and ed. Gershon Levi (Jerusalem: Magnes Press, 1980–84). chs. 10–11, 14, 19–28, passim. For a more recent and comprehensive overview of the problems and issues surrounding the Sanhedrin, see Joshua Efron, *Studies on the Hasmonean Period*, Studies in Judaism in Late Antiquity, vol. 39 (Leiden: E. J. Brill, 1987), pp. 287–338. Alon's contention that the Sanhedrin in Jerusalem was composed of priestly, aristocratic, and Pharisaic factions, whereas the postdestruction body in Yavneh (and later) was exclusively Pharisaic is used by Louis Finkelstein to date several problematic Tannaitic sources. See Finkelstein's "Beraita ḥamurah ha-mefiṣah or ʿal toledot ha-Sanhedrin" *Proceedings of the American Academy for Jewish Research Jubilee Volume* (1978–79): 97–109 (Heb. sec.).

3. Cf. Mishnah Shevuʿot 2:2 and Sanhedrin 1:5. However, Chaim Tchernowitz (*Toledot ha-Halakha* [New York: n.p., 1950], vol. 4, p. 246) considers the former to be only theoretical and the latter what was done in practice, thus positing that the two were different institutions. For a comprehensive list of the terms employed by the Tannaitic sources for the High Court or simply "court," see Hoenig, *Great Sanhedrin*, pp. 143–47; Alon, *Jews*, p. 187–88.

4. Tchernowitz, Buechler, and Zeitlin posit more than one body. For sources, see *Encyclopaedia Judaica*, s.v. "Sanhedrin."

5. Hoenig, *Great Sanhedrin*, p. 10.

6. Alon, *Jews*, p. 189.

7. See Mishnah Sanhedrin 11:2; Tosefta Sanhedrin 7:1 (Zuckermandel edition, p. 425); Tosefta, Ḥagigah 2:9 (Zuckermandel edition, p. 235); Sifre Shofetim 152 (Finkelstein edition, p. 206); PT Sanhedrin 1:19c; BT Sanhedrin 88b. Josephus confirms this as well (*Antiquities* IV:8:14).

According to Hoenig and Baer, the Sanhedrin was part of a tripartite system implemented by the Hasmoneans in 141 B.C.E. when the Commonwealth was formed. According to these scholars, the Maccabean Revolt of 167 B.C.E. resulted in a threefold separation of the political, ecclesiastical, and halakhic forces in the Jewish state, which were ultimately embodied in the monarchy, priesthood, and Sanhedrin, respectively. They posit that these offices were actually created at a formal Great Assembly, where the common people's sovereignty was recognized, and that by popular decree, the various institutions were invested with authority. See Hoenig, *Great Sanhedrin*, pp. 23–37; I. F. Baer, "Ha-yesodot ha-historiyim shel ha-Halakhah," *Zion* 18 (1952): 1–55. Salo Baron, *A Social and Religious History of the Jews* (New York: Columbia University Press, 1952), vol. 1, pp. 222–23, agrees that the Sanhedrin was a council which enjoyed widespread popular support and even served as a check on royal tyranny, but he asserts that it never really had the judicial and administrative authority Rabbinic texts claimed it had. Certainly the Rabbinic corpus never offers a constitutional image of the Sanhedrin's authority. Rather, it was rooted in the Torah's authorization of the chief court or judge, to be located in Jerusalem.

8. Mishnah Sanhedrin 11:2 (BT Sanhedrin 86b).

9. Mishnah Sanhedrin 1:5.

10. According to 2 Chron. 19:8–11, the High Court is already located in Jerusalem, although the decision may have been prompted by pragmatic concerns: the high priest was in charge of deciding issues of religious rule, while the head of the House of Judah (the capital of Judah was Jerusalem) was appointed chief judge in all civil matters.

11. The precise reasons for the choice of Yavneh are unclear. Alon argues (*Jews*, pp. 96–99) that it was a detention city for prominent citizens who turned themselves

over to the Romans during the war. By 68 C.E., a sizable community of scholars were being held there, and Rabban Yoḥanan ben Zakkai organized them into a form of protean leadership during the difficult period right after the war.

12. See Alon, *Jews*, ch. 11.

13. Alon, *Jews*, pp. 632–34, 663–73.

14. Lee I. Levine, "The Jewish Patriarch (Nasi) in Third Century Palestine," in *Aufstieg und Niedergang der römischen Welt II* (Berlin and New York: de Gruyter, 1972), vol. 19.2, pp. 649–88.

15. According to Hoenig (*Great Sanhedrin*, pp. 105ff.), the outbreak of the war in 66 C.E. had already brought about the dissolution of the Sanhedrin as an institution.

16. Baron (*Social and Religious History*, vol. 2, pp. 120) claims that Yoḥanan ben Zakkai simply arrogated the name Sanhedrin for his group in Yavneh in order to cloak it with the prestige of the original, more venerable institution. But titular continuity is a far cry from being an actual continuation of the Jerusalem Sanhedrin.

17. BT Sanhedrin 52b (*cf. Midrash Tannaim*, ed. Hoffmann, p. 102).

18. Capital punishment was explicitly linked to the Temple's presence: see *Mekhilta d'Rabbi Shimon bar Yoḥai* ed. J. N. Epstein and E. Z. Melamed (Jerusalem: Mekize Nirdamim, 1955), p. 171; PT Sanhedrin 1:18a, 7:24b; BT Ketubot 30a, BT 'Avodah Zarah 8b. It was, moreover, the standard policy of Roman occupation to deprive the native population of this judicial prerogative; see Alon, *Jews*, pp. 207–9.

19. In some cases, the third party itself may be considered a substitute of sorts. If a person is, say, mentally incompetent, and the court designates someone (relative, friend) to be that person's agent, the court may in that instance be acting as the incapacitated person's substitute. However, it may simply be acting in the position of the state to ensure that that person's rights and interests are protected, based on the Constitution's conception of the purpose of government to ensure each citizen's life, liberty, and pursuit of happiness. In any event, the "substitution" is confined to the act of designating a proxy; after that, the court's agency is ended.

20. This approach is similar to the talmudic notion of *sheliḥutaihu ka 'avdinan* (we act as their agents) as it was understood by the tosafists (BT Gittin 88b, s.v. *bemilta*). See nn. 54–60 and accompanying text.

21. BT Yoma 9b.

22. One is tempted to cite the following Rabbinic exegesis (Sifre Deuteronomy 152–53; [Finkelstein edition, pp. 205–6]): "'If a case is too baffling for you to decide . . . you shall promptly repair to the place . . .' (Deut. 17:8). 'And you shall arrive (there) . . .' (Deut. 17:9). The seemingly redundant phrase teaches us that the High Court at Yavneh is included." However, in this interpretation, the Yavneh Sanhedrin is depicted as directly authorized by the verse, not as a *substitute* for the Jerusalem High Court.

23. One could argue that in contrast to the ongoing (and contingent) nature of direct consent, investing the Rabbis as the High Court's agents might be a one-time event, similar to the public ratification of a form of government, which henceforth no longer requires formal popular consent. This model, however, is more congenial to institutional structures, where one-time authorization remains in effect as long as the structure is intact. Unless the Rabbis can be situated in such a structure, this approach remains problematic.

24. The notion of functional equivalence has a precedent in the office of the king, as David Shatz noted to me. While historically the Davidic monarchy ended with the destruction of the First Temple, other figures, both before and after, came to be seen by several halakhists as kings because of their functional equivalence.

Thus, in his *Mishneh Torah*, Maimonides treats Joshua, the Hasmoneans, and even Bar Kokhba (the leader of the revolt in 132 C.E.) as Jewish kings: (*a*) *Hilkhot Melakhim* 1:3, where Maimonides cites the case of Joshua to prove that a king must be jointly appointed by the full Sanhedrin and a prophet; (*b*) *Hilkhot Megillah ve-Ḥanukkah* 3:1, where Maimonides' depiction of the events surrounding Ḥanukkah include "the restoration of the monarchy to Israel for over 200 years"; and (*c*) *Hilkhot Ta'anit* 5:3, where Maimonides includes the capture of Betar and the killing of their "great king" among the tragedies commemorated on the Ninth of Av. In all three cases, Maimonides refers to them as "kings" even though they could not be considered as such according to the formal requirements he himself lays out in *Hilkhot Melakhim* 1. For a fuller treatment of the subject, see Gerald Blidstein, '*Eqronot mediniyim be-mishnat ha-rambam* (Ramat Gan: Bar Ilan University Press, 1983), pp. 39–45. Blidstein's focus is on the institutional continuity of the monarchy through those who led the people in battle and judged them, which were among the functions of the monarchy. Several references in Rabbinic literature may have served as precedents for Maimonides' functional focus; see BT Yoma 73b, Sanhedrin 49a, and Blidstein, '*Eqronot*, p. 39, n. 95. The issue of the functional role of a king has been of contemporary relevance in the halakhic debate revolving around the State of Israel's right to wage offensive wars. The Talmud insists that a king declare or consent to a war, a requirement R. Abraham Isaac Kook took to be satisfied by the contemporary Jewish government, since both functionally serve as the people's agent. See his responsa *Mishpat Kohen* (Jerusalem: Mossad Harav Kook, 1966), no. 144, sec. 15. Of note is Nachmanides' similar thrust in an addendum to Maimonides' *Sefer ha-Miṣvot*, no. 17, where he writes that waging war is a prerogative of "the king, the judge, or whomsoever exercises authority over the people."

25. Indeed, in a rather stark expression of this idea, Rav Amram bar Sheshnah Gaon, head of the Sura academy in the ninth century, sent a missive to the Jews of Barcelona with the following opening: "Greetings from us and from Rav Ẓemaḥ, the judge of the gate, and from the heads of the *kallah*, and from all the ordained scholars who are in the place of the Great Sanhedrin, and from the [Rabbinic] candidates who take the place of the Little Sanhedrin. . . ." The responsum is found in *Teshuvot ha-Geonim*, ed. Ya'akov Musafiyah (Lick, 1864; reprint, Jerusalem: Ḥevrat Mekiẓe Nirdamim, 1967), no. 56. The translation is by Salo Baron, in *Social and Religious History*, vol. 5, p. 20. Shelomo Dov Goitein shows that the *yeshivot* (Torah academies) of Sura and Pumbedita in Babylonia and of Geon Yaakov in Jerusalem functioned as three Sanhedrins which divided the Jewish world among themselves in terms of jurisdiction. He claims that the very name *yeshiva* was meant to be the Hebrew equivalent of the Greek word "sanhedrin." See his "Political Conflict and the Use of Power in the World of the Geniza," in *Kinship and Consent: The Jewish Political Tradition and Its Contemporary Uses*, ed. Daniel J. Elazar (Washington: University Press of America, 1983), p. 170. He does not discuss whether there was an implicit claim to the authority of the original Sanhedrin either as a substitute for or as a continuation of that body.

26. Mishnah Sanhedrin 11:2–4; in PT Sanhedrin 11:4 (30a), it appears as Rabbi Zeira's qualification of the exegesis of Sifre Deuteronomy 152–53.

27. *Mekhilta d'Rabbi Shimon bar Yoḥai*, ed. J. N. Epstein, p. 171.

28. BT Sanhedrin 52b.

29. On several occasions, Moses in fact requires divine consultation: Lev. 24:10–23; Num. 9:1–14, 27:1–11.

30. Mishnah Sanhedrin 11:2.

31. For example: "A High Priest is judged in the Court of Seventy-one. Whence do we know this? Rav Ada bar Ahava says: 'The verse states, "Every great thing will be brought to you [Moses] (Ex. 18:22)." [This means] Matters concerning a great one' " (BT Sanhedrin 16a, 18b). "Only priests, Levites, or Israelites eligible to wed their daughters to priests are entitled to judge capital crimes. What is the reason? Rav Naḥman bar Yiṣḥak says: 'The verse states, "And they will bear with you" (Ex. 18:22), they [the judges] should be similar to you' " (BT Sanhedrin 36b). " 'Listen among your brethren and judge . . . ' (Deut. 1:16). Rabbi Ḥanina said: 'This is a warning to the court that it should not listen to the words of one litigant before the other litigant arrives' " (BT Sanhedrin 7b). For others examples, see Barukh Epstein's *Torah Temimah* (New York: Hebrew Publishing Co., 1928) on the sections in Exodus and Deuteronomy for an extensive list of sources. Aaron Hyman, *Torah ha-ketuvah veha-messurah*, 2d ed. (Tel Aviv: Dvir, 1979), culls aggadic material, as well as citations from Maimonides.

32. It is the subject of extensive commentarial debate whether this episode must be read in tandem with the account in Exodus of investing judges or whether it constitutes an entirely different story. The obvious difficulty with the latter interpretation is that if the people already had thousands of local judges tending to their judicial needs (according to BT Sanhedrin 18a, there were 78,600 judges), what then was the purpose of appointing another seventy? However, it may be countered that the judges were involved only in strict litigation, when a dispute arose between two parties. There were, nevertheless, many tasks, such as listening to the people's grievances, that were not likely to be within the purview of the judges' responsibilities. Thus, these seventy were intended to function in a more bureaucratic, administrative capacity rather than a judicial one.

33. There is a dispute whether the seventy became permanent prophets or only prophesied that once, as a sign of the genuineness of their appointment, and afterward returned to their normal functioning. See Targum Onkeles on Num. 11:21 and the discussion in BT Sanhedrin 17a.

34. For example: "It was taught in a *beraita*: The great Sanhedrin was composed of seventy-one men, for it is written (Num. 11:16), 'Assemble for me seventy men from the elders of Israel.' And Moses was over them [thus arriving at a total of seventy-one]" (BT Sanhedrin 2a, 16b). " 'And they will stand there with you.' What does 'with you' imply? Similar to you—just as you [Moses] are not a convert, nor a *netin* (Gibeonite), nor a bastard, neither should [members of the Sanhedrin] be converts, nor *netinim*, nor bastards" (PT Horayot 1:4). See also David Tzvi Hoffmann, "Der Oberste Gerichtshof in der Stadt das Heiligthums," *Jahresbericht des Rabbiner Seminars für Orthodoxe Judenthum* (Berlin, 1878), p. 26. This same notion of continuity seems to underlie the talmudic comment—based on Num. 11:16, to assemble the seventy elders—that from ancestral times, the presence of a yeshiva had never ceased (BT Yoma 28b).

35. The reality of the Second Commonwealth, in which the Sanhedrin assisted the Hasmonean king, may have another parallel in the "sanhedrin" of the wilderness, in that the Sages depicted Moses as a monarch over the Israelites. Thus, the Sanhedrin always shared the administration of the people with the king. Interestingly, R. Nissim Gerondi formulates the administrative role as ideally belonging to the king; the Sanhedrin performs these functions only in the monarch's absence. That might be the equivalent of Moses' predicament, where he alone could not bear the job and was hence, to a degree, absent. See *Derashot ha-Ran*, ed. Leon A. Feldman (Jerusalem: Makhon Shalem, 1973), pp. 189–95.

36. This would be similar to the biblical prohibition against offering sacrifices to God outside the Temple, a proscription which was permanently in force only *after* the Ark was brought to Jerusalem and the Temple built. See BT Zevaḥim 119a–b, based on Sifre Deuteronomy 66 (Finkelstein edition, p. 132). This parallel would imply that until Jerusalem was chosen, the Sanhedrin existed, and enjoyed full prerogatives, wherever it was.

37. It is possible to argue that being in Jerusalem was a prerequisite for a valid Sanhedrin only so long as that option was feasible; noncompliance was then deliberate and might invalidate the institution. But when the Romans prohibited Jews from rebuilding their institutions there, the consequent inability to fulfill the requirement was imposed upon them from without and might then not necessarily delegitimize an "exiled" Sanhedrin.

38. Sifre Deuteronomy 153 (Finkelstein edition, p. 206).

39. Joseph Vining similarly sees the authoritativeness of U.S. Supreme Court decisions as stemming from the fact that they reflect the consensus of a group of highly qualified judges. See his *The Authoritative and the Authoritarian* (Chicago: University of Chicago Press, 1986).

40. Of course, the plural verbs may also imply that the vav of *ve-el ha-shofet* should be understood conjunctively, so that the judge joins the levitical priests in reaching a decision. In any event, the text as a whole assumes a collective body, not an individual judge.

41. Thus, for example, we read of eighty-five Sages seated before Rabban Gamliel in Tosefta Keilim Bava Batra 2:4 (Zuckermandel edition, p. 592), and of thirty-eight Elders in the "Vineyard at Yavneh" (*Sifre Bemidbar* 124). Apparently, the number seventy or seventy-one was not necessarily preserved in all Sanhedrins after 70 C.E.

42. A good example of this is found in BT Bava Batra 60b (Tosefta Sotah 15:11–14), where some pious groups sought to adopt an extremely severe form of asceticism in the wake of the Temple's destruction but were dissuaded by R. Joshua ben Ḥananiah due to pragmatic social considerations. See also Tosefta Sotah 15:10.

43. Tosefta Ḥagigah (2:9) gives a list of general qualities a judge should possess (based on Ex. 18:21), while other traditions (e.g., BT Sanhedrin 36b) add some technical requirements, such as age and being a father. Reuven Margaliyot sums them up in "Tena'ei minui ke-ḥaver ha-Sanhedrin" (The Requisites for Appointment to the Sanhedrin), *Sinai* 20 (1946–47): 16–26. Whether these were actually applied at some point in history is not known.

44. Judah Halevi uses the dual argument of a "consensus of scholars" when he defends the ability of the High Court to add new commandments. Among other reasons, he writes: "it is unlikely that they should agree to something which contradicts the Torah, *due to their large number*, nor will error beset them *because of their vast knowledge*, as tradition has it that the Sanhedrin was commanded to be proficient in all areas of knowledge" (*Kuzari* 3:41, emphasis added).

45. Lee I. Levine, *Ma'amad ha-ḥakhamim be-Eretz Yisrael be-tequfat ha-Talmud* (The Rabbinic Class in Palestine during the Talmudic Period)(Jerusalem: Yad Iṣḥak ben Zvi, 1985), pp. 47–52. The notes at those pages collect the various scholarly opinions that have been voiced on the issue.

46. In the Babylonian Talmud, there are only ten uses of this expression, and one instance concerns a strictly theoretical issue ('Eruvin 13b, on whether human existence is an objective good). See the Talmudic concordance of C. J. Kasovsky, *Oṣar Leshon ha-Talmud* (Jerusalem: Misrad ha-ḥinukh veha-tarbut shel Memshelet Yisrael, 1961), s.v. *ve-gamru* (vol. 9, p. 272).

47. On the pluralistic character of Halakhah at this time, see Alon, *Jews*, pp. 311–15.

48. Its emissaries, however, frequently traveled to Jewish communities outside Palestine; see Alon, *Jews*, pp. 234–48, who even suggests that some of the Sanhedrin's functions, such as intercalating the Jewish calendar, were on occasion performed in Babylonia. The Sanhedrin's seat, however, was always within Palestine.

49. David M. Goodblatt argues that during the period of the Babylonian Amoraim, study was conducted by scholars with small circles of disciples around them. See his *Rabbinic Instruction in Sasanian Babylonia* (Leiden: E. J. Brill, 1975). Isaiah M. Gafni challenges this thesis, insisting that the academies maintained a rather strict hierarchical seating; see his *Yehudei Bavel be-tequfat ha-Talmud* (Jerusalem: Zalman Shazar Center for Jewish History, 1990), pp. 190–203 and the appendix at p. 274.

50. Gafni, *Yehudei Bavel*, pp. 226–32.

51. The entire issue of the methods by which Tannaitic traditions were preserved and transmitted remains central to the study of Rabbinic literature. See Saul Lieberman, "The Publication of the Mishnah," in his *Hellenism in Jewish Palestine* (New York: Jewish Theological Seminary of America, 1950), pp. 83–99; Y. Sussman, "Kitvei-yad u-mesorot-nusaḥ shel ha-Mishnah" (Manuscripts and Text Traditions of the Mishnah), in *Proceedings of the Seventh World Congress of Jewish Studies* (Jerusalem: The Perry Foundation for Biblical Research; World Union of Jewish Studies, 1981), pp. 215–50; David Rosenthal, *Mishnah 'Avodah Zarah: mahadurah biqortit u-mavo* (Jerusalem, 1981), pp. 3–21; Martin S. Jaffee, "How Much 'Orality' in Oral Torah? New Perspectives on the Composition and Transmission of Early Rabbinic Tradition," *Shofar* 10 (1992): 53–72; Martin S. Jaffee, "Writing and Rabbinic Oral Tradition: On Mishnaic Narrative, Lists, and Mnemonics," *Journal of Jewish Thought and Philosophy* 4, no. 1 (1994): 123–46 (Jaffee's footnotes provide an extensive bibliography). Margerete Schlüter, *Auf welche Weise wurde die Mishnah geschrieben?* Texts and Studies in Medieval and Early Modern Judaism 9 (Tübingen: J. C. B. Mohr [Paul Siebeck], 1993), examines this question; see Yaakov Elman's review of her work in *AJS Review* 20 (1995): 180–86. See also Shraga Abramson, "Ketivat ha-Mishnah ('al da'at geonim ve-rishonim), in *Tarbut ve-ḥevrah be-toledot Yisrael biy-mei ha-beinayim*, ed. Menahem Ben-Sasson, Robert Bonfil, and Joseph R. Hacker (Jerusalem: Merkaz Zalman Shazar, 1989), pp. 27–52, where he argues that the position attributed to the Geonim that the Mishnah was actually written down on parchment is based on a mistranslation of the Arabic original.

52. For an English description of the Tannaitic and Amoraic enterprises, see David Weiss Halivni, *Midrash, Mishnah, and Gemara: The Jewish Predilection for Justified Law* (Cambridge: Harvard University Press, 1986), esp. chs. 3–5; David Kraemer, *The Mind of the Talmud: An Intellectual History of the Bavli* (New York: Oxford University Press, 1990). Interestingly, I. Halevy, in *Dorot ha-Rishonim* (Jerusalem, n.p. 1967), vol. 4, chs. 46ff., advances the theory that a core Mishnah existed already in the time of the Great Assembly (when the Sanhedrin existed) and that subsequent generations elaborated upon and expanded that legal nucleus, resulting in the multilayered Mishnah "sealed" by Judah I. On such a view, elaboration did not begin with the Amoraim but was already the primary Tannaitic enterprise as well, the core of the Mishnah being grounded in the Sanhedrin's authority.

53. Even a cursory look through Menachem Elon's *Ha-mishpat ha-'ivri* (Jerusalem: Magnes Press, 1973), esp. chs. 15–16, shows that legislative enactments attributed to the Tannaitic period were far more extensive than those attributed to the Amoraic period. (Elon's work does accept uncritically the historical accuracy of the dating of

these enactments.) Not all the cases that Elon cites are, however, clear examples of Amoraic legislation: the cases of an adjoining landowner's preemptive right and a debtor's right to redeem land seized to satisfy a debt are both cited as the view of the school of Nehardea and not necessarily as actual legal enactments (Elon cites a much later source that the first was indeed a *taqqanah*), and in the case of marriage law, the Amoraic "enactment" may simply have been the redactor's device to reconcile a problematic *sugya* (one, by the way, undertaken to explain a Tannaitic enactment).

54. BT Sanhedrin 2b (see also 5a).

55. BT Sanhedrin 2b.

56. See BT Gittin 88b, Bava Kamma 84b.

57. On the precise relationship of the central and local courts, see Alon, *Jews*, pp. 217–30.

58. The tosafists (BT Gittin 88b, s.v. *be-milta*), the medieval Franco-German commentators on the Talmud, raise the idea that it is presently possible to be the agents of *earlier* ordained courts which no longer exist (*shelihut de-kammai 'avdinan*). See *Beit ha-behirah*, Bava Kamma 84b, *ad loc.*, who distinguishes between the two notions of contemporaneous and transhistorical agency. However, such a claim leads to an open-ended authorization, including all post-talmudic authorities as well, an implication we already encountered at the end of the last chapter. Indeed, the tosafists use the argument to justify their own *contemporary* authority to accept proselytes, a legal procedure which, according to talmudic law, required ordained judges (*mumhim*).

59. On several occasions, Tannaim of the early postdestruction Sanhedrin rendered halakhic decisions on their travels throughout the Diaspora; see Alon, *Jews*, pp. 235ff.

60. See n. 58.

CHAPTER 4

1. Also known as *minui*, "appointment"; see PT Sanhedrin 1:3 (19a). As a term denoting appointment to the Sanhedrin, *semikhah* actually appears only once in the Mishnah: Sanhedrin 4:4.

2. On the distinction between eligibility and actual appointment to a judgeship, see Ḥanokh Albeck, "Semikhah u-minui u-veit din," *Zion* 8 (1948): 85–93.

3. *Encyclopedia Judaica* (Jerusalem: Keter Publishers, 1971), s.v. *semikhah*. See also Jeremy Cohen, "Roman Imperial Policy towards the Jews from Constantine until the End of the Palestinian Patriarchate (ca. 429)," *Byzantine Studies* 3 (1976): 1–29. Although the term came to be applied to many subsequent forms of certification, it no longer had the sense of an unbroken chain from antiquity; see Israel Schepansky, "Be-'inyan semikhat hakhamim," *Or ha-Mizrah* 44 (1995–96): 54–95, and the discussion below at nn. 18–20.

4. For a detailed study of the history of *semikhah* for most of the Rabbinic period, see Julius Newman, *Semikhah (Ordination): A Study of Its Origin, History and Function in Rabbinic Literature* (Manchester: University of Manchester Press, 1950); Schepansky "Be-'inyan semikhat hakhamim." On post-Talmudic *semikhah*, see Jacob Katz, "Rabbinical Authority and Authorization in the Middle Ages," in *Studies in Medieval Jewish History and Literature*, ed. Isadore Twersky (Cambridge, Harvard University Press, 1979), pp. 41–56.

5. Maimonides, *Mishneh Torah, Hilkhot Sanhedrin* 4:1; see also his introduction to the *Mishneh Torah*, where he actually gives the list of transmission by generation.

It is noteworthy that Maimonides states that Joshua and the original Sanhedrin were *both* ordained, although the Torah only mentions ordination in connection with Joshua's appointment; see discussion at n. 40.

6. Maimonides, *Mishneh Torah*, Hilkhot Sanhedrin 4:2. W. Bacher, in "Zur Geschichte der Ordination," *Monatsschrift für Geschichte und Wissenschaft des Judentums* 38 (1894): 122–27, argued that originally the ceremony incorporated a laying on of hands, but that was discontinued in the second century C.E.; see also Zeitlin, "The Opposition to the Spiritual Leaders Appointed by the Government," *Jewish Quarterly Review* 31 (1940):297–99. Albeck, "Semikhah," pp. 85–86, endorses Maimonides' view that the expression was always metaphoric, and hands were never used in the ceremony.

7. BT Sanhedrin 5a–b.

8. Mishnah Sanhedrin 1:3; PT Sanhedrin 1:3 (19a); BT Sanhedrin 13b.

9. Maimonides, *Mishneh Torah*, Hilkhot Sanhedrin, 4:1.

10. PT Sanhedrin, 1:3 (19a). Similarly, the Babylonian exilarch's assent was required in order to serve as a judge in Babylonia; see BT Sanhedrin 5a.

11. Leviticus Rabbah 2:4; BT Ketubot 17a; BT Sanhedrin 7b.

12. PT Bikkurim 3:3 (65d); BT Sanhedrin 14a.

13. BT Sanhedrin 14a; Maimonides, *Mishneh Torah*, Hilkhot Sanhedrin 4:6.

14. BT Bava Kamma 84b.

15. BT Bava Meṣiʿa 85a; Sanhedrin 13b.

16. See, however, Yochanan Breuer, " 'Gadol me-Rav Rabi, gadol me-Rabi Rabban, gadol me-Rabban shemo' " (*Rabbi* Is Greater Than *Rav*, *Rabban* Is Greater Than *Rabbi*, the Simple Name Is Greater Than *Rabban*), *Tarbiz* 66 (1996):41–60. Breuer argues that originally the two titles were the same, the difference resulting from a phenomenon of Eastern Aramaic which drops the final letter of a word. However, already in talmudic times, a semantic difference had evolved to explain the dialectical discrepancy, resulting in the common explanation that ordination was absent in Babylonia.

17. See n. 10.

18. Mishnah Sanhedrin 4:4.

19. BT Sanhedrin 14a. Medieval commentators (ReMaH, RaN, Meiri) suggest that since only one ordained scholar is required to ordain someone (see Maimonides, *Mishneh Torah*, Hilkhot Sanhedrin 4:3), R. Judah ben Bava simply took two of the other students present to reach the requisite three and then proceeded to ordain the others.

20. See Schepansky, "Be-ʿinyan semikhat hakhamim."

21. See Newman, *Semikhah*, pp. 155–70.

22. Yehudah Leib Maimon, *Ḥiddush ha-Sanhedrin bi-medinatenu ha-meḥudeshet* (Jerusalem: Mossad Harav Kook, 1950–51).

23. The need for state licensing in law may be greater, since the laws of each state differ, and therefore clients are entitled to know that a person knowledgeable in the laws of that state is representing them.

24. According to Maimonides (*Mishneh Torah*, Hilkhot Sanhedrin 4:2,15, and passim), ordination is strictly licensing. The formula uttered is "Behold you are ordained and you have permission to judge even matters of penalty [*qenas*]." If the candidate was unqualified, the ordination is considered null and void "as if one had sanctified a blemished animal — it never becomes sanctified."

25. BT Sanhedrin 5a–b.

26. Gedaliah Alon suggests that from time to time, bands of scholars from the Yavneh Sanhedrin actually traveled around Palestine, and even to the Diaspora, to perform the intercalation of the calendar. See his *The Jews in Their Land in the*

Talmudic Age (70–640 *C.E.*), trans and ed. Gershon Levi (Jerusalem: Magnes Press, 1980), vol. 1, pp. 246ff. On the collective nature of *semikhah*, see Katz, "Rabbinical Authority," p. 46f.

27. This notion of licensing is appropriate even after a formal judiciary has ceased to exist. Since the scholar, in his personal conduct, reflects on the entire prestige of the Jewish legal code, it was crucial for those in the profession to monitor who was allowed to decide legal issues for the people. Thus, R. Moses Isserles (mid–sixteenth century) writes in his gloss to *Shulḥan Arukh Yoreh De'ah* 242:14: "[semikhah] is so that everyone will know that he has achieved a level of competence to decide laws, and what he decides is with the permission of the person who ordained him."

28. *Haqdamah le-perush ha-Mishnah*, Sanhedrin 1:2 and Bekhorot 4:4; *Mishneh Torah*, Hilkhot Sanhedrin 4:11.

29. An individual places his hands on a sacrifice (Lev. 1:4; 3:2, 8, 13; 4:4, 15, 24, 29, 33); Aaron and his sons put their hands on sacrifices during their initiation ceremonies (Ex. 29:10, 15, 19; Lev. 8:14, 18, 22); High Priest Aaron lays his hands on the scapegoat (Lev. 16:21); and the Levites place their hands on sacrifices during their initiation (Num. 8:12).

30. Lev. 24:14.

31. Num. 8:10.

32. The usage of the word in Gen. 27:37 is figurative, mentioned in Isaac's description, to Esau, of his blessing of Jacob. Jacob's placing of his hands on the heads of Ephraim and Menasseh (Gen. 48:14, 17) is not designated as an act of *semikhah*; see n. 38.

33. See Nachmanides' commentary on Lev. 1:9.

34. See Nachmanides' commentary on Lev. 1:9.

35. Num. 3:40–51.

36. This is the elegant explanation of Hezekiah ben Manoaḥ, a thirteenth-century French commentator, in his commentary called *Ḥizkuni*. On the seriousness of the witnesses' repetition of the blasphemy, see Mishnah Sanhedrin 7:5. M. Gaster, in his article "Ordination (Jewish)" in the *Encyclopedia of Religion and Ethics*, ed. James Hastings (1917), suggests that the similarity between ordaining judges and laying hands on sacrifices was that both implied a transfer of *responsibility*: "These judges were regarded as the men upon whose authority one could rely (*samakh*), upon whom part of the responsibility for right and wrong had been devolved, just as in the case of the sacrificial animal, upon which part of the sin and responsibility of the people had been laid" (p. 553). This coheres with *Ḥizkuni*'s explanation of the witnesses' *semikhah* in the case of blasphemy.

37. Ibn Ezra (Num. 27:18) states clearly that the *semikhah* here was to denote substitution. *Ḥizkuni* (27:13) makes the connection between this ceremony and sacrifices explicit.

38. Jacob's blessing of Joseph's sons (Gen. 48), while not designated *semikhah*, is one in which the laying on of hands figures prominently. It is possible that since Jacob's intent was to grant each of Joseph's sons a full portion in the land ("Ephraim and Menasseh will be like Reuben and Simeon to me," v. 5), the laying on of hands indicated that these two grandchildren would be counted as sons, who naturally take the place of the father after his death, and therefore deserve a portion equal to the other sons. In BT Menaḥot 93b, Gen. 48:14 is cited in a discussion of *semikhah*, suggesting a connection. However, the central concern there is to determine the source for the two-hand requirement in sacrificial *semikhah*, for which various verses with the word "hand" (*yad*) are adduced.

39. Some Amoraim were such longtime disciples of their teachers that the Talmud occasionally assumes that their own opinions are in fact those of their teachers. See, e.g., BT Yevamot 12b and BT Ketubbot 18a with respect to Rav Judah and his assumed citations of Rav and Samuel. For a discussion of these, see David Weiss Halivni, "Safqei de-gavrei" (Doubtful Attributions in the Talmud), *Proceedings of the American Academy for Jewish Research Jubilee Volume* (1978–79): 69 and accompanying notes (Heb. sec.).

40. BT Sanhedrin 5b.

41. Sifre Numbers, *ad loc.* Cf. the Tanḥuma (*Be-haʿalotekha* 15), which suggests that Moses' powers were partially diminished by sharing it with the seventy elders.

42. Michael Rosenzweig, "Be-ʿinyan semikhah u-semikhat zeqeinim," *Beit Yitzḥak* 21 (1989): 91–101, argues that *semikhah*, according to Maimonides, includes one in the membership of "the scholars of Israel," which implies that they represent the interests of the Jewish people (at times even when the latter disapprove!) and are authorized to act in furtherance of those interests. However, it is not entirely clear from Rosenzweig's position how the scholars, as a group, came to possess such authority originally. His paradigm is Joshua's investment by Moses, after the latter becomes concerned about who will lead the people; the scholars are deemed to be heirs of Joshua, through ordination.

43. Samuel ben Ali, a Babylonian *gaon* (head of an academy), defended the authority of the yeshivah and its titular head against Maimonides' vocal support of allegiance to supreme scholars alone: "It is known to you, may you be blessed, that the place of the academy is the seat of Torah, which assumes the place of Moses our teacher, of blessed memory, in every era . . . for by this the religion of Israel is preserved, and their faith persists . . . and whosoever disagrees with it is indeed disagreeing with the Master of the Torah [i.e., Moses], in whose stead the yeshivah stands." The notion that the head of the academy replaces Moses is explicit. See the collection of Samuel ben Ali's letters, published by Simcha Assaf in "Qoveṣ shel iggerot R. Shmuel ben Ali u-venei doro" (A Collection of the Letters of Samuel ben Ali and His Contemporaries), *Tarbiz* 1 (1929)–30: 102–30; 2 (1930–31):43–84; 3 (1931–32):15–80; and 4 (1932–33): 146–47. The letter cited above is found at *Tarbiz* 2, pp. 63–64.

44. See Num. 12:6–8.

45. Ex. 33:17–34:8.

46. See the seventh of Maimonides' thirteen fundamentals of Jewish faith, explicated in his Commentary to the Mishnah, in an introduction to the eleventh chapter of tractate Sanhedrin.

47. E.g., Deut. 7:9–15, 11:1–25.

48. The term "being God's nation" is found in several places throughout the Hebrew Bible, beginning with the Torah, e.g., Ex. 6:7, Lev. 26:12, Deut. 26:18, 27:9, 28:9.

49. According to Rabbinic tradition, Moses himself enacted legislation that was not divinely mandated, such as reading the Torah on Sabbath and festivals (PT Megillah 4:1), learning the laws of the festivals during the festivals (BT Megillah 4a, 32a), and others. All Moses' enactments (*taqqanot*) remained in force (BT Shabbat 30a), but not all of his decrees (*gezeirot*) did; see BT Makkot 24a.

50. In both, the people are told to prepare themselves for the upcoming event, with cognates of the verb *q.d.sh.* used (Ex. 19:10 and Num. 11:18); Moses places the seventy men around (*saviv*) the Tent of Communion, just as there had been a border erected around (*saviv*) Mount Sinai (Ex. 19:12 and Num. 11:24); and God "descends" in a cloud (Ex. 19: 11,18,20 and Num. 11:17, 25).

51. Ex. 19:9. The Talmud debates (BT Sanhedrin 17a) whether the seventy con-

tinued to prophesy, or whether it was only a one-time event meant to establish their authority and nothing more. In both interpretations though, the ability to prophesy was essential to substantiate their positions as Moses' assistants.

52. Indeed, in Maimonides' list of the transmission of the Oral Law from Moses to Rav Ashi (admittedly, not a list of ordination), fully half of the links in that chain were prophets. See his *Introduction to the Mishneh Torah*.

53. In *Derashot ha-Ran*, discourse 11, the same distinction is drawn between scholar-judges, whose authority derives from the laws which they expound, and kings, who have greater latitude in what they may implement administratively but who also therefore need greater restraints.

54. This perceived equivalence may have motivated Maimonides to state that the seventy were ordained as well (see n. 5). In any event, I would argue, the supernatural circumstances had the same effect as *semikhah*.

55. Mekhilta Boʻ no. 12; BT Moʻed Qatan 25a. The limitation of prophecy to the Holy Land was imposed after the Israelites settled there.

56. The fact that the judges of Ex. 18 were organized into jurisdictions of ten, fifty, hundred, and thousand necessarily entails that their numbers would fluctuate proportionally to the population.

57. See Tosafot BT Sanhedrin 16b, s.v. *et*.

58. This orderly procedure included the overturning of one court's decision by a subsequent court, provided certain criteria were met; no individual however, is ever granted this privilege. See Maimonides, *Mishneh Torah*, Hilkhot Mamrim 2:1–3.

59. See Shaye J. D. Cohen, "The Significance of Yavneh: Pharisees, Rabbis, and the End of Jewish Sectarianism," *Hebrew Union College Annual* 55 (1984):27–53.

60. Mishnah ʻEduyot 1:5–6 states as a given that the view of the many against that of the individual should be followed, but it does not address how the Tannaitic sources that offer anonymous views, two or more attributed views, or views attributed to more than one scholar are to be used for normative practice. The rules of determining the law as set down in BT ʻEruvin 46b appear to be mere convention; see chapter 5 for a discussion of these guidelines.

61. See n. 16.

62. BT Pesaḥim 51a.

63. The Mishnah's order of transmitted tradition in Avot 1:1 (Moses received the Torah from Sinai and transmitted it to Joshua, and Joshua to the elders) suggests that Moses' *semikhah* of Joshua was meant as a unique designation of a *single* leader who would guide the people as they conquered the land and divided it among the tribes. The (seventy?) elders did not constitute the primary leadership of the people until after Joshua's death.

64. Perhaps one of the best examples of this is the early-sixteenth-century ʻEin Yaʻaqov by Jacob ibn Ḥabib, which collected all the talmudic *aggadot* (in a fashion similar to Isaac Alfasi's eleventh-century code which assembled all the halakhic portions of the Talmud).

65. See ch. 1, n. 12.

66. *Brown v. Allen*, 344 U.S. 443, 540 (1953).

67. *How to Do Things with Words*, ed. J. O. Urmson (Oxford: Clarendon Press, 1962), p. 152.

68. *Sifre* Deuteronomy 154 (Finkelstein edition, p. 207). The original version has *marʼim* (show you); most medieval quotations of this text (e.g., Rashi, Nachmanides) employ the passive form *nirʼim* (appear), which suggests that the Court indeed knows the true right and left, although it appears to the layman to be the opposite.

69. PT Horayot 1:1 (45d): "Only if they tell you that right is right and left is left, listen to them."

70. Mishnah Sheqalim 1:2.

71. See Maimonides, *Mishneh Torah*, Hilkhot Mamrim 2:5–7; Menachem Elon, *Ha-mishpat ha-ʿivri* (Jerusalem: Magnes Press, 1973), ch. 14, sec. 7.

72. This distinction of vantage points is made in *Derashot ha-Ran*, discourse 8. Cf. R. Moses Feinstein, *Iggerot Mosheh* (New York: 1959), vol. 1, in his introduction to *Oraḥ Ḥayyim*, pt. 1 (the distinction between *emet le-horaʾah*, "decision-making truth," and *emet mamash*, the "actual truth." On the variety of "double-truth" approaches to this problem, see Yitzhak D. Gilat, "'Afilu 'omer lekha ʿal yamin she-hu semol . . . shemaʿ la-hem," in his *Peraqim bi-hishtalshelut ha-Halakhah* (Ramat Gan: Bar Ilan University Press, 1992); Avi Sagi, "'Iyyun bi-shnei modelim shel musag ha-emet ha-hilkhatit u-mashmaʿutam," in *Ha-higayyon: meḥqarim bi-darkhei hashivah shel ḥazal* (Jerusalem: Bar Ilan, 1989), pp. 69–90 (translated, in an abridged form, as "Models of Authority and the Duty of Obedience in Halahkic Literature," *AJS Review* 20, no. 1 [1995]: 1–24); Avi Sagi, "Baʿayat ha-hakhraʿah ha-hilkhatit veha-ʾemet ha-hilkhatit—liqrat pilosofiah shel ha-Halakha," *Dine Yisrael* 15 (1991): 7–38.

73. Thus, the author of the *Sefer ha-Ḥinukh* writes (commandment 496): "it is better to tolerate one error, and have everyone at all times subject to their good thought, than have everyone acting as he sees fit, for this would lead to the destruction of the religion, dissension in the heart of the people, and the total loss of the nation. For these reasons the meaning of the Torah was given to the scholars of Israel." This is a theme in R. Nissim Gerondi's works as well; see his *Derashot ha-Ran*, ed. A. L. Feldman (Jerusalem, Makhon Shalem 1974), pp. 44-45, 84–85 112–14, 198ff.

74. Some preferred to see the Sifre's notions of truth and error in the application of general rules to a specific case. While most situations normally require little more than the straightforward reference to legal principles, there are cases where such strict application would yield an "incorrect" solution, as the particular circumstances demand another ruling. Gilat (*Hishtalshelut ha-Halakhah*, pp. 186–90), cites several examples throughout Jewish history where the "law" applied directly, without appreciation of mitigating circumstances, was deemed by scholars to yield the "wrong" decision.

75. See BT Ḥagigah 18a (and parallels) on the indeterminacy of the prohibitions on the intermediate days of the festivals, which the Sages had to delineate based on the indeterminacy of several biblical passages.

76. BT Bava Meṣiʿa 59b. On some of the uses of this story throughout Jewish history, see Iṣḥak Englard, "Majority Decision vs. Individual Truth: The Interpretations of the 'Oven of Achnai' Aggadah," *Tradition* 15, nos. 1–2 (1975): 137–52.

77. Louis Finkelstein considers much of the Tannaitic material on the Sanhedrin erring to be quite early and assumes that the laws were composed when the Pharisees did not control the Sanhedrin, and the High Court at times ruled contrary to Rabbinic law ("Beraita ḥamurah ha-mefitsfah or ʿal toledot ha-Sanhedrin," *Proceedings of the American Academy for Jewish Research Jubilee Volume* [1978–79]: 97–109 [Heb. sec.]). On this reading, there indeed was no case of a *Pharisaic* court making a mistake.

78. Wade L. Robison deals with the logical dilemma created by the Supreme Court reversing itself on a particular issue. His analysis yields a distinction between two senses of authority: "reasoned" authority, where the Court gives the justification for its decision in the opinion written, and authoritative "determination," where the

Court is simply the final arbiter of the constitutionality of American law. Robison claims that the writing of opinions means that the Supreme Court wants to offer the legal community the reasoning behind its decision, and in this way the decision can be adopted and applied within the American legal universe of lower courts, states' policies, etc. His thoughtful analysis, however, cannot be applied to a court whose decisions are rendered *ipse dixit*. See his "The Functions and Limits of Legal Authority," in *Authority: A Philosophical Analysis*, ed. R. Baine Harris (University, Ala.: University of Alabama Press, 1976), pp. 112–31; see also Joseph Vining, *The Authoritative and the Authoritarian* (Chicago: University of Chicago Press, 1986), who makes a similar argument about the authoritativeness of the Supreme Court. The Talmud's fervent search for the underlying reasons of Mishnaic dicta may be an effort to incorporate both senses of authoritativeness into the system of Jewish law.

PREFACE TO PART II

1. *Paul and Palestinian Judaism* (Philadelphia: Fortress Press, 1977), pt. 1, esp. pp. 180–82 and 233–38.

2. For this reason, in the nineteenth century R. Zadok of Lublin saw the cessation of prophecy as the watershed event in the history of Halakhah. See Yaakov Elman, "R. Zadok Hakohen on the History of Halakha," *Tradition* 21, no. 4 (1985): 1–26; Yaakov Elman, "Reb Zadok Hakohen of Lublin on Prophecy in the Halakhic Process," in *Jewish Law Association Studies: The Touro Conference Volume*, ed. B. S. Jackson (Chico, Calif.: Scholars Press, 1985), pp. 1–16.

3. BT Bava Meṣiʿa 59ab; see ch. 4, n. 76.

4. See Maimonides' introduction to his *Sefer ha-Miṣvot* (Book of Commandments), *shoresh rishon* (first principle), where he establishes that all Rabbinic laws fall under the single biblical commandment in Deut. 17:11. But see Nachmanides' comments, *ad loc.*

CHAPTER 5

1. On the authority of professionals, in particular within Western society, see Thomas Haskell, ed., *The Authority of Experts: Studies in History and Theory* (Bloomington: Indiana University Press, 1984).

2. Richard T. de George employs the terms "knowledge" and "competence" to distinguish between an expert offering information and one who possesses a skill. See his *The Nature and Limits of Authority* (Lawrence: University Press of Kansas, 1985), pp. 42ff. Nonetheless, the epistemic grounding of authority operates identically in both cases.

3. Richard T. de George, "The Nature and Function of Epistemic Authority," in *Authority: A Philosophical Analysis*, ed. R. Baine Harris (University, Ala.: University of Alabama Press: 1976), p. 80. A more expanded version of this paper appears in Richard T. de George, *Nature and Limits of Authority*, ch. 3.

4. BT Horayot 14a relates a debate concerning the relative superiority of various types of intellectual strength: the well-read scholar (*sinai*) versus the keen dialectician (*ʿoqer harim*). The question was raised regarding who might be the better candidate for the head of the academy. The position of the Palestinian authorities was that the well-read scholar is preferable, since "all are dependent on the owner of the wheat," presumably for the normative traditions (see Rashi's commentary, *ad loc.*). Cf. PT Horayot 3:8 (48c).

5. Thus, E. E. Urbach writes: "The activities of the Hakham [Sage] and his leading influence within the community were not necessarily related to the assumption of public office. Whether or not occupying a position of power, the Hakham felt obliged to instruct the public and guide their actions. The force of his authority derived first and foremost from his knowledge of Torah." See his "The Talmudic Sage—Character and Authority," *Jewish Society through the Ages*, ed. H. H. Ben-Sasson and S. Ettinger (London: Vallentine & Mitchell, 1971), pp. 116–47 (quotation from p. 121).

6. Thus, Carl Friedrich understands authority as "capable of reasoned elaboration"; in other words, the subject can be brought to understand and accept that which the bearer of epistemic authority stated. Friedrich's approach first appeared in his article "Authority, Reason, and Discretion," *in Authority*, ed. Carl J. Friedrich, NOMOS, vol. 1 (Cambridge: Harvard University Press, 1958), and later in his *Tradition and Authority* (New York: Praeger, 1972), ch. 1. The critiques of this notion are summarized by Mark Tushnet in "Comment on Lukes," in *Authority Revisited*, NOMOS, vol. 29 (New York: New York University Press, Press, 1987), pp. 96–101. T. D. Weldon, in *The Vocabulary of Politics* (New York: Penguin Books, 1953), also sees authority *in general* as accepting what *x* says without pressing him for reasons because there are grounds for supposing that he could produce reasons if challenged (p. 50). This is very similar to Friedrich's notion of being *capable* of reasoned elaboration.

7. The halakhic principle mentioned in ch. 4, nn. 70–71 and accompanying text—that a Rabbinic ordinance (*gezeirah*) is valid only if it can be reasonably followed by most people—seems to undermine this idea of epistemic authority in legislation. If the Sages are deemed experts, then contemporary Jews should have deferred to Rabbinic counsel and obeyed, regardless of their personal preference. However, this principle reflects only on the proposed legislation's *legal validity*, not on how well it furthers religious goals. With respect to this type of Rabbinic legislation, where Jews are distanced from transgressing the Torah by observing an additional stricture, it may still be the case that the *gezeirah* is a positive force in the religious life of the people. But legislation also has a realistic component: its observance should be feasible, a factor that the Sages can only surmise before they legislate, but that ultimately experience alone can verify. If the legislation is not widely adopted, it is seen retroactively to be only invalid, not ill-conceived. The Sages' epistemic authority regarding the ability of this ordinance to ensure the proper observance of the covenant remains intact.

8. The Jewish Publication Society translation employs the phrase "the product of *hadar* trees" (italics in original), following Nachmanides' approach that '*etz hadar* was the name of a fruit tree at the time of the Bible.

9. This position echoes the view of Ronald Dworkin that all legal systems have principles or maxims which guide judges in their decisions in hard cases. See his *A Matter of Principle* (Cambridge: Harvard University Press, 1985). In this, he opposes the school of legal positivists, represented in America by H. L. A. Hart, which maintains that valid law is simply that which is produced according to the secondary rules of a system. See H. L. A Hart, *The Concept of Law* (New York: Oxford University Press, 1961). For an application of this debate to contemporary decision making in Jewish law (*pesaq*), see Gordon Tucker, "God, the Good, and Halakhah," *Judaism* 38, no. 3 1989): 365–76. He portrays Joel Roth's *The Halakhic Process: A Systemic Analysis* (New York: Jewish Theological Seminary of America, 1986) as an exemplar of the legal positivist position.

10. See, e.g., *Kessef Mishnah* to *Mishneh Torah*, Hilkhot Mamrim 2:1, s.v. *beit din*, who argues that it was merely the convention of Amoraim not to disagree with Tannaim.

11. For an excellent analysis of this belief, and whether it was universally held in the Middle Ages, see Menachem Kellner, *Maimonides on the "Decline of the Generations" and the Nature of Rabbinic Authority* (Albany: State University of New York Press, 1996).

12. Shabbat 112b; cf. PT Sheqalim 5:1 (48c–d), which switches the attribution. For similar expressions of this idea, see BT Yoma 9b ("The earlier ones had more holiness in their small fingers than the later ones have in our entire bodies") and BT 'Eruvin 53a ("if the intellectual powers of the earlier generations can be likened to the entrance of the Temple's antechamber [which was wide], and that of the later ones to the entrance to the *hekhal*, ours are as the eye of a fine needle."). All these statements are attributed to R. Yoḥanan and his school, a phenomenon I hope to treat in a forthcoming article.

13. See, e.g., Mishnah Sotah 9:15, which enumerates all the ideal human qualities which were embodied in certain individuals from the Tannaitic period, and which after their deaths were never again so perfectly found among people. In fact, intellect is not one of the qualities mentioned, although "the glory of learning" (*ziv ha-ḥokhmah*) is listed.

14. See Mishnah Avot 6:5–6. Of the forty-eight qualities deemed most fitting for the acquisition of Torah knowledge, only a handful are related to cognitive capacity.

15. Thus, Rav Ashi, responding to a query whether his own views should be considered like codified law (*devar mishnah*) as the earlier decisions were, answered by saying, "Are we mere wood gatherers [that our views should not be held in high regard]?" See BT Sanhedrin 33a.

16. "Jephtah in his generation is like Samuel in his generation" (BT Rosh Hashanah 25b).

17. R. Isaiah Di Trani (thirteenth century), *Teshuvot ha-Rid*, ed. A. J. Wertheimer (Jerusalem, Makhon ha-Talmud ha-Yisre'eli ha-shalem 1967), no. 62, pp. 302–3. See also Shnayer Z. Leiman, "Dwarfs on the Shoulders of Giants," *Tradition* 27, no. 3 (1993): 90–94.

18. *Encyclopedia Talmudit*, s.v. *halakhah*. See also the responsum of R. Moses Feinstein, *Iggerot Moshe*, vol. 2, *Yoreh De'ah* (New York: Rabbi M. Feinstein, 1959), I, no. 101:5 (p. 186), for a clear expression of the notion that a contemporary scholar must render decisions according to his own lights, even if those who preceded him did not so rule, provided he reaches his conclusion through the most rigorous analysis and convincing proofs. Nevertheless, he must be keenly aware of the periodizational limits he must observe, allowing himself to disagree only with Aḥaronim and, on only the rarest of occasions, with Rishonim. On periodization, see Shelomo Z. Havlin, "'Al 'ha-ḥatimah ha-sifrutit' ki yesod ha-ḥaluqah le-tequfot ba-Halakhah," in Meḥqarim ba-sifrut ha-Talmudit (Jerusalem: ha-Aqademyah ha-le'umit ha-Yisre'elit le-mada'im, 1983), pp. 148–192.

19. Indeed, Rabbinic tradition perceived intelligence, to some degree, to be at odds with competence in transmission, since a bright scholar might be tempted to modify an oral tradition to accord with his own opinion. See BT Sotah 22a. This is a case where de George's distinction between knowledge and competence (n. 2) is relevant.

20. The validity of this assumption depends on the nature of talmudic discourse,

whether it is the literary invention of redactors or an actual record, even in part, of the orally preserved discussions in the academies on the various points of law. But this topic is beyond the scope of the present study.

21. This approach is best embodied in the work of Meir Leibush Malbim, the nineteenth-century traditional scholar who devoted himself to "uncovering" the rules and principles that the talmudic Rabbis employed in their exegetical derivations. According to Malbim, the laws are not the fanciful creations of ancient scholars but the necessary implications of the plain, simple meaning of the verse: "For all the words of the Oral Law are necessary and contained in the simple meaning of the written text and in the depth of the language, for the exegesis alone is the simple, plain meaning, based upon true and clear linguistic rules. Every place where the Rabbis derived some law there is a linguistic peculiarity, and through the exegesis the Scripture returns to its force according to the rules of grammar" (*Ayelet ha-shaḥar* [Bucharest, 1860], p. iii, s.v. *va-yehi*). For a historical overview of the function of *peshat* (the literal meaning) and Malbim's particular role in that history, see David Halivni-Weiss, *Peshat and Derash: Plain and Applied Meaning in Rabbinic Exegesis* (New York: Oxford University Press, 1991).

22. Thus, R. S. Peters writes: "The ultimate appeal [in spheres of knowledge] is always to reason, not to an *auctor*. . . . The pronouncements of any person who is *an* authority can always be challenged by appeal to evidence or grounds. He can always be mistaken. . . . Such authorities must always, therefore, be treated as provisional. . . . Nothing is ever *made* right because they say so, as it is in the sphere of law" (*Ethics and Education* [Atlanta: Scott, Foresman & Co., 1967], p. 152).

23. This is the view of R. Nissim of Gerondi, in his *Derashot ha-Ran*, discourse no. 8.

24. This is the implication of Judah Halevi in his *Kuzari* (3:41), when he has the rabbi say: "it is unlikely that they should agree to something which contradicts the Torah, due to their large number, nor will error beset them because of their vast knowledge, as tradition has it that the Sanhedrin was commanded to be proficient in all areas of knowledge." This is only one aspect of Halevi's position, but its emphasis on the "unlikelihood of error" is relevant to our discussion of Rabbinic expertise.

25. Perhaps one of the best examples of viewing the Rabbis as authoritative epistemically is a High Holiday message, published by the Jewish Theological Seminary of America, that appeared in the *New York Times*, Sept. 14, 1983, p. B24 (all emphases original): "*How could Akiva have known more than Moses, who met God on the mountain? Could we know more about God than Akiva? . . .*

"*The growth of understanding is God's gift to us.* If study led merely to making ourselves into the image of our ancestors we would be denying the growing body of human knowledge, the expanding conscience of the sensitive, and our own contemporary insights. . . .

"*We can understand God's message better than Akiva.* We have history, archeology, literature, philosophy, psychology, as well as Talmud and the thinking of our great scholars—the accumulated wisdom of humanity. We have to use it all. We have constantly to rethink what is expected of us as people and specifically as Jews. . . ."

Both the inherent revisability of all knowledge and the (Enlightenment) assumption of human progress (particularly in the realm of knowledge) are detectable here. Notice, also, the portrayal of Jewish law as a typical epistemic enterprise, with the accumulation of more knowledge (e.g., history, archeology) increasing over time. The conclusion that the possession of greater knowledge allows, if not mandates, a rethinking of traditional practice is one that a conservative religious tradition would find offensive, if not downright heretical.

26. Some later Amoraim were even perturbed that their perceived intellectual superiority to earlier generations did not entitle them to miracles. See, e.g., BT Berakhot 20a: "Said R. Papa to Abaye: How is it that for the former generations miracles were performed and for us miracles are not performed? It cannot be because of their [superiority in] study, because in the years of Rav Judah the whole of their study was confined to Nezikin, and we study all six Orders . . . and yet when Rav Judah drew off one shoe, rain used to come, whereas we torment ourselves and cry loudly, and no notice is taken of us!" Parallels are found in BT Ta'anit 24b and Sanhedrin 106b.

27. E. D. Watt, *Authority* (London: Croom Helm, 1982), p. 42.

28. See n. 14.

29. BT 'Eruvin 46b. A somewhat abbreviated list is given here, with no explanation. Samuel ha-Naggid's *Mavo ha-Talmud* (published in the Vilna edition of the Babylonian Talmud after the Rosh's commentary to tractate Berakhot) presents a more comprehensive list of rules of decision making.

30. A collection of comments on the principles mentioned in *Mavo ha-Talmud* (see previous note), arranged by R. Yehuda Aryeh Leib, cites several medieval commentaries that saw the rules as based on one scholar's greater Torah knowledge, to the point that, e.g., the law follows Samuel in matters concerning money because he was accustomed to rule in such cases and displayed a proficiency, and the law follows Rav in matters of prohibitions because of his experience in that field. However, certain rules cannot be explained in this manner, e.g., in a dispute between Rav and Rabbi Yoḥanan, the law follows the latter, even though the former was greater (*Yad Malakhi*, no. 556), and in a dispute between two Amoraim, if the two are in a teacher-student relationship, the law follows the teacher, up to Rava (fourth-generation Amora), after whom the rule is to follow the more recent scholar. And, of course, all rules are suspended if the Talmud explicitly states that the law accords with one opinion, regardless of their relationship—the bottom-line rule in 'Eruvin 46b.

31. BT 'Eruvin 13b.

32. BT Yevamot 14a.

33. BT Shabbat 60b; Yoma 36b; Beṣah 11a; Yevamot 47a; Bekhorot 37a; Niddah 30b and 49a. In some of the cases, the reason is presumed more logical because it is backed by a verse (or some exegesis); in others, it is merely the logic inherent in the position.

34. The story of R. Eliezer and the oven of Akhnai is perhaps the most well known example of this. See BT Bava Meṣi'a 59a–b and Isḥak England, "Majority Decision vs. Individual Truth: The Interpretations of the 'Oven of Achnai' Aggadah," *Tradition* 15, nos. 1–2 (1975): 137–52.

CHAPTER 6

1. This has been the view of various commentaries to the Pentateuch throughout history. For a summary, see Russell Jay Hendel, "Peshat and Derash: A New Intuitive and Analytic Approach," *Tradition* 18, no. 4 (1980); 327–42. Portraying the Rabbinic

project as essentially unpacking the divine message embedded in the text allows both an original revelation more minimalist in scope (i.e. the interpretations themselves were not revealed literally), and a simultaneous claim that the Sages did not invent anything new. This position, however, rests on the basic hermeneutic question of whether interpretation is an exposition of the author's view implicit in the text or a result of the reader's interaction with the text. For a debate on this issue, see David Stern's review essay of Susan Handelman's *Slayers of Moses*, "Moses-cide: Midrash and Contemporary Literary Criticism," in *Prooftexts* 4 (1984): 193–213, and the continuation of their debate in the following issue, pp. 75–103.

2. For an analysis of the various ways this notion has found expression in Jewish thought, see Shalom Rosenberg, "Hitgalut matmedet: sheloshah kivunim" in *Hitgalut, emunah, tevunah*, ed. Moshe Halamish and Moshe Schwarcz (Ramat Gan: Bar Ilan University, 1976), pp. 131–43.

3. Maimonides thus argues that Rabbi Judah the Patriarch, in arranging the Mishnah, chose to attribute the various laws only to the scholars who transmitted them most recently, since the time of Simeon the Righteous. See his *Haqdamah le-perush ha-Mishnah* ed. Y. Kapah (Jerusalem: Mossad Harav Kook, 1963), p. 33.

4. David Weiss Halivni, in *Peshat and Derash: Plain and Applied Meaning in Rabbinic Exegesis* (New York: Oxford University Press, 1991), attempts to tackle this critical historical issue by investing Ezra with a restorative function. See his most recent *Revelation Restored: Divine Writ and Critical Responses* (Boulder, Colo.: Westview Press, 1997), which expands on this theme.

5. Maimonides spells out this unbroken chain by listing the names of the forty scholars from Moses to the last of the talmudic Sages who preserved the oral tradition and transmitted it intact. See his introduction to the *Mishneh Torah*.

6. See BT Hagigah 3a–b and parallels.

7. See sources cited in ch. 4, n. 72.

8. Of the sort in BT 'Eruvin 13b: "forty-eight reasons to render clean, and forty-eight reasons to render unclean."

9. PT Pe'ah 2:6 (17a); cf. BT Megillah 19b.

10. See Yohanan Silman, "Torat Yisrael le-or hidusheha—beirur fenominologi" *Proceedings of the American Academy for Jewish Research* 57 (1990–91): 49–67.

11. BT Yoma 80a, Sukkah 44a, Megillah 3a and 18a, Temurah 16a.

12. In the third view analyzed by Shalom Rosenberg ("Hitgalut matmedet"), found in the writings of the *Shelah* (R. Isaiah Horovitz—late seventeenth century), the original Sinaitic revelation is taken to be ongoing in that the Torah is continually "revealed" in the words of the Sages. In this sense, the Rabbis and the prophets are on the same spectrum.

13. BT Yoma 9b, Sotah 48b, Sanhedrin 11a, Tosefta Sotah 13:2. On this, see Ephraim E. Urbach, "Matai pasqah ha-nevu'ah" *Tarbiz* 17 (1945–46): 1–11; Ephraim E. Urbach, "Halakhah ve-nevu'ah" *Tarbiz* 18 (1946–47): 1–27. Yaakov Elman, in "R. Zadok Hakohen on the History of Halakha," *Tradition* 21, no. 4 (1985): 1–26, offers a fine analysis of a nineteenth-century figure who saw the cessation of prophecy as the watershed event in the history of Halakhah. See also his "Reb Zadok Hakohen of Lublin on Prophecy in the Halakhic Process," in *Jewish Law Association Studies: The Touro Conference Volume*, ed. B. S. Jackson (Chico, Calif.: Scholars Press, 1985), pp. 1–16.

14. See the appendix to Urbach's article "Halakhah ve-nevu'ah" on the subject of heavenly echoes.

15. Ephraim E. Urbach, HaZaL—Pirqei emunot ve-deʿot (Jerusalem: Magnes Press, 1969), pp. 502–4, 514ff. (The Sages—Their Concepts and Beliefs, trans. Israel Abrahams [Jerusalem: Magnes Press, 1979], pp. 564–67, 577ff.)

16. BT Bava Batra 12a. Note there that the Talmud rejects the notion that after the Temple's destruction, prophecy was transferred from the prophets to scholars, concluding instead that scholars always possessed prophecy, whereas it was withdrawn from the prophets after the Temple was destroyed.

17. Nachmanides' commentary to Deut. 17:11: "And all the more so should you think that [the Sages] are saying that right is right, for the spirit of God [rests] on those who minister in his sanctuary, and he will not abandon his righteous ones; they are forever protected from error and misunderstanding."

18. Judah Halevi, in his Kuzari (3:39), suggests that the presence of prophets among the early Sages allowed them to institute new practices as commandments: "And all this is when the sacrifices and the Sanhedrin and all the other offices which contributed to the wholeness of the national life were in existence, and doubtless the divine matter clung to them, either through prophecy or through heavenly assistance and illumination, as it was throughout the period of the Second Temple. . . . Thus we were obligated in the commandments of the megillah (Scroll of Esther) reading on Purim and [the lighting of candles] on Hanukkah . . . for if these laws were created after the dispersion, they would not be called commandments and we would not be obliged to make a blessing over them, but instead they would have been deemed an ordinance or custom." Admittedly, Halevi refers only to the actual Sanhedrin, but he sees the inclusion of prophets within that body as the license to add commandments. Yair Dreyfus ("Le-she'eilat maʿamado shel ha-rav be-qehilato" Kotleinu 12 [1987]: 403–12) claims that Nachmanides saw the Sanhedrin as a source of ongoing revelation only as long as it resided near the Temple, the source of Divine Presence in the world. On the sharp difference between these views and Maimonides' view of the role of prophecy in Halakhah, see Urbach, "Matai pasqah ha-nevu'ah?"

19. The notion that there is a divine intention that a certain behavior be followed can be understood in several ways: (1) God has certain purposes in mind, and one decision realizes those better than another. This is entirely possible, but it is not clear that each and every dispute in the Talmud can be understood in this way. (2) God has a "covert reasoning" pattern, and although a certain decision is correct, it may be arrived at incorrectly. If this is what we mean, then in effect, the reference to God is entirely otiose: the error is in the human reasoning, not in the divine logic. (3) God prefers one action over another, although he has no reason. In this case, the Rabbinic project is a mere guessing game, a very undesirable conclusion. I am grateful to David Shatz for this analysis.

20. Indeed, this impulse to ground a legal position in the divine in order to render it obligatory is quite pervasive. For an extensive collection of such references as "the divine spirit," "a heavenly echo," and "Elijah revealed" over centuries of halakhic discourse, see the introduction by Reuven Margaliyot to (twelfth century) Jacob ha-Levi's She'elot u-teshuvot min ha-shamayim (Jerusalem: Mossad Harav Kook, 1957).

21. The granting of divine status to human activity bore implications beyond the issue of the level of obligation. The literary product of an author (or authors) enjoying divine assistance could be seen as possessing linguistic precision like the Torah, therefore legitimizing careful reading and exegetical inference. The extent of this was hotly debated over the centuries, particularly with respect to reading the Mishnah, since its redactor/author, Rabbi Judah the Patriarch, was viewed to possess the

Divine Spirit. On two dominant schools in this debate, see David Henschke, "Abaye ve-Rava—shetei gishot le-mishnat ha-tana'im," *Tarbiz* 49, nos. 1–2 (1979–80): 187–93; Ya'akov Speigel, "Derekh qesarah bilshon tana'im ve-'al peshat ve-drash ba-Mishnah," *Asufot* 4 (1991): 9–26. For a further discussion of this phenomenon, see chapter 8.

22. Mishnah Pe'ah 1:1.

23. I would like to thank Professor Wayne Proudfoot for raising this possibility.

24. This is precisely the opinion of Rabbi Abraham ben David of Posquières, quoted by Rabbi Shelomo ben Avraham Adret, in his novellae on 'Eruvin 16a (*Hidushei ha-Rashba le-masekhet 'Eruvin*, ed. Yaakov David Ilan [Jerusalem: Mossad Harav Kook, 1989], p. 113). The Rabad states that according to one view in the Talmud, "all the decrees [*gezeirot*] which the scholars will decree in the future were revealed to Moses at Sinai. For this reason they are referred to as 'halakha.'" Rabbeinu Nissim Gerondi quotes this position in his novellae as well, *ad loc*. My thanks to Professor David Halivni for pointing out this source to me.

25. Reflection on the presence of debate among the Sages is found, to a degree, already within Rabbinic literature, e.g., BT 'Eruvin 13b and Hagigah 3b. See Michael Rosensweig's citations in his "*Eilu ve-Eilu Divrei Elohim Hayyim*: Halakhic Pluralism and Theories of Controversy," in *Rabbinic Authority and Personal Autonomy*, ed. Moshe Sokol (Northvale, N.J.: Jason Aronson, 1992), pp. 93–122. However, to counter the Karaite charge that debate invalidated Rabbinic law, the Geonim began to deal with the subject in earnest. See, e.g., Sa'adya Gaon's polemic against Qirqisani, quoted as an appendix to A. S. Halkin's "Mi-petihat rav Sa'adya Gaon le-perush ha-Torah," in *Jubilee Volume in Honor of Levi Ginzberg* (New York: American Academy for Jewish Research, 1946), pp. 152–53 (Heb. sec.). Shemuel ben Hofni, a tenth-century Babylonian Gaon, offered eight ways that disagreement entered an entirely transmitted tradition; see Shraga Abramson, "Min ha-pereq ha-hamishi shel 'Mavo ha-Talmud' le-Rav Shemuel ben Hofni," *Sinai* 88 (1981): 210–16. See also Moshe Zucker, "Le-ba'ayat ha-mahloqet ba-masoret," in *Jubilee Volume for Salo Baron* (Jerusalem: American Academy for Jewish Research, 1974), pp. 319–29 (Heb. sec.), on Ya'aqov bar Ephraim's position. Maimonides (twelfth century) refers to Sa'adya's position in his *Haqdamah le-perush ha-Mishnah* and rejects it, offering a different view based on a catalog of Rabbinic activity.

26. See BT Hagigah 3b.

27. BT 'Eruvin 13b. See Michael Rosensweig's comprehensive analysis in "*Eilu ve-Eilu Divrei Elohim Hayyim.*"

28. On the tension between halakhic decision making and halakhic truth, see ch. 4, n. 72, and Silman, "Torat Yisrael."

29. Mishnah 'Eduyot 1:5.

30. One could argue that the divine endorsement of an opinion was conditional on the Sages' final decision; see BT 'Eruvin 13b. The subsequent status of rejected opinions would nevertheless need to be examined—did God withdraw his approval?

31. See J. D. Bleich, *Providence in the Philosophy of Gersonides* (New York: Yeshiva University Press, Department of Special Publications, 1973); Charles Raffel, "Maimonides' Theory of Providence" (Ph.D. diss., Brandeis University, 1983); see also Julius Guttmann, *Philosophies of Judaism: The History of Jewish Philosophy from Biblical Times to Franz Rosenzweig*, trans. David W. Silverman (New York: Holt, Rinehart & Winston, 1964), index, s.v. "providence"; *Encyclopaedia Judaica*, s.v. "providence."

32. See Rosenberg, "Hitgalut matmedet."

33. For a fuller discussion of the reception of texts as evidence of prophetic endowment, see Speigel, "Derekh qesarah bilshon tana'im," n. 58 and accompanying text.

34. Nahum Arieli claims that Judah Halevi held the view that what gave a law its character as commandment was its ability to cross the boundary from the realm of human activity to that of the divine. In the event that a law was under dispute, then throughout the deliberations, the law remained in the human intellectual realm, but with the vote taken, the majority rule "detached the deliberation from the realm of human discussion and transferred it into the heavenly arena." See his "Tefisat ha-Halakhah esel rabi yehudah ha-levi," Da'at 1, no.1 (1978): 43–52.

35. Thus, BT 'Eruvin 13b required a heavenly voice to decide that the law follows the school of Hillel against the school of Shammai. Presumably, the views of the schools were independently formulated and were of human provenance; only later was the heavenly decision made (according to PT Berakhot 1:7 [3b], it was made after 70 C.E. at Yavneh). It should be noted that the language of the Talmud expressly legitimizes the opinions of *both* schools, although from a practical standpoint, only one view can be normative.

36. The notion of communal acceptance is associated most often with Rabbinic legislation, where in fact the validity of the enactment depends on the people accepting it; see, e.g., *Encyclopedia Talmudit*, s.v. *gezeirah*.

37. See nn. 12 and 34.

38. See above, text accompanying nn. 22–23.

39. See David Weiss Halivni, "The Reception Accorded to Rabbi Judah's Mishna," in *Jewish and Christian Self-Definition*, ed. E. P. Sanders, with A. I. Baumgarten and Alan Mendelson, (Philadelphia: Fortress Press, 1981), vol. 2, pp. 204–12.

40. See the sources cited by Spiegel ("Derekh qesarah bilshon tana'im"), which treat several medieval works such as Maimonides' *Mishneh Torah* and Joseph Karo's *Shulhan 'Arukh* as canonical and, in retrospect, divinely inspired. On the trust in divine assistance for even the average congregational rabbi, see Ya'akov Weiss, *Rabbanut u-qehillah: bi-mishnat maran ha-Hatam Sofer* (Jerusalem: Y. Weiss, 1987), p. 47; Jeffrey I. Roth, "Three Aspects of the Rabbinate: Compensation, Competition, and Tenure," *Drake Law Review* 45 (1997): n. 235.

41. For a good overview of Rabbinic and medieval efforts to explain this difficult concept, see the entry in the *Encyclopaedia Judaica*, s.v. "providence." See also, David Berger, "Miracles and the Natural Order in Nahmanides," in *Rabbi Moses Nahmanides (Ramban): Explorations in His Religious and Literary Virtuosity*, ed. Isadore Twersky (Cambridge: Harvard University Press, 1983), pp. 107–28.

42. See Joel Roth, *The Halakhic Process: A Systemic Analysis* (New York: Jewish Theological Seminary of America, 1986), esp. pp. 7–9. Gordon Tucker ("God, the Good, and Halakhah," *Judaism* 38, no. 3 [1989]: 365–76) critiques Roth's position on this *Grundnorm*. See also Bernard S. Jackson, "Secular Jurisprudence and the Philosophy of Jewish Law: A Commentary on Some Recent Literature," *Jewish Law Annual* 6 (1987): 3–5.

43. A Rabbinic midrash claims that God consented to three things that Moses did without prior divine approval: he added a third day to the two days of preparation for the Sinaitic theophany which God had instructed; he broke the first set of tablets; and he abstained from marital relations with his wife in order to be ready at all times for prophecy from God. See BT Shabbat 87a and parallels. *Avot de-Rabbi Nattan* 4: 3 replaces one of those three with a different one.

44. For reflections on this subject from a Christian perspective, see I. A. Dorner,

Divine Immutability: A Critical Reconsideration, trans. Robert R. Williams and Clyde Welch (Minneapolis: Fortress Press, 1994). Many of his insights apply equally to the Jewish case.

CHAPTER 7

1. *Haqdamah le-perush ha-Mishnah*, ed. Y. Kapah (Jerusalem: Mossad Harav Kook, 1963), pp. 11ff.

2. Introduction to the *Mishneh Torah* (Jerusalem: Mossad Harav Kook, 1956), pp. 12–13. In his *Haqdamah le-perush ha-Mishnah* Maimonides offers a similar rationale (the people's acceptance), without any explicit historical references. (While this reasoning appears in the original Arabic of the *Haqdamah* with respect to both the fourth and fifth categories [*gezeirot* and *taqqanot*, respectively], the printed Hebrew translation mentions it only in connection with the fourth. See Y. Kapah edition, p. 12.

3. On the subject of the contemporary authority of the talmudic Rabbis, see Lee I. Levine's *The Rabbinic Class of Roman Palestine in Late Antiquity* (New York: Jewish Theological Seminary of America, 1989), where he offers several tentative conclusions. See also Lee I. Levine, "The Sages and the Synagogue in Late Antiquity: The Evidence of the Galilee" and Shaye J. D. Cohen, "The Place of the Rabbi in Jewish Society of the Second Century," both in *The Galilee in Late Antiquity*, ed. Lee I. Levine (New York: Jewish Theological Seminary of America, 1992), pp. 201–20 and 157–74, respectively.

4. In other places, however (e.g., in *Sefer ha-misvot, shoresh* 1; *Mishneh Torah*, Hilkhot Mamrim 1:2), Maimonides seems to base both the hermeneutical and the legislative authorities of the Rabbis on the verse "and you shall not deviate from what they tell you" (Deut. 17:11). Nachmanides (*ad loc.*) objects, insisting that only their exegetical authority is based on the biblical verse. For a lengthy analysis of this debate from within the tradition, see R. Elhanan Wasserman, "Quntres divrei soferim," in *Qoves Shiurim* (Petah Tiqvah: Elazar Wasserman, 1960), pp. 87ff. This apparent discrepancy may be resolved by distinguishing between the legislative acts of the High Court in Jerusalem, whose authority derives from the Deuteronomic verse, and the legislation of the post-Sanhedrin Sages, represented in the Talmud, whose legislation depends on the people's consent. Of course, seeing the talmudic Sages as a continuation of the Sanhedrin would collapse the distinction and merge the two; on this approach, see, ch. 3.

5. Largely in *Pirqoi ben Baboi* and *Iggeret Rav Sherira Gaon*, ed. B. M. Lewin (Frankfurt: ha-hevrah le-sifrut ha-yahadut, 1921).

6. Modern scholars, too, have accepted this depiction (e.g., Salo W. Baron, *The Social and Religious History of the Jews* [New York: Columbia University Press, 1952], vol. 2, pp. 204–10). However, recent archeological excavations, particularly of synagogue building in Palestine in the fifth century, are leading to a reevaluation of the notion that Palestinian Jewry was in "decline."

7. See *Iggeret Rav Sherira Gaon*, pp. 97ff.

8. Maimonides, *Haqdamah*, pp. 11ff.

9. On this view, see Joseph B. Soloveitchik, "Shenei sugei masoret" in *Shi'urim le-zekher abba mari z"l* (Jerusalem: Defus Aqiva Yosef, 1983), vol. 1, pp. 220–39.

10. Certain medieval ordinances with respect to marriage law (e.g., the ban on polygamy attributed to R. Gershom of Mayence) may qualify. While originally they spread only among European Jewry, to the exclusion of Sephardic Jewry, the mi-

gration of the latter to Israel over the course of this century has effectively meant that the ban on polygamy is universal.

11. BT Bava Batra 60b, ʿAvodah Zarah 36a, Horayot 3b. Cf. Tosefta Sheviʿit 3:13, Sanhedrin 2:13 (regarding intercalating the year), PT Shabbat 1:5 (3d).

12. According to Maimonides, "greater in wisdom" refers to the respective heads of each court, and "greater in number" refers to the number of scholars who follow each court and adhere to its rulings. See *Mishneh Torah*, Hilkhot Mamrim 2:2. R. Abraham ben David of Posquières (*ad loc.*) disagrees, stating that "greater in number" refers to the ages of the heads of the court.

13. *Mishneh Torah*, Hilkhot Mamrim 2:2 (based on Mishnah ʿEduyot 1:5), 6.

14. *Mishneh Torah*, Hilkhot Mamrim 2:7. Presumed performance, even over a considerable amount of time, is insufficient to render a decree binding, although, apparently, it does necessitate another formal act of the court to rescind the decree. This latter requirement does not necessarily indicate that the original legislation had legal standing. It may simply be a technical requirement, stemming from a concern for the original court's prestige; see Ritba on BT ʿAvodah Zarah 35b, s.v. *mikhlal*, regarding the permitting of bread baked by non-Jews (which had originally been prohibited by Rabbinic decree).

15. Tosafot Gittin 36b, s.v. *ela*. See discussion at n. 17, below.

16. Medieval commentators dispute whether the actual spread of a practice among the people is a *sign* of the people's ability to observe it (R. E. Mizraḥi, cited in *Leḥem Mishneh* on *Mishneh Torah*, Hilkhot Mamrim 1:3) or whether spread and ability are two independent factors to be considered separately (*tosafot* to BT ʿAvodah Zarah 36a, s.v. *veha-tenan*; R. Nissim and Meiri, *ad loc.*).

17. *Mishneh Torah*, Hilkhot Mamrim 2:5. Maimonides' language suggests that this is a normative rule; that is, the court must avoid issuing decrees that cannot be observed. This may be the import of the treatment in BT ʿAvodah Zarah 36b, in contrast to the Palestinian Talmud's analysis (*ad loc.*), which formulates it as a *post factum* observation—any decree issued by the court that the majority of people cannot observe is retroactively invalid. See *Siyunei MaHaRaN*, *ad loc.*

18. See Menachem Elon, *Ha-mishpat ha-ʿivri* (Jerusalem: Magnes Press, 1973), chs. 21–22; Israel Schepansky, "Minhag ve-Halakhah," *Or ha-Mizraḥ* 40, no. 91–2 (1991–92): 147–66.

19. See n. 16.

20. See Elon, *Ha-mishpat ha-ʿivri*, pp. 738–39.

21. Similarly, Nachmanides writes: "Custom is considered to be binding only when the townspeople or the communal leaders *specifically and formally adopt it*, but any custom not so adopted cannot override an existing legal rule unless the rule is doubtful" (novellae to BT Bava Batra 144b, s.v. *ha de-amrinan*, emphasis added). Without a formal act, a custom has little coercive force.

22. It seems that over the last few decades, vast improvements in travel, communications, and information technologies and their widespread availability have rendered geographical proximity much less determinative of halakhic allegiance. Moreover, in the face of increased mobility, the aim of personal consistency in one's practice has at once stretched the jurisdiction of some rabbis (who are consulted long-distance by many former students) and reduced (or even challenged) the jurisdiction of other, more local authority figures.

23. On this issue, see the important contribution made by Gerald L. Blidstein, "Le-hilkhot Ṣibbur shel yimei ha-beinayim: meqorot u-musagim" *Dine Yisrael* 9 (1978–80): 127–64. While his focus is on the medieval justifications of the commu-

nity's right to force an individual to follow certain rules and enactments of medieval communities, much of what he writes is applicable to our subject and indeed significantly informs our analysis. An English translation appeared as "Individual and Community in the Middle Ages: Halakhic Theory," in *Kinship and Consent: The Jewish Political Tradition and Its Contemporary Uses*, ed. Daniel J. Elazar (Washington: University Press of America, 1983), pp. 215–56. Menachem Elon's contribution in that same volume, "Power and Authority: Halachic Stance of the Traditional Community and Its Contemporary Implications," is also relevant to our discussion.

24. *She'elot u-teshuvot ha-Rashba*, (Bene Beraq: [n.p.], 1957–1965), vol. 3, no. 411; see also. no. 417.

25. *She'elot u-teshuvot ha-Rashba* vol. 1, no. 729.

26. E.g., the requirement that the people offer sacrificial atonement for the inadvertent errors of the High Court (Sifra on Lev. 4:13; Mishnah Horayot 1:5). Maimonides, in his commentary to Mishnah Horayot 1:6, states rather clearly, "the High Court . . . is the community of Israel as a whole." H. Cohen, in "Hefqer bet din hefqer" (in *Proceedings of the Fourth World Congress for Jewish Studies* (Jerusalem: World Union of Jewish Studies, 1967), vol. 1, pp. 185–88), claims that the right of the court to confiscate property, a right ubiquitous in talmudic law, is fundamentally based on the notion that a person's property really belongs to the collective, which is allowed to authorize specified organs to expropriate it.

27. Blidstein, "Individual and Community," p. 226.

28. There were, in fact, many cases where the leaders were not particularly knowledgeable; see Avraham Grossman, "Yahasam shel hakhmei Ashkenaz ha-rishonim el shilton ha-qahal," *Shenaton ha-Mishpat ha-'ivri* 2 (1975): 176–93; Avraham Grossman, *Hakhmei Ashkenaz ha-rishonim*, 2d ed. (Jerusalem: Magnes Press, 1988); Ephraim Kanarfogel, "Unanimity, Majority, and Communal Government in Ashkenaz during the High Middle Ages: A Reassessment," *Proceedings of the American Academy for Jewish Research* 58 (1992): 79–106.

29. R. Elijah Mizrahi (16th c. Turkey) offers the most explicit formulation: "This was the power which was granted to the High Court in Jerusalem and to every court in every generation . . . because the high court in every generation is recognized by all members of that generation. . . . and it is for this reason that they were granted the power to issue decrees and ordinances. And although it was not explicitly chosen and no specific conditions were agreed upon, it is a fact that everyone recognized it . . . and although someone may object, it is as if he explicitly gave his consent and then changed his mind" (*Responsa of R. Elijah Mizrahi* [Jerusalem: Darom, 1938], no. 57, p. 186). See Blidstein's discussion, "Individual and Community," p. 226. Note that Mizrahi employs the same rationale to ground the authority of the High Court in Jerusalem and the local court of his contemporary generation. It seems that as a whole, the scholars of this period in Turkey display a remarkable appreciation of democratic and consensual notions of government. In this connection, see 'Azriel Shohat, "'Inyanei misim ve-hanhagot sibbur be-qehillot yavvan be-me'ah ha-16," *Sefunot* 11 (1971–78): 311–39.

30. Alan John Simmons, *Moral Principles and Political Obligation* (Princeton: Princeton University Press, 1979).

31. Blidstein, "Individual and Community," pp. 227–33, treats this issue at length, in the more specific context of how medieval bans, which often accompanied enactments, could be imposed on the members of the community who opposed the legislation or subsequently violated it.

32. Nachmanides, *Mishpat ha-herem*, printed after his novellae to tractate Shevuʿot; see also Blidstein, "Individual and Community," pp. 229ff.

33. This view explains the various exceptions scholars have imposed on this rule. For instance, Maimonides (*Mishneh Torah*, Hilkhot Mamrim 2:1–2) limits this requirement to the realm of innovation and legislation, since in his view, exegetical authority is shared equally by all scholars employing the authorized hermeneutical techniques. Given the inherent equivalence of any two courts in this realm, a court is allowed to disagree with its predecessor if it reaches a different exegetical conclusion. Similarly, R. Abraham ben David of Posquières (*ad loc.*) claims that if in formulating the legislation, the earlier court actually mentioned the circumstances which motivated it to act, then the later court need not be greater than its predecessor in order to overturn it if those circumstances have since changed. The assumption of this view is that in light of the altered situation, the earlier court would not have insisted on the legislation, so there would really be no "vote." The later court is simply formally rescinding a prior legislative act, such as a law with a temporal limitation built in, which must also be formally rescinded; see Rashi, BT Beṣah 5a, s.v. *mena amina*; R. Menachem ha-meiri, *ad loc.*, *s.v. yesh.*

34. It is interesting that the sociological analysis of authority has often focussed on the communal structure which serves as the context for legitimate authority. Authority involves the individual allowing the group to define reality, making the exercise of authority in essence the activation of the members' role commitment. See Herbert C. Kelman and V. Lee Hamilton, *Crimes of Obedience: Toward a Social Psychology of Authority and Responsibility* (New Haven: Yale University Press, 1989). A philosopher who has taken a similar path in understanding authority is Yves R. Simon, *A General Theory of Authority* (Notre Dame: University of Notre Dame Press, 1962).

35. Some historians concur; see Salo Baron, *A Religious and Social History of the Jews* (New York: Columbia University Press, 1958), vol. 3, pp. 113–14. The centrality of the Jewish institutions in these regions for world Jewry, which Baron also assumes, is much harder to document.

36. The force of local custom is already treated in Mishnah Pesaḥim, ch. 5; the talmudic discussion expands it even further.

37. See Moshe Gil, "The Babylonian Yeshivot and the Maghrib," *Proceedings of the American Academy for Jewish Research* 57 (1990–91): 69–120.

38. One area of tension that could arise in this instance concerns laws that depend on Babylonia's unique geography. For example, the Sages instituted that during the rainy season the prayer for rain (*sheʾelah*) should be inserted in the ninth benediction of the silent meditation. In Palestine, the formula was included starting on the seventh of Marḥeshvan, corresponding to the rainy season there. In Babylonia, however, the climate is such that rain is not necessary until the sixtieth day of *tequfat Tishrei*, which falls in late November. The question arose in the Middle Ages whether this second date applied to all regions outside Palestine, given Babylonia's primacy in the Jewish Diaspora, or whether the date should accord with the rainy season of one's locale. In his *Perush ha-Mishnah* (*Taʿanit* 1:2), Maimonides states that the date is determined by the needs of one's own locale, a view echoed by R. Asher in his responsa (no. 4, sec. 10). The latter states unequivocally that we need follow Babylonian law only in regard to ritual matters (*ʾissur ve-heter*). When it comes to such basic needs as rainfall, there is no compelling logic to follow Babylonia.

39. There is evidence that Jews lived in Germany in the fourth century, but there is no proof of ongoing settlement. See *Encyclopaedia Judaica*, s.v. "Germany."

40. See discussion, at nn. 24–25.

41. See Yisrael M. Ta-Shma, *Minhag Ashkenaz ha-qadmon: heker ve-ʿiyyun* (Jerusalem: Magnes Press, 1992). See also Haym Soloveitchik, "Religious Law and Change: The Medieval Ashkenazic Example," *AJS Review* 12 (1987): 205–21.

42. See nn. 24–28 and accompanying text.

43. *Studies in Judaism*, ser. 1 (Philadelphia: Jewish Publication Society, 1896), pp. xvii–xix.

44. "The Talmud as Final Authority," *Judaism* 29 (1980): p. 47.

45. "A Dynamic Halakhah: Principles and Procedures of Jewish Law," *Judaism* 28 (summer 1979): 263–82.

46. See Carl J. Friedrich, *Tradition and Authority* (New York: Praeger, 1972).

47. This is not to preclude other ways of understanding communal practice. Abraham I. Kook, for instance, took the practices that the Jewish people historically accepted to be manifestations of the inexorable unfolding of the divine will. See Shalom Rosenberg, "Hitgalut matmedet: sheloshah kivunim," in *Hitqalut, emunah, tevunah*, ed. Moshe Ḥalamish and Moshe Schwarcz (Ramat Gan: Bar Ilan University, 1976), pp. 131–43.

48. Certainly, on this understanding of Maimonides, other practices could achieve similar widespread acceptance and be similarly authoritative. Indeed, one may speculate that given modern communications and transportation technology, the social forces naturally inclining communities to unify their practices will be accelerated, and more observances will likely become "accepted."

CHAPTER 8

1. E.g., Introduction to the *Mishneh Torah*, and *Mishneh Torah*, Hilkhot Mamrim 1:2.

2. Introduction to the *Mishneh Torah*, (Jerusalem: Mossad Harav Kook, 1956) pp. 13.

3. Shamma Friedman discusses how the redaction of the Babylonian Talmud in the post-Amoraic period did not "finalize" the text in the way we normally think about books in the post-printing press era. Schools of scribes continued to revise and amend the text, some aggressively, some less so, far into the High Middle Ages, some five or six centuries after what is considered the "closing" of the Talmud. See his "Le-hithavut shinuyei ha-girsaʾot be-talmud ha-bavli," *Sidra* 7 (1991): 67–102. Further discussion of this topic is contained in the introduction to his *Talmud ʿArukh: Pereq ha-sokher et ha-ʾumanin* (Yerushalayim, New York: Beit ha-midrash le-rabbanim ba-Amerika, 1996).

4. For an excellent summary of the various views on the Babylonian Talmud's redaction, see David Goodblatt, "The Babylonian Talmud," in *Aufsteig und Niedergang der römischen Welt II*, (Berlin and New York: de Gruyter, 1972), vol. 19.2, pp. 304–18.

5. See ch. 7, nn. 11–21, and accompanying text. According to the view that the force of custom is an *assumed* legislative act which has since been forgotten, if we know for certain that there was no legislative act, then compliance cannot be coerced. Accepted practice alone is insufficient to demand compliance.

6. PT Megillah 4:1 (74d); BT Gittin 60b and Temurah 14b. This subject is the focus of much current work; see the sources cited in ch. 3, n. 51, esp. Jaffee's articles.

7. E.g., PT Kilʾayim 1:1 (27a); Saul Lieberman, "The Publication of the Mish-

nah," in his *Hellenism in Jewish Palestine* (New York: Jewish Theological Seminary of America, 1950), p. 87.

8. See Martin S. Jaffee, "Writing and Rabbinic Oral Tradition: On Mishnaic Narrative, Lists, and Mnemonies," *Journal of Jewish Thought and Philosophy* 4, no. 1 (1994): 145.

9. The term is Lieberman's ("Publication of the Mishnah") (BT Megillah 28b characterizes such a person as "a basket full of books"). According to Lieberman, in each academy the master carefully formulated and revised the oral traditions after extensive deliberation with his disciples and then a tanna memorized them. This process was known as "entering the academy" (e.g., PT 'Eruvin 1:6 [19b]). The tanna was consulted in future discussions of the material (e.g., BT Bava Meṣi'a 34a; Niddah 43b). The tanna was chosen primarily for his ability to remember large amounts of material; while some tannaim were outstanding scholars, being a scholar was generally deemed a liability, since a scholar might be inclined to revise the "text" based on his own understanding. Thus, BT Sotah 22a compares "[t]he magian [who] mumbles and understands not what he says" with "the tanna [who] recites and understands not what he says."

10. Jaffee, "Writing."

11. Lieberman, "Publication of the Mishnah," p. 98.

12. Mishnah Avot 1:11.

13. BT Sanhedrin 5b.

14. BT Sanhedrin 6a. See also PT Ketubbot 9:2 (33a), where the status of the Mishnah (with respect to voiding a judge's decision) is debated between R. Yoḥanan and R. Shimon ben Laqish.

15. BT Sanhedrin 33a.

16. According to the most reliable manuscripts, Rav Hamnuna said this to Rav Ashi. This reading is corroborated by several medieval citations of this passage.

17. There is debate over the identity of Ravina, whether it is Ravina I, a contemporary of Rav Ashi, who died in 424 C.E., or whether it is Ravina II, who died in 499 C.E. See Goodblatt, "Babylonian Talmud," pp. 309–311.

18. *Iggeret Rav Sherira Gaon*, ed. B. M. Lewin (Frankfrut: ha-Ḥevra le-sifrut ha-Yahadut, 1921), pp. 69ff. For a detailed review of the traditional theory and the views of modern scholarship, see Goodblatt, "Babylonian Talmud," pp. 304–18.

19. See *Oṣar ha-geonim le-masekhet Sanhedrin*, ed. Ḥayyim Ṣvi Taubes (Jerusalem: Mossad Harav Kook, 1967), pp. 34, 311.

20. *Mishneh Torah*, Hilkhot Sanhedrin 6:1.

21. Rabad's view, as well as R. Zaraḥiah's, are cited in R. Asher ben Yeḥiel's *Hilkhot ha-Rosh*, tractate Sanhedrin, ch. 4, no. 6. The translation I used here is that of Isadore Twersky, *Rabad of Posquières: A Twelfth-Century Talmudist* (Cambridge: Harvard University Press, 1962), p. 220.

22. See Twersky, *Rabad*, pp. 218–22.

23. See n. 21.

24. *Hoshen Mishpat* 25:1 emphasis added.

25. *Hoshen Mishpat* 25:1.

26. *Terumat ha-deshen*, no. 241 of the *pesakim u-ketavim*.

27. In fact, unlike R. Isserles, two medieval rabbis link the presence of texts, not with the stability and permanence of the practice, but with the permissibility of disagreement. Thus, writing on the permission of students to disagree with their teachers, R. Aharon ha-Kohen of Lunel (thirteenth century) quotes R. Samuel of Evreaux and his brother (twelfth century) that "since the day our fathers were exiled

and our Temple was destroyed, and the lands were mixed up and the knowledge and the hearts decreased, we should no longer say 'the fear of your teacher is as the fear of heaven' and all the laws regarding how the student is to conduct himself with respect to his teacher no longer apply, for the Talmud and the commentaries, the novellae and the compositions, they are what instruct the people, and all is according to one's insight" (*Orḥot Ḥayyim, Hilkhot Talmud Torah*, no. 25). Similarly, Samuel ben Moses de Medina, writing in sixteenth-century Salonica, views much of Jewish law of his time to be a function not of the rabbi's personal decisions but of what is included in the books. Although some minor details are still debated, "nevertheless, one cannot deny that the majority of the laws are simple [i.e., are agreed upon]." See *Responsa Maharshdam* (Salonica, 1862), *Ḥoshen Mishpat*, no. 1. For an analysis of these positions, and a suggestion that their views may reflect the increased availability of printed texts, see Avi Sagi, "Models of Authority and the Duty of Obedience," *AJS Review* 20, no. 1 (1995): 9–11.

28. *Mishnah ʿim Perush Rabbeinu Moshe ben Maimon*, ed. Y. Kapaḥ (Jerusalem, Mossad Harav Kook, 1963), vol. 1, p. 34, emphasis added.

29. Sherira Gaon similarly underscores the literary distinction of the Mishnah, but only to explain why everyone accepted it as halakhically authoritative: "When everyone saw the elegance of the Mishnah's form, its truthfulness and verbal precision, they all abandoned their previous legal formulations. These laws [of the Mishnah] spread among the entire Jewish people and became our halakha. . . . All Jews accepted it faithfully when they saw it, and no one challenges it" (*Iggeret Rav Sherira Gaon*, ed. B. M. Lewin [Frankfurt: ha-Hevrah le-sifrut ha-yahadut, 1921], p. 30). The point I am underscoring is that academic attention is what determines, if not constitutive of, authoritativeness. For a fascinating analysis of the Mishnah's project from the perspective of sociology of knowledge, see Michael Robert Greenwald, *The New Testament Canon and the Mishnah: Consolidation of Knowledge in the Second Century C.E.* (Ph.D. diss., Boston University, 1989).

30. Shelomoh Z. Havlin connects periodization with the production of certain texts that prompt a change in academic curricula. See his "ʿAl 'ha-ḥatimah ha-sifrutit' ki-yesod ha-ḥaluqah le-tequfot ba-Halakhah," in *Meḥqarim be-sifrut ha-Talmudit* (Jerusalem: ha-Aqademyah ha-le'umit ha-yisre'elit le-madaʿim, 1983), pp. 148–92. At the end of the article, Havlin suggests that Maimonides' motivation for composing the *Mishneh Torah* was the self-conscious effort to close the Geonic period.

31. Thus, R. Isaiah ben Mali di-Trani writes: "The Mishnah is to the Amoraim as the Torah [was] to the Tannaim" (*Pisqei ha-Rid* on tractate Shabbat, ed. A. Y. Wertheimer [Jerusalem: Mossad Harav Kook, 1964], p. 229). Of course, this process was gradual; see David Henschke's article on the varied Amoraic approaches to reading the Mishnah ("Abaye ve-Rava—shetei gishot le-mishnat ha-tanna'im," *Tarbiz* 49, nos. 1–2 [1979–80]:187–93). It is likely that this way of reading was applied even between the generations of the Tannaim or Amoraim themselves; see n. 33.

32. But cf. Sherira Gaon's portrayal in his epistle (see n. 28), where the Mishnah's primacy is understood in normative terms. I am deliberately not taking up the issue of R. Judah's intention in composing the Mishnah, which I believe is ultimately irretrievable. As Maimonides intuited, the only evidence available to us regards how those who followed the Mishnah perceived it. Furthermore, it is highly unlikely that the Amoraim's attitude toward the Mishnah remained constant for the entire period and that its "authority" was perceived in the same way throughout the three centuries of the Amoraim. This may go far in responding to David Weiss Halivni's argument in "The Reception Accorded to Rabbi Judah's Mishna," in *Jewish and Christian Self-*

Definition, ed. E. P. Sanders, with A. I. Baumgarten and Alan Mendelson (Philadelphia: Fortress Press, 1981), vol. 2, pp. 204–12. His conclusion that "one may genuinely doubt whether R. Judah's Mishnah ever exercised binding authority" (p. 205) stems from the assumption that the Mishnah was intended as a law code, by which its success or failure must ultimately be assessed. However, how the receiving community perceived the Mishnah, or how that perception may have changed over time, is another way of examining the question of a text's "success." For an interesting analysis that highlights two schools among the Amoraim as to how the Mishnah should be read, see Henschke, "Abaye ve-Rava."

33. Thus, Barukh M. Bokser can inspect the statements of Samuel under the title *Samuel's Commentary on the Mishnah: Its Nature, Forms, and Content* (Leiden: E. J. Brill, 1975). See also Havlin, "Ha-ḥatimah ha-sifrutit," pp. 190ff. Havlin argues that this understanding of the Mishnah's authority may have led Maimonides to hope that his own code, the *Mishneh Torah*, could achieve a similar level of authoritativeness if it was accepted by Jewish communities everywhere.

34. Thus the later Amoraim might interpret their Amoraic predecessors using the same hermeneutical strategies as those applied to the Mishnah; see Yaʿakov Spiegel, "Derekh qeṣarah bilshon tanaʿim ve-ʿal peshat ve-drash ba-Mishnah," *Asufot* 4 (1991): esp. nn. 39–40 at p. 21; Richard L. Kalmin, "Changing Amoraic Attitudes toward the Authority and Statements of Rav and Shmuel: A Study of the Talmud as a Historical Source," *Hebrew Union College Annual* 63 (1992): 83–106 (reprinted in Richard L. Kalmin, *Sages, Stories, Authors, and Editors in Rabbinic Babylonia* [Atlanta: Scholars Press, 1994], pp. 43–59.

35. On the Babylonian Talmud's redaction, see Goodblatt, "Babylonian Talmud," pp. 304–18. While we know very little for certain about this process, it seems intuitive that the anonymous sections representing the redactors' voice(s) constitute an alternative to being either in the text or entirely outside it. The total absence of any attribution in these layers seems to confirm the sense that the redactors did not consider themselves to be merely a continuation of the Amoraic period. Nevertheless, the fact that they chose to create a text, or significantly edit the existing one, implies that they did not view themselves to be utterly secondary to the Amoraim, as the Amoraim were to the Mishnah. I hope to address this in a future article.

36. Havlin, "Ha-ḥatimah ha-sifrutit," focuses on periodization as manifest in the production of certain texts which prompt a change in academic curricula. Moshe Halbertal similarly reflects on this tension between "textual closure" and "hermeneutic openness." His book, *People of the Book: Canon, Meaning, and Authority* (Cambridge: Harvard University Press, 1997), came out as this work was in press, but many of the issues he addresses are connected with the contents of chapters 8 and 9 of this book.

37. "Law as Interpretation," *Critical Inquiry* 9, no. 1 (1982): 179–200. The essay was reprinted in *Texas Law Review* 60, no. 3 1982): 373–94, and in *The Politics of Interpretation*, ed. W. J. T. Mitchell (Chicago: University of Chicago Press, 1983), pp. 249–70.

38. I heard that a similar observation was made by Saul Berman with respect to the current denominational division of Jewry: Reform Judaism considers itself guided by the Bible, Conservative Judaism by the Talmud, and Orthodox Judaism by the medieval commentators (the Rishonim). Each branch ultimately justifies its positions on various matters by appeal to the text they deem authoritative. I will address this more directly in the next chapter.

39. Salo Baron charts the path which led to the Babylonian Talmud's hegemony in his *A Social and Religious History of the Jews* (New York: Columbia University

Press, 1952), vol. 3, pp. 75–119. Lawrence H. Schiffman summarizes this issue in the epilogue to his *From Text to Tradition: A History of Second Temple and Rabbinic Judaism* (Hoboken, N.J.: Ktav Publishing House, 1991), pp. 266–69.

40. One Babylonian Amora explicitly assumes a deferential posture with respect to his Palestinian colleagues, perhaps owing to their being ordained. See BT Pesahim 51a, where Abaye is recorded as saying that "we [in Babylonia] submit to them [in Palestine]," and Rashi's commentary, *ad loc.*

41. See Isaac al-Fasi's comments at the end of BT 'Eruvin, (p. 35b in the Vilna edition). But cf. Israel Isar Isserlein, *Tosefet Yerushalayim* (Vilna, 1871), pp. 1–2, where he shows that although Palestinian legal traditions were most certainly known in Babylonian academies, the talmudic corpus known as the Jerusalem Talmud did not circulate in Babylonia. See also Goodblatt, "Babylonian Talmud," pp. 285–88; Martin Jaffee, "The Babylonian Appropriation of the Talmud Yerushalmi: Redactional Studies in the Horayot Tractates," in *New Perspectives on Ancient Judaism*, vol. 4, *The Literature of Early Rabbinic Judaism: Issues in Talmudic Redaction and Interpretation*, Studies in Judaism, ed. Alan J. Avery-Peck (Lanham, N.Y.: University Press of America, 1989).

42. Shelomo Dov Goitein, "Political Conflict and the Use of Power in the World of the Geniza," in *Kinship and Consent: The Jewish Political Tradition and Its Contemporary Uses*, ed. Daniel J. Elazar (Washington: University Press of America, 1983), p. 178. Moshe Gil, "The Babylonian Yeshivot and the Maghrib," *Proceedings of the American Academy for Jewish Research* 57 (1990–91): 69–120, citing many responsa and other documents, proves that the North African and even Spanish communities of the tenth and eleventh centuries continued to consult the Babylonian Geonim and even to support the Babylonian academies financially through the early eleventh century. Thus, the decisions affecting Jewish religious and communal life were those based on the Babylonian Talmud and its traditions.

43. Gerson Cohen discusses this move by Andalusian Jewry to assert its independence legally and religiously in "The Story of the Four Captives," *Proceedings of the American Academy for Jewish Research* 29 (1960–61): 55–131 (reprinted in Gerson D. Cohen, *Studies in the Variety of Rabbinic Cultures* [Philadelphia: Jewish Publication Society, 1991], pp. 157–208).

44. That the Franco-German academies also focused on the Babylonian Talmud is not as easily explained by this account. The origins of these Jewish communities and, more important, their contact with the eastern centers remain unclear, preventing us from reaching any definitive conclusions with respect to this issue.

45. Almost all the essays in *An Introduction to the History and Sources of Jewish Law*, ed. N. S. Hecht, B. S. Jackson, S. M. Passamaneck, D. Piattelli, and A. M. Rabello (Oxford: Clarendon Press, 1996), note those developments of Jewish law which are at one level best understood in the context of the scholars' legal and political environment.

46. Louis Jacobs, "The Talmud as Final Authority," *Judaism* 29 (1980):47.

47. Louis Newman advances such an argument in his analysis of contemporary Jewish ethics, claiming that what makes such discourse "Jewish" is its reliance on and appeal to Jewish sources, even if the conclusions may differ. See his "Woodchoppers and Respirators: Interpretation in Contemporary Jewish Ethics," *Modern Judaism* 10, no. 1 (1990): 17–42.

48. See Jacob Neusner's introduction to the third edition of his *A History of the Jews in Babylonia* (Chico, Calif.: Scholars Press, 1984); Jacob Neusner, *Reading and Believing: Ancient Judaism and Contemporary Gullibility* (Atlanta: Scholars Press,

1986); David Kraemer, "On the Reliability of Attributions in the Bavli," *Hebrew Union College Annual* 60 (1989): 175–90.

49. Avraham Yeshayahu Karelitz, *Qoves Iggerot* (Collected Letters of the Hazon Ish) (Jerusalem: S. Grainiman, 1954 or 1955), vol. 1, no. 32.

50. Moshe Bleich exhaustively reviews the various contemporary positions on the status of manuscripts, concluding that while they are generally welcomed for their academic value, little weight is given to them in reaching normative conclusions. See his "The Role of Manuscripts in Halakhic Decision-Making: Hazon Ish, his Precursors and Contemporaries," *Tradition* 27, no. 2 (1993): 22–55.

51. "Contemporary Methods of the Study of Talmud," *Journal of Jewish Studies* 30, no. 2 (1979), 197 (emphasis in original).

52. *Peshat and Derash: Plain and Applied Meaning in Rabbinic Exegesis* (New York: Oxford University Press, 1991), ch. 5.

53. David Halivni notes that it was precisely the implications of historical study for Halakhah which brought him into tension with his colleagues at the Jewish Theological Seminary of America. See his autobiography, *The Book and the Sword: A Life of Learning in the Shadow of Destruction* (New York: Farrar, Straus & Giroux, 1996), p. 149.

54. On the Babylonian Talmud as an anthology, see most recently, Eliezer Segal, "Anthological Dimensions in the Babylonian Talmud," *Prooftexts* 17, no. 1 (1997): 33–61.

55. The juridical rule in Mishnah 'Eduyot 1:5, which preserves potential legitimacy for (rejected) minority opinions, may reflect this phenomenon. David Shatz pointed out to me that contemporary rabbis occasionally base the main thrust of their sermons on Rabbinic opinions that are rejected in the Talmud, another manifestation of this attitude.

56. See ch. 1, n. 12. For another implication regarding the authority of Rabbinic statements, see Mitchell First, *Jewish History in Conflict: A Study of the Major Discrepancy between Rabbinic and Conventional Chronology* (Northvale, N.J.: Jason Aronson, 1997). In that work, he classifies various medieval and modern authors regarding their views as to how to reconcile the dating of events in Jewish history, which, if Rabbinic statements are followed, leads to different dates than the standard dating of historians.

57. Thus, when the historical-critical method successfully shows the false attributions in several locations, the integrity of the entire text is challenged. See previous section.

58. It is interesting to note that some of the clearest expressions regarding treating parts of the Babylonian Talmud differently come from the Geonic period, during which the Talmud was evolving into the foundational document of halakhic discussion. External factors, however, may have influenced this phenomenon as well: the Karaite challenge may have inclined medieval scholars to treat the talmudic Rabbis as perfect in every respect. Similarly, the nineteenth-century liberal attack on talmudic Judaism, which stemmed from a growing knowledge and appreciation of the historical development of Judaism, prompted contemporary scholars to declare all Jewish law divine in origin. See Jacob Katz, "Orthodoxy in Historical Perspective," *Studies in Contemporary Jewry* 2 (1986): 3–17; Michael K. Silber, "The Emergence of Ultra-Orthodoxy: The Invention of a Tradition," in *The Uses of Tradition: Jewish Continuity in the Modern Era*, ed. Jack Wertheimer (New York: Jewish Theological Seminary of America, 1994), pp. 23–84; Moshe S. Samet, "The Beginning of Orthodoxy," *Modern Judaism* 8 (1988): 249–69.

CHAPTER 9

1. See Clifford Geertz, *The Interpretation of Cultures* (New York: Basic Books, 1973), esp. the essay "Thick Description: Toward an Interpretive Theory of Culture" (pp. 3–30).

2. Ludwig Wittgenstein, *Zettel*, ed. G. E. M. Anscombe and G. H. von Wright, trans. by G. E. M. Anscombe (Oxford: Blackwell, 1967), para. 314.

3. *Is There a Text in This Class? The Authority of Interpretive Communities* (Cambridge: Harvard University Press, 1980), pp. 303–71.

4. *Is There a Text in This Class*, pp. 303–4 (emphasis in original). While Fish does not explicitly cite Wittgenstein, the latter is palpably present. Norman Malcolm, in his article on Wittgenstein for *The Encyclopedia of Philosophy* (N.Y.: Macmillan Publishing Co. & The Free Press, 1967), summarizes Wittgenstein's view of rule-following in a way Fish would endorse: "It is this agreement that determines whether a particular action is in accordance with a rule. Rather than to say that we agree 'because' we follow rules, it is more perceptive to say that our agreement fixes the meaning of the rules, defines their content. In a sense the content of the rule grows as our practice grows. Instead of thinking of mankind as coerced by the rules of mathematics and logic, we should consider that human practice establishes what the rules are" (*The Encyclopedia of Philosophy*, 8:338). We tend to think of collective conformity as a "rule out there" which many people are following, leading them all to be acting in similar fashion. But Wittgenstein thought that such a picture was false and misleading.

5. *Is There a Text in This Class?*, p. 365 (emphasis in original).

6. In his groundbreaking *The Structure of Scientific Revolutions* (Chicago: University of Chicago Press, 1962), Thomas Kuhn made similar observations about science, referring to the revision of regnant theories as "paradigm shifts."

7. *Is There a Text in This Class?* p. 365.

8. *Ibid.*, p. 371. See his discussion in the chapter "What Makes an Interpretation Acceptable?" pp. 338–55, esp. pp. 350–55.

9. *Critical Inquiry* 9, no. 1 (1982): 179–216; reprinted in *Texas Law Review* 60 (1982): 373–94, 551–67. Most of the papers in the symposium were reprinted in a separate volume, *The Politics of Interpretation*, ed. W. J. T. Mitchell (Chicago: University of Chicago Press, 1983). All page references will be to this last volume.

10. Dworkin's "My Reply to Stanley Fish (and Walter Benn Michaels): Please Don't Talk about Objectivity Any More" appeared as a rejoinder to Fish in the volume edited by Mitchell, *Politics of Interpretation*, pp. 287–313. Fish's final serve in this volley, "Wrong Again," was offered in *Texas Law Review* 62 (1983): 299–316, where apparently Dworkin's "My Reply . . ." was to have appeared, but in the end, did not. Dworkin's *A Matter of Principle* (Cambridge: Harvard University Press, 1985) includes a chapter entitled "On Interpretation and Objectivity" (pp. 167–77), which summarizes his responses to Fish.

11. "My Reply," p. 304.

12. "Working on the Chain Gang," pp. 273ff.; "Wrong Again," pp. 304–6.

13. In "Law as Interpretation," at n. 4, Dworkin notes that "[e]ven the first novelist has the responsibility of interpreting to the extent any writer must, which includes not only interpreting as he writes but interpreting the genre in which he sets out to write." But Fish takes this admission (with which he agrees) as inconsistent with Dworkin's subsequent claim that the earlier novelists are less constrained than the later ones; see Fish (citations of previous note).

14. "Wrong Again," p. 306.

15. "Wrong Again," pp. 307–8, emphasis added.

16. *Is There a Text in This Class?*, p. 350.

17. *Is There a Text in This Class?*, p. 350.

18. Similarly, Fish writes: "in fact I am asserting an epistemological necessity . . . you [cannot] think of a meaningful utterance (even a one-word imperative like 'go!') without *already* having imagined the circumstances (including an intending agent) in which it has the meaning you're thinking of" ("Wrong Again," p. 313; emphasis in original).

19. Wade Robison offers other examples in "The Function and Limits of Legal Authority," in *Authority: A Philosophical Analysis*, ed. R. Baine Harris (Birmingham: University of Alabama Press, 1976).

20. See his letter to James Madison of September 6, 1789, in *The Writings of Thomas Jefferson*, ed. Paul Leicester Ford (New York: G. P. Putnam's Sons, 1892–99), vol. 5, p. 121.

21. This may explain the ongoing, and as yet unresolved, debate between originalism and constructionism in constitutional interpretation. Constructionists, like Karl N. Llewellyn, point to the society in which the Constitution was written and claim the impossibility of a group of agrarian aristocrats anticipating laws for an industrialized, urban nation of immigrants which they could never have imagined. The originalists, on the other hand, are expressing the feeling so many in the field of legal interpretation "feel" when they interpret a statute: that they are getting at the very essence of the law.

22. Of course, if constitution writing became a regular feature of a particular society (say, every thirty years), such that the entire form of life worked with that inevitability, it would not appear so odd. Legislation, contracts, and institutional long-term planning would all function according to where in the thirty-year cycle they stood. It is likely that the rights language of American jurisprudence, which posits certain inalienable and natural rights, contributes to most Americans' sense of the Constitution's indispensability and even immutability.

23. On Wittgenstein, see Paul Johnston, *Wittgenstein and Moral Philosophy* (London: Routledge, 1989), pp. 211–19.

24. See, e.g., Yaakov Elman, " 'It Is No Empty Thing': Nahmanides and the Search for Omnisignificance," *Torah U-madda Journal* 4 (1993): 1–83.

25. See ch. 8, n. 30.

26. See ch. 6, n. 21.

27. See the examples cited by Yaʿakov Speigel, "Derekh qeṣarah bilshon tanaʿim veʿal peshat ve-drash ba-Mishnah," *Asufot* 4 (1991): 9–26, and the views of other commentators who observed this intraperiod commentarial stance.

28. Mishnah Avot 5:22.

29. We may speculate whether this attitude was informed by Plato's conception of the Idea of the Good as producing all possible kinds of entities in actuality as an expression of its goodness. See Arthur O. Lovejoy, *The Great Chain of Being* (Cambridge: Harvard University Press, 1936), pp. 49ff.

30. Rabbinic literature ocassionally expresses this notion with the phrase *maqom hinihu li avotai le-hitgader bah* (my ancestors left room for me to excel in it) (*Mekhilta de-R. Shimon bar Yoḥai* 18:17, BT Hullin 7a).

31. For a fine catalog of the relevant Talmudic references, see Menachem Kellner, *Maimonides on the "Decline of the Generations" and the Nature of Rabbinic Authority* (Albany: State University of New York Press, 1996), pp. 8–12.

32. BT Shabbat 112b, PT Sheqalim 5:1, and parallels.

33. BT ʿEruvin 53a. R. Yohanan stands out as the Amora to whom such statements are attributed. Thus, in BT Yoma 9b, he is credited with the proverbial comparison "the fingernail of the earlier ones is better than the belly of the later ones." According to BT Hullin 137b, R. Yohanan felt this inferiority at a very early age, when as a young student in the academy, he witnessed the discussions between R. Judah the Patriarch and Rav and understood nothing of their debate.

34. Indeed, as Maimonides himself states in his introduction to the *Mishneh Torah*, the Mishnah served as his model when organizing his code.

35. *Sheʾelot u-teshuvot ha-Rashba* (Bene Braq: [n.p.] 1957–1965), vol. 4, no. 118.

36. *Migdal ʿoz*, on *Mishneh Torah*, Hilkhot Shehitah 6:8. See also his commentary to *Mishneh Torah*, Hilkhot Maʾakhalot Asurot 12:9.

37. *Milhemet miṣvah*, appended to *Qeshet u-magen*, a work composed by his father, R. Simeon ben Ṣemah Duran (Levarno, 1763).

38. *Maʿaseh Ereg* to Mikvaʾot 4:1. See also R. Meir Simhah Cohen of Dvinsk, *Meshekh Hokhmah*, Ex. 1:1.

39. See Speigel, "Derekh qeṣarah," pp. 25–26.

40. Isadore Twersky, "Shulhan ʿAruk: Enduring Code of Jewish Law," *Judaism* 16 (1967): 141–58, (reprinted in *The Jewish Expression*, ed. Judah Goldin [New Haven: Yale University Press, 1976], and in *Studies in Jewish Law and Philosophy* [New York: Ktav Publishing House, 1982]).

41. R. Zadok of Lublin, *Mahashavot haruṣ* (1912), p. 3c; cf. p. 57c, where he cites the author of the *Tumim*, who made a similar point.

42. See Kellner, *Maimonides*, pp. 7–26.

43. This observation dovetails with Menachem Kellner's claim in *Maimonides* that the view of the "decline of generations" was not universally held in either the period of the Talmud or the period of the early medieval scholars. Nevertheless, the longer the interpretive enterprise continued, and as more and more scholars found themselves writing expositions of their predecessors' commentaries, this theory became more pervasive and normative in traditional culture. By the late Middle Ages, it is hard to find a scholar who does not endorse the general view of *hidardarut ha-dorot*.

44. On this, see David Weiss Halivni, *Peshat and Derash: Plain and Applied Meaning in Rabbinic Exegesis* (New York: Oxford University Press, 1991), esp. chs. 1–3.

45. This is particularly the strategy of the nineteenth-century Meir Leibush Malbim, who devoted himself to "uncovering" the rules and principles that the Rabbis used in their exegetical derivations, thus revealing the simple, plain meaning (*peshat*) of the verse. See ch. 5, n. 21.

46. See Michael K. Silber, "The Emergence of Ultra-Orthodoxy: The Invention of a Tradition," in *The Uses of Tradition: Jewish Continuity in the Modern Era*, ed. Jack Wertheimer (New York: Jewish Theological Seminary of America, 1994), pp. 47ff.

47. See Silber, "Ultra-Orthodoxy," for a full catalog of the ideological and theological tactics taken by Hungarian Ultra-Orthodox Jews in the 1860s and 1870s.

48. Thus, Louis E. Newman, who writes on various philosophical issues in Jewish ethics, observes: "With rare exceptions . . . these authors [on Jewish ethics] have not attempted to defend their particular way of selecting and reading the sources against other possible or actual readings. Much less have they found it necessary to articulate a view of the coherence of the Jewish tradition as a whole in terms of which they

have chosen to make interpretive decisions in one way as against another. As a result, it could be said that much contemporary Jewish discourse resembles a conversation in which the participants are talking past, rather than to, one another" ("Woodchoppers and Respirators: The Problem of Interpretation in Contemporary Jewish Ethics," *Modern Judaism* 10, no. 2 [1990]: 41). The article was reprinted in *Contemporary Jewish Ethics and Morality: A Reader*, ed. Elliot N. Dorff and Louis E. Newman (Oxford: Oxford University Press, 1995).

49. See the Jewish Theological Seminary New Year message (quoted in ch. 5, n. 26) as an excellent example of this.

50. See Joseph B. Soloveitchik, *U-viqashtem mi-sham* (Jerusalem: World Zionist Organization, 1979), pp. 230–32.

51. While there is widespread consensus within Orthodox circles that boys should study the Talmud, there is significant variety regarding the appropriate curriculum for women. This, in itself, is connected to the particular community's form of life and its attitude about the role of women in contemporary society. The respective defenses offered—all, by the way, citing Rabbinic and traditional sources—are further evidence of the rootedness of authority in specific social and historical settings. For the various positions, see Elyakim Ellenson, *Bein ha-'isha le-yoṣrah* (Jerusalem: World Zionist Organization, Department of Torah Education and Culture in the Diaspora, 1974), pp. 158–62.

52. Mishnah Avot 5:21, the opinion of R. Judah ben Teima. The present rationale given for deviating from the Rabbinic prescription is that Mishnah study is, according to the Mishnah, to commence at age ten, and Gemara is indispensable in understanding Mishnah.

53. This seems to be the point of Wittgenstein's critique of "private language." See Saul A. Kripke, *Wittgenstein on Rules and Private Language: An Elementary Exposition* (Cambridge: Harvard University Press, 1982).

54. Indeed, the desire of many Ultra-Orthodox Jews to live together in homogeneous communities comes not from an ethnic snobbery but from a belief that their values are durable only as long as communal practices, both inside and outside the home, reflect those values. The relatively recent efforts to homogenize religious practice among the Orthodox, despite the acknowledgment of legitimate historical diversity of praxis, underscore the challenges of living in an open secular society: if meaning is public, no effort can be spared at ensuring that the public nature of observances reinforces the same message. See Haym Soloveitchik, "Rupture and Reconstruction: The Transformation of Contemporary Orthodoxy," *Tradition* 28, no. 4 (1994): 64–130. See also Isaac Chavel's response, "On Haym Soloveitchik's 'Rupture and Reconstruction . . . ,' a response," *Torah U-Madda Journal* 7 (1997): 122–136, and Haym Soloveitchik's "Clarification and Reply," pp. 137–49. It is interesting that this homogenization has accelerated in recent years, owing perhaps to the ease of travel, rapid communications, and the widespread dissemination of printed material with respect to practical application of the law. If a hundred years ago, the eastern European *shtetl* (village) conducted its collective life in a uniform way, then the "global village" has created similar expectations of Ultra-Orthodox Jews worldwide. Uniformity of practice renders Rabbinic authority, or any of the other values of Ultra-Orthodoxy, "obvious" wherever one may turn.

55. This might be one way of reading the High Holiday message of the Jewish Theological Seminary cited earlier (ch. 5, n. 26).

Bibliography

Abramson, Shraga. "Ketivat ha-Mishnah ('al da'at geonim ve-rishonim)." In *Tarbut ve-ḥevrah be-toledot Yisrael biy-mei ha-beinayim*, ed. Menahem Ben-Sasson, Robert Bonfil, and Joseph R. Hacker. Jerusalem: Merkaz Zalman Shazar, 1989.

Adret, Solomon ben Abraham. *She'elot u-teshuvot ha-Rashba*. Bene Braq, [n.p.] 1982.

Albeck, Ḥanokh. "Semikhah u-minui u-veit din." *Zion* 8 (1948): 85–93.

Alon, Gedaliah. *Toledot ha-Yehudim be-Erets-Yisrael bi-tequfat ha-Mishnah veha-Talmud*. 2 vols. Jerusalem: Magnes Press, 1954–55. Subsequently published as *The Jews in Their Land in the Talmudic Age (70–640 C.E.)*, 2 vols., trans. and ed. Gershon Levi (Jerusalem: Magnes Press, 1980–84).

———. *Meḥqarim be-toledot Yisrael*. 2 vol. Tel Aviv: ha-Kibutz ha-meuḥad, 1957–58.

Arendt, Hannah. "What Is Authority?" In *Between Past and Future: Six Exercises in Political Thought*. New York: Viking Press, 1968.

Assaf, Simcha. "Qoveṣ shel iggerot R. Shmuel ben Ali u-venei doro." *Tarbiz* 1 (1929–30): 102–30; 2 (1930–31): 43–84; 3 (1931–32): 15–80; 4 (1932–33): 146–47.

"Authority." *Aristotelian Society Supplement* 32 (1958), pp. 207–60.

Bacher, W. "Zur Geschichte der Ordination." *Monatsschrift für Geschichte und Wissenschaft des Judentums* 38 (1894):122–27.

Baer, Yitzhak. *A History of the Jews in Christian Spain*. Vol. 2. Philadelphia: Jewish Publication Society of America, 1966.

Baron, Salo W. *A Social and Religious History of the Jews*. 18 vols. New York: Columbia University Press, 1952–.

Berger, David. "Miracles and the Natural Order in Nahmanides." In *Rabbi Moses Nahmanides (Ramban): Explorations in His Religious and Literary Virtuosity*, ed. Isadore Twersky. Cambridge: Harvard University Press, 1983.

Berger, Michael Seth. "The Authority of the Babylonian Talmud: Analysis of Its Justifications and a Proposal for a Contemporary Model." Ph.D diss., Columbia University, 1992.

Bleich, J. D. *Providence in the Philosophy of Gersonides*. New York: Yeshiva University Press, Department of Special Publications, 1973.

Bleich, Moshe. "The Role of Manuscripts in Halakhic Decision-Making: Hazon Ish, His Precursors and Contemporaries." *Tradition* 27, no. 2 (1993): 22–55.

Blidstein, Gerald. "Le-hilkhot ṣibbur shel yimei ha-beinayim: meqorot u-musagim." *Dine Yisrael* 9 (1978–80): 127–64. Subsequently published as "Individual and Community in the Middle Ages: Halakhic Theory," trans. Sarah Lederhendler, in *Kinship and Consent: The Jewish Political Tradition and Its Contemporary Uses*, ed. Daniel J. Elazar, pp. 215–56. (Washington: University Press of America, 1983).

———. "Masoret ve-samkhut mosdit le-raʿayon torah she-be-ʿal peh bi-mishnat ha-rambam." *Daʿat* 16 (1986): 11–27.

———. "Maimonidean Structures of Institutional Authority: Sefer Hamitzvot Aseh 172–177." *Dine Yisrael* 17 (1993–94): 103–26.

Boyarin, Daniel. *Intertextuality and the Reading of Midrash*. Bloomington: Indiana University Press, 1990.

Brody, Baruch A., ed. *Readings in the Philosophy of Religion: An Analytic Approach.* Englewood Cliffs, N.J.: Prentice-Hall, 1974.

Cassuto, Umberto. *Torat ha-teʿudot vi-siduram shel sifrei ha-Torah*. Jerusalem: Magnes Press, 1941. [Subsequently published as *The Documentary Hypothesis and the Composition of the Pentateuch: Eight Lectures*. Jerusalem. Magnes Press, 1961.]

Cohen, Gerson. "The Story of the Four Captives." *Proceedings of the American Academy for Jewish Research* 29 (1960–61): 55–131. Reprinted in Gerson D. Cohen, *Studies in the Variety of Rabbinic Cultures* (Philadelphia: Jewish Publication Society, 1991).

Cohen, Mark R. *Under Crescent and Cross: Jews in the Medieval Period*. Princeton, N.J.: Princeton University Press, 1994.

Cohen, Shaye J. D. "The Significance of Yavneh: Pharisees, Rabbis, and the End of Jewish Sectarianism." *Hebrew Union College Annual* 55 (1984): 27–53.

———. "The Place of the Rabbi in Jewish Society of the Second Century." In *The Galilee in Late Antiquity*, ed. Lee I. Levine. New York: Jewish Theological Seminary of America; distributed by Harvard University Press, 1992.

Cohen, Stuart A. *The Three Crowns: Structures of Communal Politics in Early Rabbinic Jewry*. Cambridge: Cambridge University Press, 1990.

de George, Richard T. *The Nature and Limits of Authority*. Lawrence: University Press of Kansas, 1985.

Dorner, I. A. *Divine Immutability: A Critical Reconsideration*. Trans. Robert R. Williams and Clyde Welch, with intro. by Robert R. Williams. Minneapolis: Fortress Press, 1994.

Dreyfus, Yair. "Le-sheʾeilat maʿamado shel ha-rav be-qehilato." *Kotleinu* 12 (1987): 403–12.

Ducasse, C. J. *A Critical Examination of the Belief in Life after Death*. Springfield, Ill.: Charles C. Thomas, 1961.

Dworkin, Ronald. "Law as Interpretation." *Critical Inquiry* 9, no. 1 (1982): 179–200. Reprinted in *Texas Law Review* 60, no. 3 (1982): 373–94, and in W. J. T. Mitchell, ed., *The Politics of Interpretation*, (Chicago: University of Chicago Press, 1983).

———. "My Response to Stanley Fish (and Walter Benn Michaels): Please Don't Talk about Objectivity Any More." In *The Politics of Interpretation*, ed. W. J. T. Mitchell. Chicago: University of Chicago Press, 1983.

———. *A Matter of Principle*. Cambridge: Harvard University Press, 1985.

Efron, Joshua. *Studies on the Hasmonean Period*. Studies in Judaism in Late Antiquity, vol. 39. Leiden: E. J. Brill, 1987.

Eider, Shimon D. *Halachos of Shabbos*. 4 vols. Lakewood, N.J.: S. D. Eider, 1970.

Elman, Yaakov. "R. Zadok Hakohen on the History of Halakha." *Tradition* 21, no. 4 (1985): 1–26.

———. "Reb Zadok Hakohen of Lublin on Prophecy in the Halakhic Process." In *Jewish Law Association Studies: The Touro Conference Volume*, ed. B. S. Jackson. Chico, Calif.: Scholars Press, 1985.

———. " 'It Is No Empty Thing': Nahmanides and the Search for Omnisignificance." *Torah U-madda Journal* 4 (1993):1–83.

Englard, Ishak. "Majority Decision vs. Individual Truth: The Interpretations of the 'Oven of Achnai' Aggadah." *Tradition* 15, nos. 1–2 (1975): 137–52.

Feinstein, Moses. *Iggerot Moshe*. Vol. 2, *Yoreh De'ah*. New York: Rabbi M. Feinstein, 1959.

Finkelstein, Louis. "Beraita hamurah ha-mefisah or 'al toledot ha-Sanhedrin." *Proceedings of the American Academy for Jewish Research Jubilee Volume* (1978–79): pp. 97–109 (Heb. sec.).

First, Mitchell. *Jewish History in Conflict: A Study of the Major Discrepancy between Rabbinic and Conventional Chronology*. Northvale, N.J.: Jason Aronson, 1997.

Fish, Stanley. *Is There a Text in This Class? The Authority of Interpretive Communities*. Cambridge: Harvard University Press, 1980.

———. "Working on the Chain Gang." *Critical Inquiry* 9, no.1 (1982): 201–16. Reprinted in *Texas Law Review* 60 (1982): 551–67.

———. "Wrong Again." *Texas Law Review* 62 (1983): 299–316.

Flew, Antony, and Alasdair, MacIntyre, eds. *New Essays in Philosophical Theology*. New York: Macmillan, 1955.

Friedman, Shamma. "Le-hithavut shinuyei ha-girsa'ot be-Talmud ha-bavli." *Sidra* 7 (1991): 67–102.

Friedrich, Carl J. "Authority, Reason, and Discretion." In *Authority*, ed. Carl J. Friedrich. NOMOS, vol. 1. Cambridge: Harvard University Press, 1958.

———. *Tradition and Authority*. New York: Praeger, 1972.

Gafni, Isaiah M. *Yehudei Bavel be-tequfat ha-Talmud*. Jerusalem: Zalman Shazar Center for Jewish History, 1990.

Geach, P. "Praying for Things to Happen." In *God and His Soul*. London: Routledge & Kegan Paul, 1969.

Geertz, Clifford. "Thick Description: Toward an Interpretive Theory of Culture." In *The Interpretation of Cultures*. New York: Basic Books, 1973.

Gerondi, Nissim ben Reuben. *Derashot Ha-Ran*, ed. A. L. Feldman. Jerusalem: Makhon Shalem, 1973.

Ghiselin, Michael T. *Intellectual Compromise: The Bottom Line*. New York: Paragon House, 1989.

Gil, Moshe. "The Babylonian Yeshivot and the Maghrib." *Proceedings of the American Academy for Jewish Research* (1990–91): 69–120.

Gilat, Yitzhak D. "Bet Din matnin la'aqor davar min ha-Torah." *Bar Ilan* 7–8 (1970): 117–32.

———. *Peraqim bi-hishtalshelut ha-Halakhah*. Ramat Gan: Bar Ilan University Press, 1992.

Goitein, Shelomo Dov. "Political Conflict and the Use of Power in the World of the Geniza." In *Kinship and Consent: The Jewish Political Tradition and Its*

Contemporary Uses, ed. Daniel J. Elazar. Washington: University Press of America, 1983.

Goldberg, Chaim B. *Mourning in Halakhah*. New York: Mesorah Publications, 1991.

Goodblatt, David. "The Babylonian Talmud." In *Aufstieg und Niedergang der römischen Welt II*, vol. 19.2, Berlin and New York: de Gruyter, 1972. Reprinted in Jacob Neusner, ed., *The Study of Ancient Judaism* (Hoboken, N.J.: Ktav Publishing House, 1981).

Gordis, Robert. "A Dynamic Halakhah: Principles and Procedures of Jewish Law." *Judaism* 28 (1979): 263–82.

Greenwald, Michael Robert. "The New Testament Canon and the Mishnah: Consolidation of Knowledge in the Second Century C.E.". Ph.D. diss., Boston University, 1989.

Greenwald, Y. Y. *Kol Bo 'al Aveilut*. New York: Feldheim Publishers, 1973.

Grossman, Avraham. *Hakhmei Ashkenaz ha-rishonim*. 2d ed. Jerusalem: Magnes Press, 1988.

———. "Yahasam shel hakhmei Ashkenaz ha-rishonim el shilton ha-qahal." *Shenaton ha-Mishpat ha-ivri* 2 (1975): 176–93.

Guttmann, Julius. *Philosophies of Judaism: The History of Jewish Philosophy from Biblical Times to Franz Rosenzweig*. Intro. by R. J. Zwi Werblowsky, trans. David W. Silverman. New York: Holt, Rinehart & Winston, 1964.

Halbertal, Moshe. *People of the Book: Canon, Meaning and Authority*. Cambridge: Harvard University Press, 1997.

Halevy, Isaac. *Dorot ha-rishonim*. 6 vols. Reprint, Jerusalem: n.p., 1967.

Halivni, David Weiss. "Safqei de-gavrei." *Proceedings of the American Academy for Jewish Research Jubilee Volume* (1978–79): 67–84 (Heb. sec.).

———. "Contemporary Methods of the Study of Talmud." *Journal of Jewish Studies* 30, no. 2 (1979): 192–201.

———. "The Reception Accorded to Rabbi Judah's Mishna." In *Jewish and Christian Self-Definition*, vol. 2, Ed. E. P. Sanders, with A. I. Baumgarten and Alan Mendelson. Philadelphia: Fortress Press, 1981.

———. *Midrash, Mishnah, and Gemara: The Jewish Predilection for Justified Law*. Cambridge: Harvard University Press, 1986.

———. *Peshat and Derash: Plain and Applied Meaning in Rabbinic Exegesis*. New York: Oxford University Press, 1991.

———. *The Book and the Sword: A Life of Learning in the Shadow of Destruction*. New York: Farrar, Straus & Giroux, 1996.

———. *Revelation Restored: Divine Writ and Critical Responses*. Boulder, Colo.: Westview Press, 1997.

Harris, R. Baine, ed. *Authority: A Philosophical Analysis*. University, Ala.: University of Alabama Press, 1976.

Hart, H. L. A. *The Concept of Law*. New York: Oxford University Press, 1961.

Haskell, Thomas, ed. *The Authority of Experts: Studies in History and Theory*. Bloomington: Indiana University Press, 1984.

Havlin, Shelomo Z. "'Al 'ha-hatimah ha-sifrutit' ki-yesod ha-haluqah le-tequfot ha-Halakhah." In *Mehqarim be-sifrut ha-Talmudit*, pp. 148–92. Jerusalem, ha-Aqademyah ha-le'umit ha-Yisre'elit le-mada'im 1983.

Heinemann, Isaak. *Darkei ha-Aggadah*. Jerusalem: Hebrew University, 1970.

Heinemann, Joseph. *Aggadot ve-toledoteihen*. Jerusalem: Keter, 1974.

Hendel, Russell Jay. "Peshat and Derash: A New Intuitive and Analytic Approach." *Tradition* 18, no. 4 (1980): 327–42.

Henschke, David. "Abaye ve-Rava—shetei gishot le-mishnat ha-tana'im." *Tarbiz* 49, nos. 1–2 (1979–80): 187–93.

Hirsch. E. D. *Dictionary of Cultural Literacy.* Boston: Houghton Mifflin, 1988.

Hoenig, Sidney B. *The Great Sanhedrin.* New York: Dropsie College, 1953.

Isserlein, Israel Isar. *Tosefet Yerushalayim.* Vilna, 1871.

Jackson, Bernard S. "Secular Jurisprudence and the Philosophy of Jewish Law: A Commentary on Some Recent Literature." *Jewish Law Annual* 6 (1987): 3–44.

Jacobs, Louis. "The Talmud as Final Authority." *Judaism* 29 (1980): 45–48.

Jaffee, Martin. "Oral Torah in Theory and Practice: Aspects of Mishnah-Exegesis in the Palestinian Talmud." *Religion* 15 (1985): 387–410.

———. "The Babylonian Appropriation of the Talmud Yerushalmi: Redactional Studies in the Horayot Tractates." In *New Perspectives on Ancient Judaism,* vol. 4, *The Literature of Early Rabbinic Judaism: Issues in Talmudic Redaction and Interpretation,* ed. Alan J. Avery-Peck. Studies in Judaism. Lanham, Md.: University Press of America, 1989.

———. "How Much 'Orality' in Oral Torah? New Perspectives on the Composition and Transmission of Early Rabbinic Tradition." *Shofar* 10 (1992): 53–72.

———. "Writing and Rabbinic Oral Tradition: On Mishnaic Narrative, Lists, and Mnemonics," *Journal of Jewish Thought and Philosophy* 4, no. 1 (1994): 123–46.

Johnston, Paul. *Wittgenstein and Moral Philosophy.* London: Routledge, 1989.

Kalmin, Richard. *The Redaction of the Babylonian Talmud: Amoraic or Saboraic?* Cincinnati: Hebrew Union College Press, 1989.

———. "Changing Amoraic Attitudes toward the Authority and Statements of Rav and Shmuel: A Study of the Talmud as a Historical Source." *Hebrew Union College Annual* 63 (1992): 83–106. Reprinted in Richard L. Kalmin, *Sages, Stories, Authors, and Editors in Rabbinic Babylonia* (Atlanta: Scholars Press, 1994).

Kanarfogel, Ephraim. "Rabbinic Attitudes toward Nonobservance in the Medieval Period." In *Jewish Tradition and the Nontraditional Jew,* ed. Jacob J. Schacter. Northvale, N.J.: Jason Aronson, 1992.

———. "Unanimity, Majority, and Communal Government in Ashkenaz during the High Middle Ages: A Reassessment." *Proceedings of the American Academy for Jewish Research* 58 (1992): 79–106.

Karelitz, Avraham Yeshayahu. *Qoveṣ Iggerot.* Jerusalem: S. Grainiman, 1954 or 1955.

Katz, Jacob. *Emancipation and Assimilation: Studies in Modern Jewish History.* Farnborough: Gregg, 1972.

———. *Out of the Ghetto: The Social Background of Jewish Emancipation, 1770–1870.* Cambridge: Harvard University Press, 1973.

———. "Rabbinical Authority and Authorization in the Middle Ages." In *Studies in Medieval Jewish History and Literature,* ed. Isadore Twersky. Cambridge: Harvard University Press, 1979.

———. *Jewish Emancipation and Self-Emancipation.* Philadelphia: Jewish Publication Society, 1986.

———. "Orthodoxy in Historical Perspective." *Studies in Contemporary Jewry* 2 (1986): 3–17.

———. *Tradition and Crisis: Jewish Society at the End of the Middle Ages.* Trans. and with an afterword and bibliography by Bernard Dov Cooperman. New York: New York University Press, 1993.

Kellner, Menachem. *Maimonides on the "Decline of the Generations" and the Nature of Rabbinic Authority.* Albany: State University of New York Press, 1996.

Kelman, Herbert C., and V. Lee. Hamilton. *Crimes of Obedience: Toward a Social Psychology of Authority and Responsibility*. New Haven: Yale University Press, 1989.

Kermode, Frank. *The Classic*. London: Faber & Faber, 1975.

———. *Forms of Attention*. Chicago: University of Chicago Press, 1985.

Kook, Abraham Isaac. *Mishpat Kohen*. Jerusalem: Mossad Harav Kook, 1966.

Kraemer, David. "On the Reliability of Attributions in the Bavli." *Hebrew Union College Annual* 60 (1989): 175–90.

———. *The Mind of the Talmud: An Intellectual History of the Bavli*. New York: Oxford University Press, 1990.

———. "The Formation of Rabbinic Canon: Authority and Boundaries." *Journal of Biblical Literature* 110, no. 4 (1991): 613–30.

Kugel, James. *In Potiphar's House*. San Franscisco: Harpers, 1990.

———. "Two Introductions to Midrash." In *Midrash and Literature*, ed. Geoffrey H. Hartman and Sanford Budick. New Haven: Yale University Press, 1986.

Lamm, Maurice. *The Jewish Way in Death and Mourning*. New York: Jonathan David, 1969.

Leiman, Shnayer Z. "Dwarfs on the Shoulders of Giants." *Tradition* 27, no. 3 (1993): 90–94.

Levine, Lee I. "The Jewish Patriarch (Nasi) in Third Century Palestine." In *Aufstieg und Niedergang der römischen Welt II*, (vol. 19.2. Berlin and New York: de Gruyter, 1972).

———. *Ma'amad ha-hakhamim be-Eretz Yisrael be-tequfat ha-Talmud*. Jerusalem: Yad Izhak ben Zvi, 1985. Subsequently published as *The Rabbinic Class of Roman Palestine in Late Antiquity*.(New York: Jewish Theological Seminary of America, 1989.)

———. "The Sages and the Synagogue in Late Antiquity: The Evidence of the Galilee." In *The Galilee in Late Antiquity*, ed. Lee I. Levine. New York: Jewish Theological Seminary of America, 1992.

Lewin, B. M., ed. *Iggeret Rav Sherira Gaon*. Berlin, 1921. Reprint, Jerusalem: Makor, 1972.

Lieberman, Saul. *Hellenism in Jewish Palestine*. New York: Jewish Theological Seminary of America, 1950.

Maimon, Yehudah Leib. *Ḥiddush ha-Sanhedrin be-medinatenu ha-meḥudeshet*. Jerusalem: Mossad Harav Kook, 1950–51.

Mantel, Hugo. *Studies in the History of the Sanhedrin*. Harvard Semitic Series, no. 17. Cambridge: Harvard University Press, 1961.

Margaliyot, Reuven. "Tena'ei minui ke-ḥaver ha-Sanhedrin" (The Requisites for Appointment to the Sanhedrin). *Sinai* 20 (1946–47): 16–26.

Meyer, Michael A. *The Origins of the Modern Jew: Jewish Identity and European Culture in Germany, 1749–1824*. Detroit: Wayne State University Press, 1967.

———. *Response to Modernity: A History of the Reform Movement in Judaism*. New York: Oxford University Press, 1988.

Mitchell, W. J. T., ed. *The Politics of Interpretation*. Chicago: University of Chicago Press, 1983.

Montefiore, C. G., and H. Loewe. *A Rabbinic Anthology*. Philadelphia: The Jewish Publication Society of America, 1960.

Neusner, Jacob. *A History of the Jews in Babylonia*. 3d ed. Chico, Calif.: Scholars Press, 1984.

————. *Torah: From Scroll to Symbol in Formative Judaism*. Philadelphia: Fortress Press, 1985.

————. *Reading and Believing: Ancient Judaism and Contemporary Gullibility*. Atlanta: Scholars Press, 1986.

Neuwirth, Y. Y. *Shemirat Shabbat ke-hilkhatah*. Jerusalem: F. Feldheim, 1964 or 1965.

Newman, Julius. *Semikhah (Ordination): A Study of Its Origin, History and Function in Rabbinic Literature*. Manchester: University of Manchester Press, 1950.

Newman, Louis. "Woodchoppers and Respirators: Interpretation in Contemporary Jewish Ethics." *Modern Judaism* 10, no. 1 (1990): 17–42.

Penelhum, Terence. *Survival and Disembodied Existence*. London: Routledge & Kegan Paul, 1970.

Pennock, J. Roland, and John W. Chapman, eds. *Authority Revisited*. NOMOS, vol. 29. New York: New York University Press, 1987.

Phillips, D. Z. *The Concept of Prayer*. London: Routledge & Kegan Paul, 1965.

Pinchuk, Ben Zion. *Shtetl Jews under Soviet Rule: Eastern Poland on the Eve of the Holocaust*. Oxford: Blackwell, 1990.

Price, H. H. *Essays in the Philosophy of Religion*. London: Oxford University Press, 1972.

"Providence." *Encyclopaedia Judaica*. Vol. 13:1279–86. Jerusalem: Keter Publishers, 1971.

Rabinowich, Nosson. *The Iggeres of Rav Sherira Gaon*. Brooklyn: Moznaim, 1988.

Raffel, Charles. "Maimonides' Theory of Providence." Ph.D. diss.: Brandeis University, 1983.

Redner, Harry. *The Ends of Science: An Essay in Scientific Authority*. Boulder: Westview Press, 1987.

Robison, Wade L. "The Functions and Limits of Legal Authority." In *Authority: A Philosophical Analysis*, ed. R. Baine Harris. University, Ala.: University of Alabama Press, 1976.

Rosenberg, Shalom. "Hitgalut matmedet: sheloshah kivunim." In *Hitgalut, Emunah, Tevunah*, ed. Mosh Halamish and Moshe Schwarcz. Ramat Gan: Bar Ilan University, 1976.

————. "Emunat Hakhamim," in *Jewish Thought in the Seventeenth Century*, ed. Isadore Twersky and Bernard Septimus. Cambridge: Harvard University Press, 1987.

Rosenzweig, Michael. "Be-ʿinyan semikhah u-semikhat zeqeinim." *Beit Yitzḥak* 21 (1989): 91–101.

————. "*Eilu ve-Eilu Divrei Elohim Hayyim*: Halakhic Pluralism and Theories of Controversy." In *Rabbinic Authority and Personal Autonomy*, ed. Moshe Sokol. Northvale, N.J.: Jason Aronson, 1992.

Rosner, Fred. *Medicine in the Bible and Talmud: Selections from Classical Jewish Sources*. New York: Ktav, 1977.

Roth, Joel. *The Halakhic Process: A Systemic Analysis*. New York: Jewish Theological Seminary of America, 1986.

Sagi, Avi. "ʿIyyun bi-shnei modelim shel musag ha-emet ha-hilkhatit u-mashmaʿutam." In *Ha-higayyon: meḥqarim bi-darkhei hashivah shel ḥazal*. Jerusalem, Bar Ilan 1989.

————. "Baʿayat ha-hakhraʾah ha-hilkhatit veha-emet ha-hilkhatit—liqrat pilosofia shel ha-Halakha." *Dine Yisrael* 15 (1991): 7–38.

———. "Models of Authority and the Duty of Obedience in Halahkic Literature." *AJS Review* 20, no. 1 (1995): 1–24.

Sanders, E. P. *Paul and Palestinian Judaism*. Philadelphia: Fortress Press, 1977.

"Sanhedrin." *Encyclopaedia Judaica*. vol. 14:836–39. Jerusalem: Keter Publishers, 1971.

Saperstein, Marc. *Decoding the Rabbis: A Thirteenth-Century Commentary on the Aggadah*. Cambridge: Harvard University Press, 1980.

Schechter, Solomon. *Studies in Judaism*. Series 1. Philadelphia: Jewish Publication Society, 1896.

Schepansky, Israel. "Minhag vi-Halakhah." *Or ha-Mizrah* 40, no. 2 (1991–92): 147–67.

———. "Be-ʿinyan semikhat hakhamim." *Or ha-Mizra* 44 (1995–96): 54–95.

Schiffman, Lawrence H. *From Text to Tradition: A History of Second Temple and Rabbinic Judaism*. Hoboken, N.J.: Ktav Publishing House, 1991.

Schreier, S. "Le-toledot ha-sanhedriyah ha-gedolah biyrushalayim." Ha-Shiloah 31 (1914–15): 404–15.

Segal, Eliezer. "Anthological Dimensions in the Babylonian Talmud." *Prooftexts* 17, no. 1 (1997): 33–63.

"Semikha." *Encyclopaedia Judaica*. Vol. 14:1140–47. Jerusalem: Keter Publishers, 1971.

Shilat, Y. *Haqdamot ha-Rambam la-Mishnah*. Jerusalem: Maʿaliyot, 1992.

Shapley, Deborah, and Roy, Rustum. *Lost at the Frontier: U.S. Science and Technology Policy Adrift*. Philadelphia: ISI Press, 1985.

Shatz, David, ed. *Contemporary Philosophy of Religion*. New York: Oxford University Press, 1982.

Silber, Michael K. "The Emergence of Ultra-Orthodoxy: The Invention of a Tradition." In *The Uses of Tradition: Jewish Continuity in the Modern Era*, ed. Jack Wertheimer. New York: Jewish Theological Seminary of America, 1994.

Silman, Yohanan. "Torat Yisrael le-or hidusheha—beirur fenominologi." *Proceedings of the American Academy for Jewish Research* 57 (1990–91): 49–67.

Simmons, Alan John. *Moral Principles and Political Obligation*. Princeton: Princeton University Press, 1979.

Simon, Yves R. *A General Theory of Authority*. Notre Dame: University of Notre Dame Press, 1962.

Sokol, Moshe Z., ed. *Rabbinic Authority and Personal Autonomy*. Northvale, N.J.: Jason Aronson, 1992.

Soloveitchik, Haym. "Religious Law and Change: The Medieval Ashkenazic Example." *Association for Jewish Studies Review* 12 (1987): 205–21.

———. "Rupture and Reconstruction: The Transformation of Contemporary Orthodoxy." *Tradition* 28, no. 4 (1994): 64–130.

Soloveitchik, Joseph B. *Shiʿurim le-zekher abba mari z"l*. Vol. 1. Jerusalem: Defus Aqiva Yosef, 1983.

Spiegel, Yaʿakov. "Derekh qeṣarah bilshon tanaʾim ve-ʿal peshat ve-drash ba-Mishnah." *Asufot* 4 (1991): 9–26.

Stern, David. "Moses-cide: Midrash and Contemporary Literary Criticism." *Prooftexts* 4 (1984): 193–213. Debate with Susan Handelman in *Prooftexts* 5 (1985): 75–103.

Swinburne, Richard P. *Responsibility and Atonement*. New York: Oxford University Press, 1989.

Ta-Shma, Yisrael M. *Minhag Ashkenaz ha-qadmon: heqer ve-ʿiyyun*. Jerusalem: Magnes Press, 1992.

Tucker, Gordon. "God, the Good, and Halakhah." *Judaism* 38, no. 3 (1989): 365–
   76.
Tucker, Robert C. "The Theory of Charismatic Leadership." *Daedalus* 97 (fall 1968):
   731–56.
Twersky, Isadore. "Shulhan ʿAruk: Enduring Code of Jewish Law." *Judaism* 16 (1967):
   141–58. Reprinted in Judah Goldin, ed., *The Jewish Expression* (New Haven:
   Yale University Press, 1976); and in Isadore Twersky. *Studies in Jewish Law and
   Philosophy* (New York: Ktav Publishing House, 1982).
Urbach, Ephraim E. "Matai pasqah ha-nevu'ah?" *Tarbiz* 17 (1945–46): 1–11.
———. "Halakhah ve-nevu'ah." *Tarbiz* 18 (1946–47): 1–27.
———. *HaZaL—Pirqei emunot ve-deʿot*. Jerusalem: Magnes Press, 1969.
———. "The Talmudic Sage—Character and Authority." In *Jewish Society through
   the Ages*, ed. H. H. Ben-Sasson and S. Ettinger. London: Vallentine & Mitchell,
   1971.
———. *The Sages—Their Concepts and Beliefs*. Trans. Israel Abrahams. Jerusalem:
   Magnes Press, 1979.
Vining, Joseph. *The Authoritative and the Authoritarian*. Chicago: University of Chi-
   cago Press, 1986.
Weldon, Thomas D. *The Vocabulary of Politics*. Baltimore: Penguin Books, 1953.
Wertheimer, A. J., ed. *Teshuvot ha-Rid*. Jerusalem: Makhon ha-Talmud ha-Yisre'eli
   ha-shalem.
Wittgenstein, Ludwig. *Zettel*. Ed. G. E. M. Anscombe and G. H. von Wright. Trans.
   G. E. M. Anscombe. Oxford: Blackwell, 1967.
———. *Philosophical Investigations*. Trans. G. E. M. Anscombe. Oxford: Blackwell,
   1968.
———. *On Certainty*. Ed. G. E. M. Anscombe and G. H. von Wright. Trans. Denis
   Paul and G. E. M. Anscombe. Oxford: Blackwell, 1974.
Zeitlin, Solomon. "The Opposition to the Spiritual Leaders Appointed by the Gov-
   ernment." *Jewish Quarterly Review* 31 (1940): 287–300.
Zucker, Moshe. "Le-baʿayat ha-maḥloqet ba-masoret." In *Jubilee Volume for Salo
   Baron* (Heb. sec.). Jerusalem: American Academy for Jewish Research, 1974.

Index

Speigel, Yaʿakov, 202n.27
Stammaim, 17, 116
Substitution, 43–45, 57–62, 171n.19
Supreme Court, U.S. *See* U.S. court
  system

Talmud, 6, 17, 82. *See also* Babylonian
  Talmud; Palestinian Talmud
Tanna, 118, 196n.9
Tannaim
  Amoraim's reverence for, 144, 146,
    184n.10
  authority of, 49
  compared with Amoraim, 49–50, 52,
    142, 197n.31
  and *devar mishnah*, 121
  halakhic decisions by, on travels
    through Diaspora, 176n.59
  and hermeneutical rules, 142
  ideal human qualities of certain
    individuals, 184n.13
  legislation by, 175–76n.53
  and Mishnah, 175n.52
  multiple or anonymous views and
    normative practice, 180n.60
  ordination of, 60
  and Sanhedrin, 46, 48, 181n.77
Taqqanot (regulations), 19, 24, 34, 75,
  106, 176n.53, 179n.49
Tchernowitz, Chaim, 170n.3
Temple in Jerusalem, 174n.36
Textual authority
  acceptance of text in Jewish law, 115–
    16
  attitude toward historical-critical
    study, 127–29
  "authority spreading to fill its
    container," 129–31
  and commentarial traditions, 122–23
  and community of scholars, 126–27
  and *devar mishnah*, 118, 119–21, 123–24
  discussion of, 116–24
  general discussion of, 12–13
  and historical contingency, 125–26
  implications of, 125–31
  and "independence" of texts, 117
  Ḥazon Ish on study of manuscripts,
    127–28
  medieval views of, 196–97n.27
  and Mishnah, 197n.29

overview of Rabbinic authority as, 38–
  39, 98, 154
and periodization, 197n.30, 198n.36
summary on, 131
Torah. *See also* Oral Torah; Written
  Torah
  authorship of, 143–44
  commandments in, 166–67n.11
  as compilation of documents, 4
  dual Torah as Written Torah and
    Oral Torah, 5, 16–17, 20, 159nn.13,
    15
  as given by God at Sinai, 95
  Rabbinic interpretation of, as divinely
    grounded, 5, 160n.17
  reading of, 143–44, 148–49
  Sages and authority of, 5, 159n.13
  study of, by women, 204n.51
Tosafists, 110, 142, 176n.58
Tosefta, 39, 131
Traditionalists, 6, 158n.3, 160n.22
Transformed authority
  authority of publicly accepted
    practice, 98, 101–13, 154
  conclusion on, 154–55
  interpretive communities, 15, 132–52,
    154
  introduction to, 97–99
  textual authority, 98, 114–31, 154
Transmission, 84–85, 168n.22, 180n.52,
  187n.5
Transmitted traditions, 18

Ultra-Orthodox Judaism, 6, 204n.54
U.S. Constitution, 13, 139, 202nn.21–22
U.S. court system, 33, 64, 138, 174n.39,
  181–82n.78
Urbach, E. E., 183n.5

"Verdictive" authority, 64
Vining, Joseph, 162n.42, 174n.39

Weldon, T. D., 183n.6
Wellhausen, 4, 159n.11
Will of God. *See* Divine will
Wissenschaft des Judentums (Science of
  Judaism), 111, 149, 160n.24
Witness analogy, and epistemic
  authority, 79–80

DATE DUE
